Money, Markets, and Merit

OXFORD STUDIES IN THE HISTORY OF ECONOMICS

Series Editor:

Steven G. Medema, PhD, University Distinguished Professor of Economics, University of Colorado Denver

This series publishes leading-edge scholarship by historians of economics and social science, drawing upon approaches from intellectual history, the history of ideas, and the history of the natural and social sciences. It embraces the history of economic thinking from ancient times to the present, the evolution of the discipline itself, the relationship of economics to other fields of inquiry, and the diffusion of economic ideas within the discipline and to the policy realm and broader publics. This enlarged scope affords the possibility of looking anew at the intellectual, social, and professional forces that have surrounded and conditioned economics' continued development.

Money, Markets, and Merit

The Economic Thought of Leonardus Lessius

WIM DECOCK

OXFORD
UNIVERSITY PRESS

OXFORD
UNIVERSITY PRESS

Oxford University Press is a department of the University of Oxford. It furthers the University's objective of excellence in research, scholarship, and education by publishing worldwide. Oxford is a registered trade mark of Oxford University Press in the UK and in certain other countries.

Published in the United States of America by Oxford University Press
198 Madison Avenue, New York, NY 10016, United States of America.

CIP data is on file at the Library of Congress.

ISBN 9780197827314

DOI: 10.1093/9780197827345.001.0001

Printed by Integrated Books International, United States of America

MIX
Paper
FSC FSC® C183721

The manufacturer's authorized representative in the EU for product safety is Oxford University Press España S.A., Parque Empresarial San Fernando de Henares, Avenida de Castilla, 2 – 28830 Madrid (www.oup.es/en or product.safety@oup.com). OUP España S.A. also acts as importer into Spain of products made by the manufacturer).

What the great religious epoch of the seventeenth century bequeathed to its utilitarian successor was, however, above all an amazingly good, we may even say a pharisaically good, conscience in the acquisition of money, so long as it took place legally.

Max Weber[1]

Contents

Acknowledgements

"He already had it all figured out." These are the words often used by scholars and business professionals alike when they first encounter Lessius' thoughts on money, markets, and merit. Over the years, I have been fortunate to meet experts from various disciplines who shared my enthusiasm for the man his contemporaries called the "Oracle of the Low Countries."

One of them is Alexandre Laumonier—anthropologist, author of books about algorithmic decision-making in financial markets, and founding editor of Zones Sensibles, a boutique publishing house in Brussels. Many years ago, he suggested that I write a book on Lessius that would provide a comprehensive yet accessible overview of his economic ideas, set against the broader context of his work as a spiritual counsellor, legal expert, and professor of theology. A visiting professorship at the École des hautes études en sciences sociales in Paris in 2017, at the invitation of Sylvain Piron, gave me the opportunity to refine my ideas and receive valuable feedback on early drafts of some chapters. The result was the publication of a French monograph on Lessius' legal and economic thought : *Le marché du mérite. Penser le droit et l'économie avec Léonard Lessius* (Zones Sensibles, 2019).

Another scholar whose path I have been fortunate to cross is Steven G. Medema. Back in 2009, he published my first international article on Lessius in the *Journal of the History of Economic Thought.* More than fifteen years later, he has generously accepted to publish a revised English version of *Le marché du mérite* as part of Oxford Studies in the History of Economics. Without his support, this book would not have come to fruition. I am also grateful to the anonymous reviewers whose insightful suggestions improved the work, leading to the drafting of an entirely new introductory chapter. Throughout the publication process, I benefited from the professional assistance of the editors at Oxford University Press and Integra, particularly James Cook, Phoebe Aldridge-Turner and Hemasankar Amurugam. Preparing an English edition of the French book has also made me appreciate the remarkable capabilities of DeepL Pro. At the same time, my experience with AI-assisted translation has reinforced my impression that human beings should always have the final say over algorithms.

I owe much to conversations I have had with colleagues and friends over nearly two decades, in many different languages. In this brief section, I cannot do justice to them all. However, I must mention the early encouragements by Toon Van Houdt, who supervised my master's thesis in classical philology at KULeuven in 2005 and introduced me to Lessius. Likewise, without the support of Laurent Waelkens and Emanuele Conte, who supervised my doctoral dissertation in law at KULeuven and Roma Tre University (2011), I would not have grasped the juridical framework underpinning scholastic economics. My understanding of Lessius would also have remained one-sided, had I not had to opportunity to engage with leading scholars in early modern studies and the history of philology, philosophy and theology—especially in the context of LECTIO (KULeuven's Institute for the Study of the Transmission of Texts, Ideas, and Images) and GEMCA (UCLouvain's Group for Early Modern Cultural Analysis). I am also indebted to my colleagues and students at the Faculties of Law and Criminology at UCLouvain and ULiège, for constantly challenging me to translate the wisdom of the past into the language of the present.

Without the financial support of numerous institutions and funding agencies, the research endeavours that lie behind this book would not have been possible. The EU's Marie Skłodowska-Curie Research Program enabled me to spend unforgettable years at the Max Planck Institute for Legal History and Theory in Frankfurt, the Istituto Italiano di Scienze Umane in Florence, and the École des hautes études en sciences sociales in Paris. The Belgian Historical Institute provided a stipend for my research at the Academia Belgica in Rome. The Flemish Fund for Scientific Research (FWO) funded my doctoral scholarship at KULeuven. Between 2012 and 2014, the LOEWE Research Focus on the history of conflict resolution at Goethe University and the Max Planck Institute for Legal History and Legal Theory in Frankfurt gave me the opportunity to lead a junior research group on canon law and business. KULeuven enabled me to hold a research professorship at the university's Faculty of Law and Criminology from 2014 to 2021. Finally, the ongoing support of the Flemish Fund for Scientific Research (FWO) and the Belgian Fund for Scientific Research (FNRS) has been instrumental in sustaining both my research and that of many of my doctoral and postdoctoral researchers at KULeuven, ULiège, and UCLouvain.

Over the years, I have greatly benefited from the feedback I received on numerous presentations about Lessius, delivered at invited lectures around the world—from Helsinki to Beijing and from Malibu to Oxford. I am especially grateful to Noah Feldman and Charlie Donahue Jr. for inviting me to the Finance in Religious Law workshop at Harvard Law School in 2013, to Luisa Brunori and Olivier Descamps for their invitation to The Economy without Work workshop in Paris in 2015, and to Günther Wassilowsky and Christoph Strohm for welcoming me to Augsburg in 2023 for the Religion and Economics in the Early Modern Period conference. I have also had the privilege of lecturing on Lessius as a visiting professor at the Universities of Bayreuth, Bergen, Bonn, Catania, Clermont-Auvergne, Paris Panthéon-Sorbonne, Toulouse-Capitole, and the East China University of Political Science and Law in Shanghai. These opportunities were made possible through the generous invitations of Rudolf Schüßler, Jörn Sunde, Mathias Schmoeckel, Orazio Condorelli, Nicolas Laurent-Bonne and Cyrille Dounot, Pierre Bonin, Florent Garnier, and Lihong Zhang, respectively, to whom I am deeply grateful.

As Aristotle and the scholastics knew, the intellectual, personal, and institutional debts one accumulates over the years are immeasurable. There is no market where they can be repaid entirely. They serve as a reminder that every claim to individual merit must not ignore the common good.

Fig. 0.1 *Leo Belgicus*, map of the Low Countries, by Claes Jansz Visscher, colour engraving, Amsterdam, 1650 (first version, 1609)

Fig. 0.1 Continued

Introduction
Leonardus Lessius and the History of Economics

In his monumental *History of Economic Analysis*, published posthumously in 1954, the Austrian American economist Joseph Alois Schumpeter (1883–1950) stated that three scholastic doctors came nearer than anyone else to having been the "founders of scientific economics."[1] One of them is central to the argument developed in this book: Leonardus Lessius (1554–1623; Fig. I.1). A polymath from Brecht, a little town close to the city of Antwerp in the Duchy of Brabant, Lessius served as a well-renowned professor of theology at the Jesuit College in Louvain. He acquired great fame as an advisor to merchants and princes in the Spanish Netherlands and the Principality of Liège. Through regular contacts with men of practice and careful observation of trade and finance in Antwerp, he became familiar with business practices in a formative stage of modern capitalism. Schumpeter affirmed that his treatise *On Justice and Law* (*De iustitia et iure*, first published in Louvain in 1605) contained "a body of analytical tools and propositions that was sounder than much subsequent work." The same judgement applied to similar works at the crossroads of theology, law, and economics published by Luis de Molina (1535–1600) and Juan de Lugo (1583–1660), prominent Jesuit scholars like Lessius, whom Schumpeter considered as the two other founding fathers of modern economics.

Theories on economic value, money, interest, and business profits elaborated by late nineteenth-century economists could have been developed more quickly, according to Schumpeter, if only they had immediately taken the insights of these scholastic doctors as their basis. By way of example, he affirmed that Molina, Lessius, and Lugo had been as wise as Carl Menger (1840–1921), one of the founders of the "Austrian School of Economics,"[2] to point out that "utility was not a property of the goods themselves or identical with any of their inherent qualities, but the reflex of the uses the individuals under observation proposed to make of these goods."[3] Though admitting "that we are not as a rule in the habit of looking to the scholastics

Money, Markets, and Merit. Wim Decock, Oxford University Press. © Oxford University Press (2025).
DOI: 10.1093/9780197827345.003.0001

Fig. I.1 Portrait of Leonardus Lessius, attributed to Boëtius Adams Bolswert, engraving, 1623

for the origin of the theories that are associated with nineteenth-century laissez-faire liberalism,"[4] Schumpeter interpreted the scholastics' wariness of price-fixing or their view on business losses as either the result of bad luck or a penalty for incompetence as signs of the liberal outlook of their economic ideas. He was also impressed by their analysis of money as the merchant's tool and of pure interest as the result of business profit rather than risks and transaction cost.[5]

Schumpeter's interest in Molina's, Lessius', and Lugo's economic thought received further impetus through the work of Bernard William Dempsey (1903–1960), a Jesuit priest and economist.[6] Dempsey was one of Schumpeter's pupils at Harvard University in the late 1930s and early 1940s, around the time that Schumpeter wrote the chapter on "the schoolmen" of his *History of Economic* Analysis.[7] Dempsey wrote a doctorate on the development of scholastic teachings on money and interest. When it was published in 1943, Dempsey's *Interest and Usury* was prefaced by his mentor. The latter warned readers that they would be surprised by the "modernity" of the scholastic doctors.[8] Schumpeter knew they were not equipped with the mathematical and statistical tools of modern economics, but he was convinced that "if those schoolmen rose from the dead today, they would readily understand our world and be quite prepared to take part in the discussion of its problems." Moreover, their statements on the economy were based on empirical evidence, rational inquiry, and methodological rigour.[9] This was possible, he explained, because despite the fundamentally moral nature of their endeavour, they were convinced that a sound moral judgement presupposed an analysis of the economic facts of the case at hand. While in his own time, religious leaders were allegedly driven by a morality of good intentions, "this was not so with the great Jesuits of the sixteenth and seventeenth centuries."[10]

The reappraisal of late scholasticism in Schumpeter's and Dempsey's economic writings inspired other researchers. In 1952, Marjorie Grice-Hutchinson (1909–2003) published a seminal essay on *The School of Salamanca. Readings in Spanish Monetary Theory*. It recalled historians of economic thought that Molina, Lessius, and Lugo were part of a much wider renewal in scholastic economics in the sixteenth century. That revival was connected to the renaissance of Thomistic thought at the faculties of theology, canon law, and civil law of the University of Salamanca, which flourished during Spain's Siglo de Oro. An example discussed by

Grice-Hutchinson are the ideas on money expressed in the treatise *On Justice and Law* (published in 1553 in Salamanca) by Domingo de Soto (c. 1495–1560), a Dominican friar teaching theology at the University of Salamanca and a resident of San Estebán, the Dominican convent in the same city. Even if the title of her work did suggest otherwise, Grice-Hutchinson nevertheless acknowledged that the renaissance of scholastic economic thought was not limited to places like Salamanca. For example, the innovative monetary ideas of Martín de Azpilcueta (1492–1586, also known as Dr Navarrus), especially concerning the purchasing-power-parity theory of exchange rates and the quantity theory of money, were formulated at the University of Coimbra, where Azpilcueta taught canon law.[11]

In the acknowledgements section of her book, Marjorie Grice-Hutchinson expressed gratitude to Friedrich Hayek (1899–1992) and Raymond de Roover (1904–1972) for reading her draft manuscript. In their turn, Hayek and De Roover played a substantial role in advancing research on scholastic economics. During his 1974 Nobel Prize lecture, Hayek hailed the scholastics of the sixteenth century as "remarkable anticipators of modern economics."[12] Hayek's positive appreciation of scholastic economic thought found resonance among economic libertarians. For example, a synthesis of late scholastic economic thought was published in 1987 by Alejandro Chafuen, an Argentinian economist, member of the Mont Pelerin Society and long-time president of the libertarian Atlas Network.[13] In the meantime, the late scholastics grew increasingly popular with advocates of the Austrian school of economics, which, building on the work of the likes of Carl Menger and Ludwig von Mises (1881–1973), held individual freedom in high regard. Murray Rothbard (1926–1995), a pupil of von Mises, dedicated an entire chapter of *An Austrian Perspective on the History of Economic Thought* (1995) to the "late Spanish scholastics."[14] He held Lessius in high regard. According to Rothbard, Lessius "had an insight into how all economic markets are interrelated" and "engaged in the most sophisticated analysis yet achieved of the workings of wages and the labour market."[15] Lessius' appreciation of "entrepreneurial industry" and his accommodating views on the morality of business were praised for their "liberating effect on trade."[16]

Raymond de Roover, a Belgian American historian of business, published several articles on scholastic economics in the 1950s which were eventually collected by Julius Kirshner in *Business, Banking and Economic Thought in Late Medieval and Early Modern Europe* (Chicago University Press, 1974).

De Roover's work covers different aspects of the economic ideas of the scholastics, ranging from their ideas on competition, monopolies, interest, and usury to the just price. De Roover was eager to connect Adam Smith's economic thought on free markets to the legacy of the scholastics.[17] He also advanced the notion that scholastics did not adhere to a so-called cost-of-production theory of value, as Richard Tawney had argued, but to a notion of economic value based on subjective utility.[18] While highlighting the innovative character of economic ideas expressed by scholastics from Peter of John Olivi to Lessius, he still acknowledged the gap between scholastic economic thought and modern economics.[19] The scholastics were not primarily interested in economic growth but in the salvation of souls. In a 1955 article in the *Quarterly Journal of Economics*, he criticized scholastics for their continued reliance on the usury doctrine.[20]

Just two years after De Roover's negative remarks about the late scholastics' backward-looking attitude to money and interest, John T Noonan Jr (1926–2017) published *The Scholastic Analysis of Usury*. In the acknowledgements section of his book, Noonan thanked De Roover for his "criticism and comment." In this unparalleled work, the second part of which was entirely dedicated to "Criticism and Revision of the Usury Theory, 1450–1750," Noonan revealed the astonishingly clever and unconventional observations on interest in the work of scholastic theologians such as Lessius.[21] A jurist by training, Noonan was perhaps more inclined than De Roover to appreciate the sophisticated contractual schemes used to circumvent the traditional prohibition on interest-taking. These legal techniques ranged from the triple contract (a combination of insurance, sale, and partnership contracts) to mutually redeemable rent contracts (*census*) and exchange banking (*cambium*). In each of these instances, Noonan showed, scholastics such as Lessius proved themselves to be fine observers of daily banking practices, simultaneously justifying those practices from a normative point of view by using their knowledge of contract law. In the process, they developed innovative ideas on the productive nature of money, the establishment of the market price for money, and the economic value of risk-taking and hard work (*industria*).

In Noonan's view,[22] continuing "the tradition of intelligent comprehension of business problems," Lessius is the theologian "whose views on usury most decidedly mark the arrival of a new era." Noonan's final judgement about Lessius speaks volumes: "careful, perceptive, boldly logical, modest, and sure of himself, Lessius is a master of scholastic economic analysis." This flattering account of Lessius led Barry Gordon, an Australian economist, to dedicate no fewer than thirty pages to Lessius in *Economic Analysis Before Adam Smith*, his influential handbook on pre-Smithian economic thought, the subtitle of which read *Hesiod to Lessius*. Drawing on Schumpeter, Dempsey, De Roover, and Noonan, it offered an account of Lessius' analysis of money and interest, loans and exchanges, prices and markets, labour and salaries, and monopolies. Gordon was of the opinion that an original element in Lessius' economic thought was that he broke with the medieval view of treating monetary transactions such as loans as merely happening in an isolated way.[23] Lessius saw that individual transactions were occurring in the context of a market where the just price of goods, including that of money, was established by common estimation of a number of price determinants (including the number of buyers and sellers, the availability of money, the abundance or scarcity of the good, its usefulness, and the average costs incurred by sellers), independently of subjective circumstances or intentions specific to the individual contracting parties.

Gordon credited Lessius with fully recognizing the existence of a market in money loans, based on his empirical observations of mercantile customs at the Antwerp exchange. This insight altered the traditional morality of interest-taking, according to Gordon, since demonstrating the presence of specific circumstances allowing for the charging of interest in an isolated case now became immaterial. "What is material," Gordon explained,[24] "is the presence in the community of an objectively stated and just price for loss of liquidity." Lessius' detailed description of the establishment of a price for the privation of money foreshadowed modern theories on "liquidity preference." This was a new normative basis, referred to by Lessius in Latin as "lack of money" (*carentia pecuniae*), that could justify interest-taking in all loans. Gordon rightly stressed that the presence of a preference for liquidity was a recurring theme throughout Lessius' treatment of commercial dealings.[25] It made the traditional theory of extrinsic titles for charging interest all but redundant. The radical nature of Lessius' ideas was recognized by Juan de Lugo, who rejected, or rather reformulated, them in more traditional terms, through an extensive interpretation of "profits foregone" (*lucrum cessans*).[26]

Lessius' market-based approach to economic analysis and business morality drew special attention in Odd Inge Langholm's seminal book *The Legacy of Scholasticism in Economic Thought. Antecedents of Choice and Power*. Published with Cambridge University Press in 1998, this book was one of many groundbreaking contributions by Langholm to the reappraisal of scholastic economic thought, including his magistral *Economics in the*

Medieval Schools: Wealth, Exchange, Value, Money and Usury according to the Paris Theological Tradition, 1200–1350 (Brill, 1992). Contemplating the transition from medieval to early modern forms of scholastic economics, Langholm saw at least two major developments at work. Firstly, a kind of analytical "depersonalization" that was the corollary of the depersonalization of economic institutions themselves in the early modern world. "The individual exchanger would be seen less and less as involved in a personal relationship but as confronting a system," Langholm explained.[27] As a result, contracting parties were seen as confronting economic laws that were abstract and impersonal in character. For example, a patient's fear of death does not render an excessive doctor's fee invalid, because that fear of death is no one else's concern. "Faced with an impersonal economic system," Langholm pointed out,[28] "each person is on his own." A second development noted by Langholm concerned a shift of emphasis from duties to rights. In Langholm's view, this evolution could be seen clearly at work in Francisco Suárez (1548–1617). Incidentally, Suárez was one of Lessius' mentors at the Jesuit college in Rome.

Drawing on Langholm's insights, I have tried to illustrate the depersonalization of economic ethics in Lessius' *On Justice and Law* by examining his analysis of the case of the Merchant of Rhodes.[29] A merchant shipping grain from Alexandria to the island of Rhodes, where there is a grain dearth, wants to know whether it is morally licit to sell his goods at a high price, even though he knows that the price will go down very soon because of other grain merchants setting sail to Rhodes. Inherited from Stoic philosophy, it became a standard case in scholastic economics through its inclusion in Thomas Aquinas' *Summae Theologiae*. The case was discussed by scholastic authors in the sixteenth and seventeenth centuries in more abstract terms ("Can I sell a good at the current price even if I know, privately, that the price is going to decrease?"). It was the starting point for dealing with a range of questions related to profit-making, self-interest, just pricing, speculation, information asymmetry, lying, insider trading, and dominant positions. While some doctors argued that, due to the information advantage of the seller, there was a fundamental imbalance between the personal conditions of the buyer and seller, Lessius argued otherwise. He thought that exploiting information advantages was part of the business game. Moreover, the market is governed by the virtue of justice in exchange, not by charity. Businessmen have the right to take advantage of their private knowledge.

As noted, the contrast between medieval and early modern scholastic approaches to the market is something that struck Gordon and Langholm.

The discontinuity becomes even more clear if we consider some of the characteristics usually attributed to what one could call a "scholastic paradigm" in economic ethics. It can be derived from the work of expert scholars on medieval scholastic economics such as Oscar De-Juan and Fabio Monsalve, or, more recently, Paolo Evangelisti.[30] Drawing on an article by De-Juan and Monsalve in *The European Journal of the History of Economic Thought*, a non-exhaustive list of distinguishing features of the scholastic paradigm in economic ethics could include the following:[31] (1) market relations are personal and morally ruled by the virtues of charity and justice; (2) intention matters, and one cannot account for a deed by appealing to impersonal forces; (3) merchants have a sense of duty towards other merchants and the community as a whole. However much these characteristics apply to most medieval scholastics, they are no longer helpful to understand Molina, Lessius, and Lugo. That was reason enough for Joseph Schumpeter to consider them, rather than previous generations of schoolmen, as "founders of scientific economics."

From the point of view of the history of economic science, the interesting point is that the depersonalized view of the market that can be observed in the moral writings of Molina, Lessius, and Lugo has to do not only with the fact that they were living in the first era of global capitalism, but that they also had a much firmer grasp of the impersonal laws underlying trade and finance than any of their predecessors. To be sure, among the medieval scholastics, some could be seen as having anticipated these evolutions. Many of them were Franciscan friars working as moral counsellors in the thirteenth and fourteenth centuries. Stimulating studies by Giacomo Todeschini and Sylvain Piron, both medievalists, have shown the pre-eminence of Peter of John Olivi's thinking in this regard.[32] His economic thought has been qualified as "proto-liberal," for instance by Richard Sturn, an Austrian economist.[33] Still, Olivi's commentaries on sale, moneylending, and restitution, inspired by his practice as a moral advisor to merchants in Narbonne, remain short and schematic compared to the depth and breadth of the voluminous treatises *On Justice and Law* written by the Jesuit theologians of later centuries. After all, Olivi's world was still limited to the Mediterranean economy. The early modern scholastics were confronted with trade and finance on a global scale, following the worldwide expansion of the Iberian kingdoms. Portuguese merchants traded from Lisbon to Goa and Macao, and their Spanish counterparts from Seville to Puebla and Manila.

Despite this promising strand of literature and regardless of the occasional references to scholastic economics in modern textbooks on the history of economics,[34] in-depth analyses remain scarce. Mark Blaug's (1927–2011) influential textbook *Economic Theory in Retrospect* sums up scholastic economic analysis in rather broad terms, without mentioning Lessius or any of his fellow Jesuits. It takes Blaug just two pages to jump to the conclusion that scholastic theology is of little or no use in trying to understand Adam Smith.[35] In contrast, the *Handbook of the History of Economic Analysis* edited by Gilbert Faccarello and Heinz Kurz contains a full-fledged chapter on scholastic economics, essentially focusing on thirteenth century authors such as Thomas.[36] Specialized journals, however, such as *The European Journal of the History of Economic Thought*, *Journal of the History of Economic Thought*, and *History of Political Economy*, have continued to publish papers that deal with aspects of the scholastic legacy in economic thought. For example, the changing nature of the scholastic analysis of usury, interest, and just pricing was revisited in several articles by Fabio Monsalve.[37] Other experts, such as André Lapidus, have investigated the (dis)continuities between the late scholastics and Hugo Grotius (1583–1645).[38] Edd Noell has thoroughly investigated scholastic wage theory, also in comparison with Adam Smith.[39] In the meantime, important impulses for further study of Luis de Molina's economic thought were offered by Francisco Gómez Camacho, Diego Alonso Lasheras, and Rudolf Schüßler.[40]

Because of his groundbreaking insights on the nature of money, interest, and markets, Lessius earned an eminent place in *Great Economic Thinkers from the Classicals to the Moderns*, a standard work in the field published in 2016 by Bertram Schefold.[41] In fact, already back in 1999 Schefold had published a collected volume on Lessius' economic thought, which was included in the prestigious German series Klassiker der Nationalökonomie. It included seminal contributions on Lessius' economic thought by Bertram Schefold, Louis Baeck, Barry Gordon, and Toon Van Houdt.[42] In an article published in 1998 in *The European Journal of the History of Economic Thought*, Van Houdt offered fresh insights on Lessius' development, and, ultimately, fundamental recasting of the scholastic doctrine of extrinsic titles for interest-taking.[43] Louis Baeck (1928–2014), a development economist from the University of Leuven, viewed Lessius as a late protagonist of what he considered to be a typically Mediterranean tradition in economic thought.[44] Contrary to the Atlantic tradition, he thought that this tradition was characterized by the prevalence of a moral view on economics. Incidentally, Baeck's paper in Schefold's volume dwells on the juridical and moral theological roots of Lessius' economic thought.

Baeck's insistence, as an economist, on the need to revisit the juridical framework of Lessius' economic thought is a caveat I have tried to consider over the years in my research on Lessius' economic thought. As a matter of fact, after publishing an article in the *Journal of the History of Economic Thought* on Lessius' quite liberal analysis of the Merchant of Rhodes, I have had the opportunity to study the contractual framework of scholastic economic thought in *Theologians and Contract Law: The Moral Transformation of the Ius Commune*.[45] At the same time, collaboration with other scholars has offered avenues for exploring the astonishing heterogeneity of scholastic thinking in early modern times.[46] What has struck me are the manifold cross-fertilizations between theological, legal, and economic arguments in scholastic thought. This feature of scholastic thinking came to a climax in the early modern period. The interactions go in many ways, from theology to economics and law, but also the other way around. For instance, the theological debate on the relationship between divine grace and free will—a central topic in the age of Reformations—was articulated, by scholastic theologians, in legal and economic terms. As will be explained further in this book (chapter 9), the relationship between God and man was often analysed in terms of an employment contract. The quest for eternal life was described by Lessius in economic terms like a contest that could be won through the accumulation of merit.

The methodological specificities of scholastic economic analysis, particularly its connections with legal concepts and arguments, was something that Joseph Schumpeter was still very much aware of. Trained as a jurist—he received the degree of *doctor utriusque juris* (doctor of both Roman law and canon law) from the University of Vienna in 1906[47]—Schumpeter had no problems acknowledging that "the motive of scholastic analysis was manifestly not pure scientific curiosity but the desire to understand what they were called upon to judge from a moral standpoint."[48] Moreover, to quote a recent paper by Tristan Velardo, Schumpeter was convinced that the rise of capitalism should be seen "as not only an economic phenomenon but also an institutional and cultural one."[49] In some ways, Schumpeter's intellectual formation and scholarly intuitions resembled those of other great thinkers of his era, not in the least Max Weber (1864–1920), a jurist by training who became more famous as a sociologist and economist, as will be discussed below (chapter 2). To understand the genesis of economic thought and practice, Weber, too, was inclined to study the normative foundations of the economy. Although less interested in unravelling the origins of economic analysis in the technical sense, Weber tried to establish connections between religiously informed strands of moral and legal literature on the economy, on the one hand, and the creation of the psychological and institutional preconditions for the emergence of capitalistic types of economy, on the other.

In recent years, there has been a remarkable revival of interest among economists in Max Weber's *Protestant Ethic and the Rise of Capitalism* (1905), especially amongst institutional economists investigating the cultural determinants of economic prosperity. "Religion and Growth," a paper by Sascha O. Becker, Jared Rubin, and Ludger Woessmann published in the September 2024 issue of the *Journal of Economic Literature*, offers a remarkable synthesis of the existing literature on the subject. Considering Weber's thesis of a Protestant ethic underlying capitalism as "probably the first major social science argument that connects religious belief to economic development,"[50] it spends long pages dealing with Weber and the importance of the connections he established between economic growth, thriftiness, saving, and capital accumulation. Often, this leads to literature engaging in a rather reductionist way with the so-called Weber thesis, allegedly claiming that there is a monocausal relationship between the Protestant reformation and the rise of capitalism. A thorough, critical review of this type of literature was offered in 2023 in *Capitalism: A Journal of History and Economics* by Francesca Trivellato, an early modern historian at Princeton's Institute for Advanced Study.[51] In her thought-provoking piece, Trivellato calls for a disciplinary dis-enclosure of economists' engagement with Weber, which should be more respectful of the unfinished, incoherent quality of his work and the legal-political bend of his thought.

While the second chapter in this book offers a critical reading of popular, yet caricatural views of *The Protestant Ethic and the Rise of Capitalism*, its goal is not primarily to shed new light on Max Weber. In this book, Weber is taken as a starting point for reflection because of a basic, yet often neglected, methodological intuition that lies at the heart of his research endeavours. That basic intuition, almost as unknown as *The Protestant Ethic* is famous, is that one of the best ways to get a glimpse of the interaction between religious beliefs and economic behaviour is to read the "cases of conscience" literature. This literature, written by religious pastors and spiritual leaders, offers moral guidance to Christians confronted with difficult cases in different spheres of life, such as the family and the economy—think of the case of the Merchant of Rhodes. In each instance, the case is carefully analysed from the perspective of Roman law, canon law, divine law, and natural law to make sure that the individual Christian can navigate his way through this world while remaining on the right track to heaven.[52] The Jesuits played a particularly important role in providing this spiritual guidance, with Luis de Molina, or, for that matter, Leonardus Lessius, addressing his treatise *On Justice and Law* explicitly to judges not just in the external courts, but also in the internal forum or court of conscience.

The first chapter of this book takes us back to Lessius and his life as a confessor and spiritual advisor—a task he accomplished so well that he became known among his contemporaries as "the Oracle of the Netherlands." This opening chapter is also the occasion to present Lessius' writings in theology other than his famous treatise *On Justice and Law*. Some of these writings, for instance his *De perfectionibus moribusque divinis* (*On the divine perfections and morals*, 1620), are taken as the starting point for the expositions in chapters 9 and 10 of this book, which highlight the theological views of Lessius, particularly with regards to divine grace and free will, but also related to Christian soberness and discipline, as expressed in his *Hygiasticon*, a dietary treatise on remaining healthy even in old age. The objective of showing that Lessius was more than just a "master of economic analysis" is to provide a more holistic and contextually sensitive picture of the Jesuit from Brecht. As Richard Sturn has shown with regards to the scholastics, or, for that matter, Benjamin Friedman regarding Adam Smith's thought,[53] putting economic ideas in their wider philosophical-theological context often leads one to new insights. That is exactly the case with Lessius. A look at his theological ideas reinforces the conclusions reached by economists such as Gordon and Rothbard, namely that he was a proto-liberal, entrepreneurial-minded thinker.

Seeing the individual as a morally responsible agent who should be empowered by spiritual leaders to actively shape both his material and spiritual destiny by accumulating "merit," Lessius can rightly be considered not just as a proto-liberal economist, but also as a premodern advocate of a proto-form of "meritocracy." As will be shown, the vocabulary of merit (*meritum*) is particularly strong in Lessius' theological writings. It is one of the clearest testimonies, if need be, to the religious origins of the politics and economics of meritocracy in modern times—a storyline that received attention in recent years through the writings on meritocracy by Eric Nelson, Michael Sandel, and Daniel Markovits.[54] His proto-meritocratic tendencies may help us understand why Lessius became so popular with economists belonging to the "Austrian school"—for whom, at the core of the economy, there are entrepreneurial individuals, not collective entities or the state.[55] Yet, investigating the theological background of Lessius' economic thought also results in a better understanding of the fundamental differences between his opinions and those of, for instance, present-day anarcho-capitalists. Because of his Christian background, Lessius warned against limitless occupation with material interests and a view of human merit that did away entirely with notions of predestination, grace, and luck. Clearly, for Lessius, the spiritual imperatives of the Christian faith were also there to temper man's lust for money, prestige, and worldly pleasures.

As will be shown in chapter 8, recalling principles of Aristotelian-Thomistic political philosophy, Lessius thought that the common good prevailed over the individual good. At some point, he even stated that individuals were born for the public good. This does not mean that Lessius was an advocate of collectivism. Quite the opposite, we will see how Lessius arrived at justifying, from a moral-juridical point of view, controversial techniques to stimulate entrepreneurship, facilitate public finance, commercial lending, and investment practices, precisely on account of the argument that these techniques promoted the common good. Following other scholastic theologians, he thought that innovative commercial and financial practices such as the triple contract and the Mounts of Piety (also known as the Mounts of Charity) had to be promoted for the sake of the salvation of the economy. Through the example of the Mounts of Piety, the mutual reinforcement of spiritual salvation and the salvation of the economy becomes clear, as investors can gain spiritual credit and accumulate merit in heaven by making donations to the public pawn-bank, in turn improving material conditions for the poor. The harmonious conjunction of spiritual and material interests as envisaged by Lessius and other scholastic theologians is something that may well look more "medieval" than "modern" to readers today.

Protection of public interest is at the heart of Lessius' combat against all kinds of distortionary market practices that lead to the concentration of economic power in the hands of the few: cartels, monopolies, dominant positions, trade barriers. The smooth functioning of competitive markets, free from fraud and monopolies, was seen by him and other scholastics as a fundamental prerequisite for justice in transactions, since it prevented the weak and poor from being systematically exploited by the rich and powerful. As chapter 7 will show, Lessius' appraisal of the entrepreneurial spirit made him nevertheless doubt whether all forms of dominant positions could be considered as unjust. From the point of view of commutative justice, it appeared difficult for him to condemn traders who had done their best, through intelligence and hard work (*industria*), to reach a position enabling them to dominate the market. Those merchants could surely be condemned by criminal laws enacted for the sake of the common good, but in the absence of such positive laws, it was difficult, in Lessius' opinion, to bring a natural law case against excessive industry. As will be shown in chapters 5 and 6, he considered that the diligent and prudent merchant was expected to be industrious, to be able to make profits by exploiting information advantages, by making less costs than his competitors did on average, by speculating on price differences, and by anticipating market evolutions more quickly than others. These qualities were particularly required of merchants and investors active in insurance and secondary debt markets.

As Gordon and Langholm already pointed out, Lessius conceived of individual economic transactions, probably more radically than any scholastic theologian before him, as subject to impersonal laws that every contracting party was allowed to exploit at his advantage. The increasingly depersonalized view of markets played a role in Lessius' innovative view of interest as the price of the privation of money—a notion that undermined the basic principles of the traditional scholastic usury doctrine. The latter relied on technical legal distinctions such as the difference between external and internal titles for charging interest in a loan for consumption (*mutuum*), or the difference between simple loans and contractual schemes that were based on the exchange of money (*cambium*) or the sale of debt paper (*census*). In chapter 3, which highlights Lessius' views on money, lending, and interest, his exceptional knowledge of these technical legal distinctions will become clear. Since legal categories, especially as derived from contract law, were the lens through which Lessius dealt with business and finance, in "Keeping Promises" (chapter 3) this book deals with scholastics' contributions to contract law. It will show that Lessius, a Jesuit theologian, was not just "a master of economic analysis" but also "a master of laws."

1

The "Oracle of the Low Countries"

A leading theologian, Lessius travelled from the lectures halls in Louvain to Antwerp to converse with merchants.

—Franciscus Zypaeus

There remains a theological logic at the heart of Western economic reason, and a return to scholastic economics—taught in medieval and modern universities, colleges, and schools—allows us to grasp its historical underpinnings. This contention, put forward by Sylvain Piron in *L'Occupation du monde* (Zones Sensibles, 2019), will be built on in the present work, the aim of which is to present the exceptional contribution of Leonardus Lessius (1554–1623), professor at the Jesuit College of Louvain, to the moral justification of mercantile activity and the principle that industry, in the sense of hard work, engenders merit that must be rewarded in this world and the hereafter. Attracted by the sermons of Robert Bellarmine, a leading figure in the Counter-Reformation, the young Lessius joined the Society of Jesus, whereas his family had plans for him to join the world of business once he had finished his studies at the University of Louvain. Nevertheless, he was not completely cut off from mercantile practice. He rapidly earned a reputation as a moral counsellor to businessmen and he was soon referred to as the "Oracle of the Low Countries" on account of the brilliance of the advice he offered to the economic and political elites of his day. Regarding his famous treatise *De iustitia et iure ceterisque virtutibus cardinalibus* (*On Justice, Law and the Other Cardinal Virtues*), published in 1605 and republished until the end of the nineteenth century, Archduke Albert of Austria, who ruled the Low Countries at the beginning of the seventeenth century, is said to have carried a copy with him everywhere he went. And with good reason: Lessius' consultations and writings were based on an extraordinary knowledge of mercantile practices, combined with a deep understanding of the scholastic masters, in particular the theologians and canonists linked to the University of Salamanca.

Money, Markets, and Merit. Wim Decock, Oxford University Press. © Oxford University Press (2025).
DOI: 10.1093/9780197827345.003.0002

Economist, Saint, or Jurist?

It was in Salamanca, indeed, in the heart of the vast Spanish empire that the economic thought of the scholastics reached its apogee.[1] In long treatises on justice, law, commerce, and contracts, hundreds of Augustinian, Dominican, Franciscan, and Jesuit friars attempted to address the various challenges of early modernity—the discovery of the New World, the status of indigenous peoples, the Protestant Reformation and the schism within Christianity, the invention of printing, the emergence of the modern state, welfare for the poor, the globalization of trade, the invention of new investment techniques, risk management, and the transformation of credit and finance. Conscious of guiding souls so that as many individuals as possible could attain the Christian ideal in their daily lives, they developed a framework of thought at the intersection of law and theology that has fascinated modern observers ever since.

Admiring the sophistication of Leonardus Lessius' economic thought, but also that of Luis de Molina and Juan de Lugo, two other of Lessius' Jesuit contemporaries, the Austrian economist Joseph Alois Schumpeter remarked in 1954, in his famous *History of Economic Analysis*, that "it is within their systems of moral theology and law that economics gained definite if not separate existence, and it is they who come nearer than does any other group to having been the 'founders' of scientific economics."[2] Schumpeter's interest in the scholastics was undoubtedly aroused by the work of Bernard Dempsey, a Jesuit with a PhD in economics from Harvard, where Schumpeter taught from 1932 until his death in 1950. In his introduction to Dempsey's work on interest and usury, Schumpeter noted that the reader is struck by the "modernity" of the economic analyses proposed by Molina, Lessius, and Lugo: "If those schoolmen rose from the dead today, they would readily understand our world and be quite prepared to take part in the discussion of its problems. . . . They were no doubt judges and directors of consciences. Their fundamental system of belief was the same as that of the *Doctor Angelicus*. But, to put it bluntly, they always knew what they were talking about."[3]

The Jesuits of the time knew what they were talking about, something that, according to Schumpeter, set them apart from most of the religious leaders of his day. Schumpeter's introduction prompted other economists to take a closer look at the works of Leonardus Lessius. In 1975, Barry Gordon concluded in his overview of Adam Smith's precursors with a profound analysis of the Jesuit's philosophy, whom he regarded as "a leading innovator."[4] Murray Rothbard, a leading figure of the Austrian school of economics, believed that Lessius' thought had a "liberating effect" on trade and money.[5] A monograph by Raymond de Roover, originally from Antwerp and professor of economic history in New York, was the basis for a revival of scientific interest in Lessius' economic work in the 1950s and 1960s.[6] In the following decades, Robert Beutels and Louis Baeck drew the attention of Belgian economists to Lessius' contribution to market analysis. This renewed interest led to the presentation of a doctoral thesis in 1995 by Toon Van Houdt, a classical philologist from the University of Leuven, on the scholastic conception of money-lending and interest-taking.[7] Van Houdt was subsequently involved in the publication of a vade-mecum on Lessius in a collection directed by Bertram Schefold and devoted to the leading lights in economic thought.[8]

The depiction of Lessius as an economist, while interesting, does not cover all of his various facets. At the turn of the twentieth century, Victor Brants, a jurist and professor of political economy in Louvain, made a significant contribution to the rediscovery of Lessius' social and economic philosophy. In the midst of the revival of scholastic thought following the publication, in 1879, of Pope Leo XIII's encyclical *Aeterni patris*, he regarded Lessius as the model of the great Catholic jurist. In his book on the history of the faculty of law at Louvain, Brants took the opportunity to highlight Lessius' influence on the great contemporary jurists. There are so many references to Lessius in his work that, in the index of proper names, Brants omitted Lessius' name, explaining that "some names recur so often that it would be tiresome to assign them a page in the table."[9] While the links between Lessius and the jurists in Louvain often remain less clear than Brants would have wished, Lessius' significant contribution to various branches of legal thought is well established. At the start of the twenty-first century, following in the footsteps of eminent legal historians such as Robert Feenstra and James Gordley, Laurent Waelkens revived legal studies on Lessius at the faculty of law at Louvain, highlighting Lessius' crucial role in the development of contract law.

Although for the past century the image of Lessius as an economist and jurist has been added to his reputation as a theologian, it would be remiss not to mention the recurrent attempts to present him as one of the most devout defenders of the Catholic Church. Efforts to have him beatified, already initiated immediately after his death, were revived in the early twentieth century.[10] As Pope Pius XI, faced with the rise of increasingly authoritarian political regimes in the 1930s, sought to strengthen ecclesiastical power, he rediscovered the Jesuits' contribution to the ancient doctrine of the indirect power of the Church in temporal affairs. On the occasion of the three hundredth anniversary of Lessius' death, Belgian Jesuits launched an offensive to put the beatification of their illustrious predecessor back on the agenda. In 1923, Karel Van Sull published a biography of Lessius that was nothing short of a hagiography.[11] His account focused less on the virtuosity of Lessius' economic thought and more on the mystical circumstances of his consecration as a priest and the absolute sanctity of his exemplary conduct. For Van Sull, Lessius was more of "a new Saint Paul returned from the third heaven." His work referenced the miracles said to have occurred after Lessius' death in the vicinity of the Jesuit church in Kortrijk.

Nevertheless, Van Sull's attempts to beatify, or even canonize, Lessius failed. In 1923, Pope Pius XI decided to elevate Robert Bellarmine to the ranks of the Beatified. The theologian was even declared a saint in 1930, then a Doctor of the Church the following year. The publication of the French version of the biography of Lessius written by Van Sull, that same year, did nothing to change the situation. It came too late to have any influence and failed to promote Lessius' cause. Owing to his too-strong opinions, Lessius' cause may have been compromised by the fact that he was caught up in the controversy over grace and free will at the turn of the seventeenth century (see chapter 9). Lessius' obstinacy in defending a theory of justification based on the merits of man, an obstinacy considered to undermine the sovereignty of the divine will, had already cost him his beatification in the decades following his death (in 1640, Lessius' first biography, which revived this doctrine, was put on the index of prohibited books for this reason).

A Conscious Life Choice

Faced with the danger of anachronisms, it is worth recalling some factual elements in the life of the Oracle of the Low Countries.[12] Born on 1 October 1554 in Brecht, near Antwerp, Lessius lost his parents at the age of six and was put under the guardianship of his uncle Huibrecht, who planned to send him to Antwerp to learn the merchant trade. Nevertheless, Lessius obtained a scholarship in 1567 to study at the University of Louvain. In February 1572, he graduated first in his year and obtained the degree of master of arts, a generalist training that gave access to higher faculties where it was possible to study civil and canon law, medicine, or theology. To the dismay of his family, Lessius decided not to go into business in Antwerp nor to pursue higher education. He joined the Society of Jesus in June 1572. Founded in 1540 by Ignatius of Loyola with the approval of Pope Paul III, the Jesuit order had been present in Louvain since 1542, where it actively recruited among students. It is not inconceivable that Lessius decided to join the young Society following the sermons of Robert Bellarmine, a renowned preacher who was attached to the Jesuit College in Louvain from 1569 to 1576. The sources do not provide any clues as to possible encounters between Lessius and Bellarmine, but given the esteem in which college professors were held by university students, it cannot be ruled out that Lessius attended one or other of his lectures. One can even imagine that Lessius listened to Bellarmine's famous sermon on death, in which he exhorted the Belgians not to neglect spirituality in their lives: "Oh Louvain, Oh Brabant, Oh Belgium, make sure that the cares and worries of this world do not make you forget about death and the Last Judgment!"[13]

In the spiritual literature that he would subsequently produce, Lessius frequently returned to considerations in the same vein, urging young people not to pay too much heed to the advice of their family regarding their life choices. He warned against people's tendency to worry about appearances and material comfort. Since the people around us (family and friends) are mainly haunted by such considerations, we should not pay them too much heed, Lessius warned in his *Disputatio de statu vitae deligendo et religionis ingressu* (*Disputation on the Choice of a State of Life and Entry into Religion*, 1613). The same applies in making life choices as in performing a scientific demonstration: the slightest error in the premise leads to colossal errors in the conclusions.[14] Along with Lessius' other spiritual books, the *Disputation on the Choice of a State of Life* makes it possible to understand the motivations that may have prompted Lessius not to follow his uncle's advice, and thus to join the Jesuits. "The ineptitude of the human mind," he explained in his *Quae fides et religio sit capessenda consultatio* (*Consultation on the Choice to Be Made in Matters of Faith and Religion*, 1609), "consists in its unconcern for anything that touches eternal salvation, while its preoccupations and inventiveness in temporal and fleeting things are beyond the imagination."[15] Invoking the wisdom of pagan philosophers such as Plato, he considered the Christian religion to be the supreme philosophy, in that it prompts us to renewed meditation on our mortal condition: "The best way to deliberate on what we must do begins with a consideration of death and eternal judgment."[16]

Lessius would have had plenty of opportunities to meditate on death during his novitiate at Saint-Omer, which he left in October 1574 to go to the college of Anchin, at Douai. At the time, this city played a major role in King Philip II's efforts to form an intellectual front against Protestantism. He founded a new Catholic university there in 1562 to rival the university in Louvain, which was considered too exposed to the Protestant threat. The Jesuits made their contribution to the building by founding the college of Anchin. The burial of Boetius Epo, a renowned professor of law, in the Jesuit church at Douai, testifies to the close ties that must have existed between the elites there. It cannot be ruled out that Lessius met Epo in person in Douai, whose motto was "working hard, the trident is nevertheless happy." Epo was also the author of an edition of the *Προγνωστικῶν* (*Prognosticon futuri saeculi*) by Archbishop Julian of Toledo (ca. 642–690), a fundamental work in the history of the development of Christian dogma concerning death, the hereafter, and the last judgment.[17] Even if the sources do not provide any clues as to possible encounters between Lessius and Epo, it has been established that his journey to Douai allowed Lessius to learn the basics of civil and canon law, while teaching Aristotelian philosophy at the college of Anchin.

The School of Salamanca

From 1582, Lessius continued his theological studies at the Jesuit college in Liège, a city within a principality that was a haven of peace compared to the Netherlands, which was in the grip of revolution against Spanish dominance. Between May 1583 and April 1584, he stayed at the *Collegio Romano*, the Jesuit college in Rome, which received support from Pope Gregory XIII. His master's degree in theology, considered the queen of sciences, opened the door to a career as a professor at the Jesuit College of Louvain. From 1585 to 1600, Lessius taught courses based on the various parts of the famous *Summa Theologica* of Thomas Aquinas, of which the second part of the second volume (*Secunda secundae*) is devoted to questions of law and Christian morality. This commentary formed the basis of his works, including the treatise *On Justice and Law*. Notes from the lectures taken between 1593 and 1595, when Lessius was dispensing his commentaries on the *Secunda secundae*, testify to the prominent role of Spanish authors in the efforts to update

Thomistic theology. In this regard, Lessius followed the approach of Bellarmine, whose teachings in Louvain were based on a reading of the *Summa Theologica* combined with an analysis of the treatise *On Justice and Law* by Domingo de Soto and the *Manual for Confessors* by Martín de Azpilcueta (also known as Dr. Navarrus).

The works of de Soto and Azpilcueta take us back to the epicentre of the renewal of sixteenth-century scholastic theology in the School of Salamanca. Even more than other European universities, Salamanca witnessed the renaissance of a hybrid Thomism. Characterized by a more practical approach to resolving moral questions, this theology strengthened the legal foundations of moral reasoning. While this phenomenon was particularly strong in Spain, it was not the preserve of the most powerful empire of the day.[18] Around 1500, Konrad Summenhart, a theologian from Tübingen, published his voluminous *Opus septipertitum de contractibus* (*Treatise in Seven Parts on Contracts*). The synthesis between legal and moral traditions, already typical of the medieval summas for confessors and of the *Tractatus de contractibus* (*Treatise on Contracts*, 1294), of the Franciscan Peter of John Olivi,[19] manifested itself with a new vigour. Summenhart became one of the favourite authors of Francisco de Vitoria, a Dominican theologian regarded as the founder of the School of Salamanca in the 1520s.[20] Vitoria taught Domingo de Soto in Salamanca, where they met at the Convento de San Estebán, the magnificent convent of Dominican friars, many of whom taught at the nearby university.

By replacing Peter Lombard's *Libri IV Sententiarum* (*Four Books of Sentences*) with Thomas Aquinas' *Summa Theologica* as the basic textbook for theology courses, the Dominican friars contributed to the revival of their illustrious predecessor's philosophy. This phenomenon emerged at the end of the fifteenth century, before being given a boost when Tommaso de Vio, commonly known as Thomas Cajetan, took over the reins of the Dominican order. Besides having based his teaching of theology in Pavia between 1497 and 1499 on Thomas Aquinas, Cajetan published a commentary on the *Summa Theologica* between 1508 and 1523 which is still a reference today. As for Vitoria, he witnessed this renewal of the discipline when he studied theology in Paris, under the auspices of Peter Crockaert. In 1512, Vitoria contributed to the publication of Crockaert's commentaries on the *Secunda secundae*.

When he began teaching in Salamanca in 1526, Francisco de Vitoria adopted the new Thomistic methods he had learned in Paris, while combining them with the Scotist theological traditions and the heritage of medieval canon law. Although Thomistic currents had already been present in Salamanca since the fifteenth century, the arrival of Vitoria led to an unprecedented passion for Thomas Aquinas, which gave rise to the revival of a hybrid Thomism relayed by Vitoria and his many direct and indirect pupils, who ended up establishing a veritable school: the so-called School of Salamanca, of which Vitoria and his pupil, Domingo de Soto, were among the founding teachers. Soto joined the faculty of theology in 1532, after studying philosophy and theology in Paris and at Alcalá de Henares. With the publication of his treatise *De iustitia et iure* (1553–1554), taken from his commentaries on the *Secunda secundae*, Soto laid the foundations of a new literary genre that would be highly successful, in particular among the Jesuits.

Far from being confined to the field of theology, the revival of the Thomistic current driven by Vitoria and de Soto quickly crossed the boundaries of disciplines. Martín de Azpilcueta, a major source of inspiration for Lessius, is a good example. A doctor of canon law, Azpilcueta taught this subject in Salamanca from 1524, before being transferred to the University of Coimbra in 1538, at the request of Emperor Charles V. An expert in high demand among the Portuguese elite, he was subsequently appointed advisor to the popes and to the Apostolic Penitentiary in Rome, the supreme tribunal where cases of conscience were heard. Azpilcueta's legal works are full of references to the moral theology characteristic of the School of Salamanca. A quarter of his famous *Manual for Confessors and Penitents* is devoted to economic ethics. Within the Society of Jesus, his *Manual* circulated as one of the most popular works in the training of future priests for their pastoral mission. The book was a gold mine for Leonardus Lessius, who drew directly from it in his commentaries on the *Summa Theologica* and in the organization of practical sessions for resolving cases of conscience.

Following the example of Bellarmine, Lessius worked assiduously to bring the ideas of Soto, Azpilcueta, and the other theologians of Salamanca to the Low Countries. Together with his friend Johannes Hamelius, a lawyer by training who had studied theology at the *Collegio Romano* at the same time as Lessius, he decided to use the *Summa Theologica* as a reference manual, while drawing inspiration from reading the great thinkers of Salamanca. The friction between the Jesuit College and the university theologians, caused by both conflicts of interest and doctrinal differences, continued to grow. In any event, Lessius was making an impression. Confronted with the painful realization that more and more students were attending his lectures, the university's Faculty of Theology also decided in 1596 to adopt the *Summa Theologica* as a reference manual. A new professorship in scholastic theology was created, entrusted to Johannes Malderus. Officially enrolled in the Faculty of Theology, Malderus had attended Lessius' lectures. His *Commentaries on the Theological Virtues, Justice, and Religion according to the* Secunda secundae *of Thomas Aquinas*, published in Antwerp by Plantin-Moretus in 1616, bears witness to this. When Malderus left the scholastic theology professorship to become bishop of Antwerp, his successor Johannes Wiggers, a major proponent of the theology of Augustine and defender of the famous bishop of Ypres Cornelius Jansenius, continued the tradition. In contrast, in Wiggers' treatise *On Law, Justice and the Other Cardinal Virtues*, references to Lessius are rare, or even non-existent. Wiggers was indeed fiercely opposed to the Jesuits, and to Lessius in particular. The striking similarities between his treatise and Lessius', at least in terms of their structure, are no less remarkable.

A Jesuit

The conflict between Leonardus Lessius and the theologians of the university went back to the origins of his teaching at Louvain. In a nutshell, Lessius' concern with the value of personal liberty and his meritocratic instincts quickly irritated theologians, who were more attracted by the anthropological pessimism of Augustine than by the positive affirmation of human nature typical of Thomas Aquinas. This tension came to a head in 1587–1588, when Lessius was forced to defend himself against accusations of "semi-Pelagianism" hurled at him by the theologians—Pelagius (ca. 350–ca. 420), whose contentions were deemed heretical, claimed that mankind could attain salvation by itself, thereby relativising the role of divine grace (see chapter 9, p. 143). The rivalry between the Jesuit college and the university in attracting the largest number of students only exacerbated these doctrinal tussles, which required papal intervention.[21] The Pope forbade the theologians of Louvain from continuing to condemn each other, without proposing a real solution to the problem of the relationship between grace and free will.

Faced with the dangers of Protestantism, the Jesuits insisted above all on the essential role of human freedom in obtaining eternal salvation. They proposed a general, optimistic vision of humankind, which had the capacity to "merit" its salvation. As Ignatius of Loyola noted in his *Spiritual Exercises* (1548), the Protestant doctrine of predestination without consideration for merit (*merita*) carried with it the risk of defeatism.[22] It is worth underlining here the extent to which Lessius was an advocate of a meritocratic idea of spiritual salvation. In his eyes, God can only save the chosen based on an evaluation of their merits. As such, Lessius tried to reconcile God's omniscience with his respect for human freedom. This is the central theme of his apologetic disputation *De gratia efficaci, decretis divinis, libertate arbitrii et praescientia Dei conditionata* (*On Efficacious Grace, Divine Decrees, Free Will, and God's Conditioned Prescience*, 1610), which contained in appendix two disputations, respectively *De praedestinatione et reprobatione angelorum et hominum* (*On the Predestination and Reprobation of Angels and Men*) and *De praedestinatione Christi* (*On the Predestination of Christ*). This major book was published by Jean Moretus in Antwerp, in 1610, after several years of debate with the censor, and it continued to prompt controversy thereafter. Bellarmine, who had defended Lessius against the accusations made by Janssonius in the late 1580s, was sceptical. Claudio Acquaviva, the Superior General of the Society of Jesus, believed that Lessius' opinions were even more difficult to defend than those of Luis de Molina.[23]

But Lessius was not about to change his opinions. Despite the criticism, he repeated his viewpoint in the treatise *De perfectionibus moribusque divinis* (*On the Divine Perfections and Morals*, 1620). Here, as was the case regarding his views on the morality of the market, he continued to defend a vision of humankind based on the rewarding of merit.[24] This attention to the work of man is also reflected in his innovative opinions on the inspired character of biblical writings. According to Lessius, it is possible, and even historically proven, that texts written by man, based on his own industry, can become true holy and biblical texts after subsequent validation by the Holy Spirit—he was thinking in particular of the second book of Maccabees.[25]

Undoubtedly, Lessius promoted a vision of man that made him master of his own destiny. It is a vision that he defended all the more vigorously because he believed it was necessary in the fight against the heresies of his day. In various writings with an apologetic slant, he attempted to demonstrate the superiority of Catholicism over the Protestant sects, while defending the privileges of the Supreme Pontiff, to whom, it should be remembered, the Jesuits are bound by a specific vow of obedience. In addition to his *Consultation on the Choice to Be Made in Matters of Faith and Religion*, already mentioned above, Lessius confronted Lutherans, Calvinists, and Anglicans in *De Antichristo et eius praecursoribus*, a disputation *On the Antichrist and His Predecessors* (1611) to which he added an appendix *De Calvino* (*On Calvin*). The major subject of this work is the refutation of the accusation of King James I of England against the pope, whom he claimed was the reincarnation of the antichrist. In addition, Lessius produced a *Defence of Papal Power* (*Defensio potestatis Summi Pontificis*, 1611), which he also developed through an analysis of the importance of the Fourth Lateran Council (*Discussio decreti Magni Concilii Lateranensis*, 1613) concerning the cure of souls and the regular practice of confession.

To stimulate the virtuous industry of Christians in their daily lives, Lessius found it important to emphasize the mystical nature of existence. In 1613 he published a manifesto highlighting the divine character of nature and its providential government: in the apologia *De providentia numinis et animi immortalitate* (*On Divine Providence and the Immortality of the Soul*), which incorporates Neoplatonic and Stoic ideas, he urged his readers to observe the mystical character of nature, in particular the cosmos, the stars, the plants, the animals, and man, creatures worthy of all glory and admiration. This mystical tone is also found in his treatise *De summo bono et aeterna beatitudine hominis* (*On the Supreme Good and Eternal Beatitude of Man*, 1616). After his death in 1623, a summary of his mystical philosophy was published under the title *Quinquaginta nomina Dei seu divinarum perfectionum compendiaria expositio* (*The Fifty Names of God*, 1640), the title alone recalling the work on the divine names of Pseudo-Dionysius the Areopagite, a spiritual author of the early fifth century, some of whose works Lessius is said to have translated. Moreover, Lessius authored an *Apologia pro scriptoribus mysticae theologiae* (*Apologia of the Authors of Mystical Theology*) which has been lost to posterity.

True to the message of Ignatius of Loyola, Lessius was first and foremost a Jesuit who did everything he could to help humanity perceive the divine signature in Creation. In the prefaces to his works, it is often a question of reaching the reader via feelings and emotions, "affects," rather than overwhelming him or her with speculative and dry reasoning. This intimacy touches the deepest part of Ignatian spirituality.[26] The aim is simple: to move humankind, to get in touch with the most intimate space inside its being, so that we are moved and are ready to act. With our will and strength, in effect, humankind must actively cooperate with divine grace in order to do good works, by offering succour to the poor, giving thanks to God, and renouncing ourselves. In short, it is a question of encouraging everyone to be just, prudent, moderate, and courageous, and to participate in the economy of salvation (see chapter 9). For Lessius, a sober life was highly conducive to achieving this ideal. In his *Hygiasticon* of 1613, a book on nutrition translated into several languages, he proposed recipes for healthy eating and drinking in order to grow old without losing mental and physical capacities (see chapter 10). At the same time, these recipes for sobriety made it possible to regain the physical condition that is essential for leading a spiritual life. As an analysis of how to combine this spirituality with participation in active life, Lessius wrote his great treatise *On Justice and Law*. It is this major work that we will extensively draw on in the following chapters to decipher the economic thought of the Oracle of the Low Countries.

2

The Shadow of Max Weber

I expressly reject the possibility of the absurd thesis that the Reformation alone . . . created the capitalist spirit.

—Max Weber

We cannot embark on an investigation of the theological foundations of economic thought without evoking the name of Max Weber, the great German jurist and legal historian who is regarded as the founding father of modern sociology.[1] His linking of the relationship between religion and economics in the world's great cultures remains impressive, by its breadth as much as by its scientific rigour.[2] But it is above all Weber's work on the impact of the English Puritan sects on the rise of capitalism in the West, set out in *The Protestant Ethic and the Spirit of Capitalism* (1904–1905), that has most appealed to the collective imagination. The tidal wave of controversies and the widely diverging interpretations of this work mean that the ins and outs of the Weberian assertions cannot be analysed in detail here.[3] Nor can we dwell on Weber's exceptional essays on the workings of political careers, the intrigues of academic life, or the functioning of the law in modern Western societies. Instead, we propose returning to the sources in the double sense of a rediscovery of some key fragments of *The Protestant Ethic* and a reappraisal of its methodological intuition. Weber's methodological intuition has received little consideration in the literature, but it primarily consists of examining the literature of cases of conscience, considered by Weber as the royal road to rediscovering the religious foundations of the rise of capitalism.

"Protestantism" and "Capitalism"

The fascination which *The Protestant Ethic* holds for readers has often misled them. Contrary to the pervasive image, Max Weber did not try to establish a monocausal or an exclusive relationship between the Protestant faith and the rise of the capitalist system. As the quotation at the

Money, Markets, and Merit. Wim Decock, Oxford University Press. © Oxford University Press (2025).
DOI: 10.1093/9780197827345.003.0003

beginning of this chapter, taken from a letter to Karl Fischer,[4] one of his critics, shows, he was fully aware of the existence of other factors—material and spiritual—which may have contributed to the rise of the capitalist spirit. Weber admitted that essential forms of capitalist activity preceded the Reformation, just as he recognized the contribution of certain scholastics, even Jesuits, to the development of the capitalist spirit. In the second edition of his work, published in 1920, Weber inserts explicit references to Bernardine of Siena and Antonine of Florence, two medieval scholastic theologians.[5] Weber acknowledged the "relatively friendly" positions of Bernardine and Antonine to industry and capital.[6] By way of comparison, he characterizes Martin Luther's anti-capitalist ideas as "definitely backward."[7] On the other hand, he sees in Bernardine and Antonine the precursors of the Jesuits, whose "liberal utilitarian compromise with the world"[8] he highlights. He also admits that rationalized asceticism found its full strength in the Jesuit order.[9] In his study "On the Psychophysics of Industrial Work," which was based on his empirical observations in 1908 of how the textile factory belonging to his wife's family operated, he suggests that modern Catholicism, unlike the situation in the Middle Ages, can clearly have the same effect on the conduct of life—and more precisely on what he calls "the domestication of workers"—as Protestant asceticism.[10]

Weber's assertion was therefore more nuanced than the caricature that has been made of it suggests. Moreover, his understanding of Protestantism did not start from a homogeneous vision of the Reformation. Only Protestant sects of an "ascetic" nature, such as the English Puritans, were considered by Weber as vectors of a "conduct of life" adequate to the spirit of capitalism. The reference to the Protestant ethic in the title of his book does not include Lutheranism or German pietism. Despite his fundamental contribution to the Protestant ethic through his revolutionary concept of the profession as a vocation, Weber did not regard Martin Luther and his followers as promoters of the spirit of capitalism, because they were not sufficiently "ascetic." For Weber, a jurist by training, this asceticism is synonymous with system, order, formalism, method, and rationalism, as Peter Ghosh[11] has shown. Taking as an example the treatise *Ta Askètika sive exercitia pietatis* (*Ascetic Practices or Exercises of Piety*, 1664) by Gijsbert Voet, founder of the "Nadere Reformatie" (an even more rigorous form of Calvinism in the Netherlands), Weber believes that the rationalization of the conduct of life, a prerequisite for the rise of the capitalist spirit, reached its apogee in the Puritan ascetic experience. While in the first instance he encountered this asceticism in medieval monasteries, which explained their economic success,[12] he believed that it was not until the emergence of the Puritan sects that asceticism spread to the outside world, in the exercise of professional activities: "And this asceticism was no longer an *opus supererogationis*, but something which could be required of everyone who would be certain of salvation. The religious life of the saints, as distinguished from the natural life, was—the most important point—no longer lived outside the world in monastic communities, but within the world and its institutions. This rationalization of conduct within this world, but for the sake of the world beyond, was the consequence of the concept of calling of ascetic Protestantism."[13]

While the notion of "Protestantism," in Weber's thought, deserves a nuanced approach, this is also (or even more so) the case when it comes to understanding what he intended to express by the term "capitalism." Despite the conspicuous absence of a definition of the "spirit of capitalism," Weber takes the opposite view of a rather popular concept of capitalism as the insatiable pursuit of money, unbridled consumption, and unlimited pleasure. He considers that those unscrupulous businessmen who submit to the desire to make money as to an uncontrolled impulse lead an irrational life, incompatible with what he conceives as the ascetic spirit of capitalism. Even if he avoids giving a clear and unambiguous definition, Weber offers an illustration of what he means by the "spirit of capitalism" by referring to Benjamin Franklin's *Advice to a Young Tradesman* (1748). These recommendations are full of references to the need for virtuous, sober, and controlled living, so that the tradesman can enhance his credibility. As such, the tradesman must above all be a prompt payer and a disciplined man. He must ensure that promises are kept and that he observes his contracts with the greatest fidelity: "After industry and frugality, nothing contributes more to the raising of a young man in the world than punctuality and justice in all his dealings. Therefore, never keep borrowed money an hour beyond the time you promised, lest a disappointment shut up your friend's purse forever."[14]

For Weber, the unscrupulous merchant does not embody the spirit of capitalism. The "sacred hunger for gold," *auri sacra fames*, is, in his own words, as old as the history of man, and is not unique to the modern spirit of capitalism. It has existed in all periods of history, in all places, and in all possible ways, without constituting the distinctive mark of modern capitalism as a mass phenomenon.[15] The type of man who has made modern capitalism possible pursues the endless accumulation of his wealth not to enjoy it without limits, but to give expression to his obedience to his professional calling, understood as the commandment of God. For this man, the accumulation of capital is not the result of a frantic race towards a life without concerns and full of luxury. It is the fruit of the faithful fulfilment of the task that God has set for him, for his glory and that of humanity. It is a work conceived as a duty, accomplished in a rational way, and not a passion, propelled by uncontrolled impulses. For this man, every idle hour is taken away from work dedicated to the glory of God.[16] On the other hand, a man should not waste his time doing work that does not correspond to his calling: "What God demands is not labour in itself, but rational labour in a calling. In the Puritan concept of the calling the emphasis is always placed on this methodical character of worldly ascetism, not, as with Luther, on the acceptance of the lot which God has irretrievably assigned to man."[17]

Work, conceived as a calling, is a service to God. Thanks to his devotion and asceticism, the Puritan manages to work hard to enhance both the glory of God and his wealth, without taking advantage. Possessions are not regarded as suspicious in themselves, but only insofar as they involve the risk of a form of idle inactivity.[18] As Weber underscores, Puritan moralists oppose enjoying possessions, but not accumulating them.[19] They denounce the consumption of goods, not their increase per se. The result is the accumulation of colossal capital by continual saving.[20] As such, the spirit of Christian asceticism, reserved for monks in the medieval tradition, but generalized to the population as a whole under the effect of the Reformation, is one of the constitutive elements of the modern capitalist spirit.[21] According to Weber, there is nevertheless a difference between a Puritan and a modern individual: the former submitted to the disciplined fulfilment of his professional calling according to his own will and beliefs, while the latter is forced to submit to a capitalist logic now stripped of all reference to a divine Providence.[22]

Political-Ideological Considerations

While the conduct of a rational and methodical life, the deeply theological roots of which he highlighted, is seen by Weber as a necessary condition for the rise of the modern capitalist ethos, the controversy generated by his work was anything but sober and ascetic. Criticism and counter-criticism were quickly forthcoming. Weber personally responded to two German controversialists, Karl Fischer and Felix Rachfahl, on two occasions. He deemed it necessary to conclude his second reply to a second attack by Fischer with a quote from the economist Georg Friedrich Knapp: "I certainly don't like to see it written in black and white that I am an ass. But I also take no pleasure when someone believes that it should be printed that I am not an ass."[23] Clearly, the debates around *The Protestant Ethic* quickly took an emotional and polemical turn. Beyond questions of ego, which do not only afflict academics, the political climate also certainly made a contribution, at a time when nationalist fervour, often accompanied by religious identity, was raging. Regardless of the true nature of his religious and nationalist sentiments, which are often put forward as crucial in reading Weber's works.[24] it is important to consider the general atmosphere in which Weber's great work on the links between capitalism and Protestantism saw the light of day.

At the end of the nineteenth century, various texts emerged which explained economic progress according to whether or not the nations of Europe had adopted the Protestant religion. One of the leading figures of this movement was the Belgian jurist Émile de Laveleye, whose pioneering work is acknowledged by Weber in his introduction to *The Protestant Ethic*.[25] The scion of a wealthy family in Bruges, de Laveleye earned his reputation as co-founder of the Institute of International Law and as a professor of political economy at the University of Liège,[26] but he was also the author of a controversial article entitled "Le protestantisme et le catholicisme dans leurs rapports avec la liberté et la prospérité des peuples"[27] (*Protestantism and Catholicism in Their Relation to the Liberty and Prosperity of Nations*). Published in 1875, five years after the first Vatican Council, at which Pope Pius IX successfully established the principle of papal infallibility as an official dogma against the backdrop of the decline of the Church's temporal power, the article was an opportunity for de Laveleye to reiterate his wish that Belgium abandon its allegiance to Rome. But the reasons for Laveleye's aversion to Rome go beyond the simple fear of civil liberties being oppressed by a Roman theocracy. The interest in Protestantism also reflects the trauma prompted by the defeat of France in the Franco-Prussian War of 1870. This debacle was attributed after the fact to the excessive ideological influence of Catholics on the French politics of the Second Empire.[28] Terrified of witnessing the "decadence of the Latin races" that he observed in France, Italy, and Spain, de Laveleye was of the opinion that it was not "on account of the blood that flows in their veins" that "the Latin races" were condemned to economic decline, but rather because of their adherence to the Catholic faith.[29] In order to safeguard the material prosperity of "the Latin races," it is therefore necessary that these countries abandon their Catholic faith and replace it with the Protestant religion: "Wherever the two religions exist together in the same country, the Protestants are more active, more industrious, more economical, and consequently richer, than the Catholics. . . . In the presence of all these concurring facts, it is difficult not to confess that it is religion, and not race, which is the cause of the extraordinary prosperity of certain nations."[30] By his own admission, it was the observation of the economic superiority of the Protestant regions that led Max Weber, in turn, to analyse the religious foundations of economic prosperity. The very first sentence of *The Protestant Ethic* testifies to this: "A glance at the occupational statistics of any country of mixed religious composition brings to light with remarkable frequency a situation which has several times provoked discussion in the Catholic press and literature, and in Catholic congresses in Germany, namely, the fact that business leaders and owners of capital, as well as the higher grades of skilled labour, and even more the higher technically and commercially trained personnel of modern enterprises, are overwhelmingly Protestant."[31]

Max Weber seems to have wanted to limit himself to a scientific explanation of this discrepancy between Catholic and Protestant cultures, without any obvious ambition to demonstrate, at all costs, the superiority of Protestantism over Catholicism. But the context of rivalry among confessional denominations and political nations in which the first version of the first and second parts of his work were published, in 1904–1905, meant that they couldn't help prompting controversy. It would be vain to mention even the tip of the iceberg of these endless debates, which have been the subject of a vast scholarly literature. Let us recall that Sylvain Piron asserted that "certain Protestant theologians could resent being associated with the rise of the cult of Mammon, while Catholic historians, frustrated at feeling left out of modernity, tried to assert the existence of a spirit of capitalism in medieval Christianity."[32]

Among the Catholics critical of Weber's overlooking of the Catholic spirit of capitalism was the economist Hector Menteith Robertson, author, in 1933, of a study on the fundamental contribution of the Jesuits to the spirit of capitalism. In it, he demonstrates, in detail, that the Jesuits approved of modern financial practices still considered usurious by Calvinists.[33] But the reception of Robertson's book in Catholic circles speaks volumes about how little interest there was, and still is, in regarding Catholics as the first advocates of capitalism. In 1934, the Irish Jesuit James Brodrick published a book that sought to destroy Robertson's contentions.[34] Brodrick welcomed the popularity of Weber's assertion that Catholics and his order in particular had nothing to do with the origin of the spirit of capitalism. In the 1930s, the Catholic Church was happy to distance itself from a system which, a few years earlier in 1929, had led to an unprecedented financial crisis. In *Quadragesimo Anno*, Pope Pius XI's 1931 encyclical written in response to the Great Depression, solidarity was put forward as the supreme virtue of Catholic social thought. Written by the German Jesuit Oswald von Nell-Breuning, the assertions of *Quadragesimo Anno* did not fit well with Robertson's observations regarding the individualistic and capitalist tendencies of Jesuit economic ethics at the turn of the seventeenth century. Similarly, in his influential 1934 book, *Catholicism, Protestantism and Capitalism*, the young Catholic Amintore Fanfani, a leading figure in Italian Christian democracy after the Second World War, was happy to blame Protestants for blind capitalism. That was the opinion of Michael Novak, an American Catholic theologian praising the spirit of capitalism, which he understood essentially as an economic system that gives free rein to man's creativity.[35] There are therefore divergent conceptions of capitalism, not only with regard to its origins, but also its very definition.[36]

An Unfinished Methodology

The controversies prompted by *The Protestant Ethic* invite us to return to a methodological instinct that underpins the book. Regardless of the validity or invalidity of the conclusions Weber makes, it is worth drawing attention to the sources that constitute the starting point of his scientific approach. To understand the relationship between religious beliefs and economic ideas, Weber explains,[37] "it is necessary to examine with special care such writings as have evidently been derived from ministerial practice." In the German original, the term "ministerial practice" (*seelsorgerische Praxis*) refers more clearly to literature that reflects pastors' care of souls. Moreover, the original text calls this literature theological in nature (*solche theologische Schriften*), whereas Parsons' translation has wiped out the explicit reference to theology. As examples of this theological literature, Weber mentions the literature on cases of conscience (*casus conscientiae*). He insists that pastoral practice, the fruit of premodern man's preoccupation with the afterlife, has had a lasting effect on Western culture. To this observation he adds, somewhat disillusioned, that the reason of modern man lacks the strength to grasp the enormous impact that the religious imagination has had on daily life. At the end of *The Protestant Ethic*, he even admitted that "the modern man is in general, even with the best will, unable to give religious ideas a significance for culture and national character which they deserve."[38] He repeated this observation in 1906 in an article on "Protestant Churches and Sects in North America," stating that modern men lack a "musical ear" for religion: they are barely able to imagine or simply to believe what a powerful role these religious factors played in the periods when the "characters of the high cultured nations of modern times" were forged. And, yet, he warned that in those times when concern for the afterlife was the most real thing for men, these religious aspects cast their shadow over everything.[39]

As mentioned, Max Weber refers here to the *responsa* and *casus conscientiae* literature, the collections of responses to cases of conscience, as privileged witnesses of this concern and of the major impact of pastors as experts and spiritual advisors. An analysis of this literature is at the heart of Weber's methodology. For example, Weber criticizes Karl Fischer for not understanding the results of his investigation, due to his lack of understanding of this methodological basis: "He simply does not know that the sources that were decisive for my analysis of the influence on the conduct of life . . . are derived from collections of *responsa* that refer directly to highly concrete questions addressed to a priest (who was at the time by far the most universal advisor that any period of history had ever known)."[40] The methodology proposed by Weber may take the modern, Western reader, who is often no longer used to religious references, away from his comfort zone, but it has the merit of bringing us closer to the soul that has inspired European society and its economic thought for centuries. In this light, the relevance of the methodological precaution of Giorgio Agamben is revealed, for whom any intellectual historical investigation must take into account the possibility that the genealogy of a concept can be located in a sphere quite different from that envisaged at the outset.[41] The vast literature on cases of conscience, from medieval *summae confessorum* to the directories of Puritan pastors to the manuals *On Justice and Law* of the theologians of the School of Salamanca, lays bare what Harold Berman referred to as the "belief systems" that underpinned economic life prior to the modern era.

However, in *The Protestant Ethic*, Weber only lifts the tip of the veil concealing the hundreds of thousands of pages of literature on cases of conscience that has been bequeathed to us.[42] Far from exhausting the enormous potential of his methodology, he limits himself to a preliminary investigation based on a small selection of authors belonging to Puritanical-leaning Protestant sects. By his own admission, Weber confined himself essentially to reading the *Christian Directory* (1673) of the Presbyterian minister Richard Baxter, a book he considered "the most complete compendium of Puritan ethics."[43] While Weber does not go any further, it is nevertheless interesting to note that this work bears witness to his intense reading of Jesuit casuistry, a sign of the circulation of Catholic casuistic literature across denominational boundaries in England.[44] Baxter openly admits that the rules of his own ascetic life are directly inspired by the advice dispensed by Catholic moral theologians. Moreover, he expressly refers to Leonardus Lessius' *Hygiasticon*.[45] In his list of recommended authors at the end of the third part of his book, Baxter includes Juan Azor, a Jesuit and author of the *Moral Institutes*, a seminal handbook of Catholic moral theology, and Martín de Azpilcueta, author of the *Manual for Confessors and Penitents*, one the most successful penitential handbooks in the Catholic tradition.

Weber was aware of the limits of his undertaking. On several occasions, he refers to the publications of his colleague and friend Ernst Troeltsch on the historical development of the social doctrines of the Christian churches, to delve deeper into the subject in question. Conversely, apart from the few references to Bernardine of Siena and Antonine of Florence in the second edition of *The Protestant Ethic*, the vast Catholic literature on cases of conscience generally remained a blind spot. The ideological struggles between Protestants and Catholics in the Germany of his day, which gave rise to a veritable "culture war" (*Kulturkampf*), as well as the assertion that Protestant churches were superior, are also relevant. With little in the way of nuance, Weber looks down upon the writings of Catholic scholars such as the jurist Wilhelm Endemann, author of two volumes of studies on the history of economic and legal doctrines in the Catholic Church, which have become "obsolete in certain points."[46] Is it possible, however, that beyond his antipathy to Catholics, Weber was simply discouraged by the enormous body of literature on cases of conscience at the dawn of the modern age? Writing his history of Christian morality in 1808, the Lutheran theologian Karl Friedrich Stäudlin admitted that the mere confrontation with this huge quantity of texts discouraged even the most tenacious individual from investigating the literature of cases of conscience in the Catholic countries of the sixteenth and seventeenth centuries.[47] Yet this is what we have to do in order to complete Max Weber's investigation.

3

Keeping Promises

One binds oxen by the horns,
and men by words.

—Antoine Loysel

When addressing the question of what the spirit of capitalism looks like, Max Weber avoids giving an abstract definition. Yet the passages he quotes from Benjamin Franklin's *Advice to a Young Tradesman*—where we find the famous phrase "time is money"—are meant to illustrate what he understood by the "spirit of capitalism." Franklin insisted on the fact that success in business is a matter of trust and credibility: the credit that the merchant enjoys is the result of his respecting his commitments. By scrupulously keeping his promises, the young tradesman quickly learns that a word given and kept is trust earned, and therefore money. "Remember this Saying," explains Franklin, "That the good Paymaster is Lord of another Man's Purse."[1] Respecting conventions gives the merchant more credibility. As such, this is where we see the intimate, but fragile, link between credit and trust, contracts and commerce, fidelity and prosperity. This link leads us to the heart of the economic and legal thought of the scholastic theologians. Fully aware that the market is first and foremost an edifice built on the dogma of keeping promises, it is through the law of contracts that these theologians grasped commercial exchanges. This chapter proposes exploring the religious roots of what Alain Supiot described as one of the great dogmatic foundations of the market economy: the belief in the power of keeping promises.[2] This belief is manifested in the imperative that agreements must be kept: *pactum serva.*

The Binding Force of Promises

It was in 1188, in commentaries written by Huguccio and Bernard of Pavia on Gratian's *Decretum*, that the classic adage *pacta sunt servanda* first

Money, Markets, and Merit. Wim Decock, Oxford University Press. © Oxford University Press (2025).
DOI: 10.1093/9780197827345.003.0004

appeared: "Agreements must be kept." In its more complete version, *pacta quantumcumque nuda servanda sunt*, it states that "agreements, however 'naked,' must be respected." In this form, the adage appears at the head of the canon *Antigonus* in the *Liber Extra*, the collection of canon law promulgated in 1234 by Pope Gregory IX, which incorporated decisions and laws by medieval councils and popes. The clergy gathered at the Council of Carthage (348) were called upon to settle a dispute between Antigonus and Optantius, two bishops involved in a dispute over the boundaries of their respective dioceses. According to the council, an agreement concerning these boundaries, made a few years earlier between Antigonus and Optantius, had to be honoured, as peace could only be guaranteed on the condition of strict compliance with the agreements.[3] The inclusion of this decision in the medieval canon law tradition marks the point where canon law broke away from the civil law tradition. Civil law was based on the Roman law of the Emperor Justinian, which dated back to the early sixth century. In effect, the "nakedness" of the agreements referred to in the full version of the adage (*pacta quantumcumque nuda servanda sunt*) refers to a passage in Justinian's Digests where binding force is denied to simple agreements, also referred to as "naked agreements."[4] Roman law reserves the binding force of simple exchanges of consent to a highly specific category of agreements, namely *contractus consensu*: sale, hire, partnership, and mandate. It does not provide for contracts in a generic and abstract way. To be effective before the courts, agreements other than *contractus consensu* require "clothing" beyond consent, such as the transfer of the promised item, or the use of certain solemn formulas. According to a metaphor widely used among medieval jurists to explain Roman contract law, naked agreements became rigid, like a naked body. They could only protect themselves from the immobilizing effects of the cold by warming themselves with the help of the heat provided by clothing. When Roman law was received in medieval universities, long lists of "clothes" capable of "warming" and therefore "substantiating" the binding force of simple agreements were drawn up.

Among the most popular clothing suitable for warming up naked agreements is the oath, considered by many medieval civil law practitioners to be the most appropriate garment for giving binding force to all kinds of naked agreements. By invoking God as a witness of the promise made, the effectiveness of the promise could be ensured in all circumstances. The oath had the power to bring the contractual domain into the religious domain. As such, God could be invoked as the guarantor of simple agreements. At the same time, a shift in the understanding of simple promises and oaths was about to take place. Indeed, medieval canonists were less and less inclined to see oaths as "clothes" existing purely outside of simple agreements. Instead, in the light of the Gospel, they felt that in the eyes of God, the simple promise included the force and credibility of a sworn promise. Therefore, there was no reason to differentiate the binding force of the oath from the simple promise. For religious reasons, the legal value of the simple promise of a Christian had to be the same as that of an oath—otherwise the Christian was in danger of lying, and therefore of committing a mortal sin. In accordance with the Lord's words in the Gospel of Matthew (5:33–37), a higher degree of reliability was required on the part of Christians, whose "yes" has to be a "yes" and "no" a "no." Consequently, it was no longer necessary to assert the necessity of adding clothing, such as an oath, to a simple agreement, since the simple promise was already supposed to have the force of a sworn undertaking. Jesus called on his disciples to no longer make any oaths, and to undertake to honour their promises without invoking the name of God. The simple exchange of words was enough for the agreement to become strong, stable, and effective: "And this is the reason why God does not want there to be any difference between our oath and our word: just as perfidy is not appropriate in the oath, so lies must be absent from our words. According to the biblical phrases, perjury and lying are punishable by divine judgement: 'a lying mouth destroys the soul.'"[5]

Drawing on Gratian's *Decretum*, which was itself influenced by biblical texts, the canonists established consensualism as a general principle of contract law. By virtue of the promise made, agreements must be respected, no matter how naked. Every agreement based on free consent is identified by canonists and theologians as a contract binding the individuals involved, before the law. It has the binding force of a sworn agreement. Conscious of tackling lies, rooting out sin, and promoting peace, the canonists reversed the Roman principle that naked agreements have no binding force.

Of course, the Romans recognized the moral value of keeping one's word. The writings of the major Roman rhetoricians and writers are full of references to the idea that keeping one's word is an essential moral requirement for living together. Cicero's famous words, "the foundation of justice, moreover, is good faith—that is, truth and fidelity to promises and agreements,"[6] were quoted hundreds of times by medieval canonists and theologians. From a strictly legal perspective, however, the Romans refused to admit that every agreement could give rise to legal action. Only canon law and its courts were concerned with the legal effectiveness of the simple agreement. In this way, the canonists made a significant contribution to putting in place a fundamental belief on which the market economy is based. As noted by Alain Supiot with great acuity, "it is because people believed in the existence of one God, who sees everything, and before whom lies must never be uttered, that the simple agreement (the naked agreement) ended up being identified with the contract." And Supiot goes on to explain that "the modern notion of a contract could not have developed without faith in a universal guarantor of a promise made." Although, as Western culture becomes more secularized, the State takes the place of the Church as guarantor of exchanges, it remains the case that "this secularization does not mean that the contract can do without faith from now on, without the belief in a guarantor of a promise made."[7]

From the beginning of the sixteenth century, when Christianity was being torn apart and powerful princes sought to establish themselves as new popes in their respective territories, secular courts replaced ecclesiastical courts and assimilated various principles derived from canon law. The assimilation of the principle of *pacta sunt servanda* is a good example. In France, the Ordinance of Villers-Cotterêts of 1539 removed all jurisdictional power from the ecclesiastical courts in contractual matters. At the same time, the great jurist Charles Dumoulin, one of the founding fathers of modern French law, affirmed the application of the principle of *pacta sunt servanda* in the civil courts, while acknowledging its canonical origins. As such, the spirit of canon law was perpetuated at a time when States were taking over the role of the Church as universal guarantors of promises made. Among the new priests of national law were jurists who claimed to be drawing on customary traditions proper to their region or nation. They doubted the universal validity of Roman and canon law. However, in practice they continued to adhere to some of the major principles of canon law. Thus, the principle of keeping one's word was increasingly affirmed by jurists in the early modern period, even though some of claimed that it was just a question of observing local custom. For example, Antoine Loysel, author of a collection of maxims of French customary law, wrote: "One binds oxen by the horns and men by words."[8] In doing so, he provided the French translation of a medieval Latin gloss that was imbued with Christian, canon law values.[9] While the reference to canon law remained concealed, in some posthumous editions of Loysel's maxims, the overturning of Roman law by the canonists was made more explicit by adding the following phrase: "And a simple promise or agreement is worth as much as the stipulations of Roman law."[10]

From Consensualism to Freedom of Contract

The moral theology of the early modern scholastics, which Pierre Legendre has described as "a second canon law,"[11] welcomed this adoption by sixteenth-century secular law of the consensualist principle of the medieval canonists. The Jesuit Luis de Molina, heir to the School of Salamanca and friend of Leonardus Lessius, called for an adaptation of civil law to the requirements of canon law and natural law, on the grounds that this would be beneficial for promoting peace. Henceforth, he noted with satisfaction that in the Kingdom of Spain the civil jurisdictions had abandoned the subtle distinctions, "introduced by heathens," between nominate and innominate contracts, or between naked and clothed agreements.[12] Moreover, his own treatise *De iustitia et iure*, published in three large volumes between 1593 and 1609, was expressly addressed to both confessors and judges. For Molina, the ultimate criterion for evaluating the rules of law, including those of canon law, was natural law. From the perspective of this natural law, the essential element of the contractual obligation was the simple exchange of the free consent of the parties. Similarly, Leonardus Lessius explained that "every agreement, even a naked one, produces a natural obligation, that is, an obligation in the conscience, provided that it is freely and willingly concluded by parties who have the capacity to contract, so that you cannot dissolve the contract without the consent of the other, unless the agreement is invalid due to a provision of positive law or you have been granted the power to invalidate it."[13] Even more than in the canonical tradition, the perspective of natural law and the practice of confession prompted theologian-jurists to reject the subtleties of Roman law and to focus on consent as the intimate foundation of the contractual bond. Molina insisted that "from the perspective of natural law and the jus gentium, that is, before the introduction of civil law, the distinction between nominate and innominate agreements, and that between naked and clothed agreements, was pointless. It follows that in conscience, having regard to the very nature of the thing, all these agreements generated an obligation which is qualified as 'natural' to differentiate it from that referred to as 'civil,' which is the basis of the legal action granted by civil law."[14]

Natural law makes it possible to think of contracts in a generic and abstract way, based on the intimate will of the parties. Within this concept of contracts, the theologians confirmed, man rediscovered his original natural freedom (*libertas restituta*). These are the words used by the Jesuit Pedro de Oñate, author of a voluminous treatise (1646–1654), several thousand pages long, on contract law, to summarize the joint contribution of canon law and natural law to the development of contract law over the centuries.[15] This freedom was considered to be conducive to the common good to the extent that the principle of keeping one's word is the foundation of a peaceful and prosperous society. Here we see an overturning of the logic of Roman law. The civil lawyers started from the premise that the universal actionability of agreements is harmful to the public interest, owing to a possible multiplication of litigation. On the other hand, Oñate, like Molina, assumed the opposite: that a shared belief in keeping one's word will lead to fewer legal disputes and more prosperity. Rather than disturbing the public peace, *pacta sunt servanda* encourages the trust necessary for trade and business. Thanks to freedom of contract, people can dispose of their goods as they wish. They can use earthly goods as creatively as the Creator. The creation of man in the image of God implies freedom of action and the power to dispose of one's goods through reason and free will.[16] The development of the theological dogma of man being created in God's image refers directly to one of the dogmatic foundations of Western law. Returning to Alain Supiot, "it is only in the West that it was thought that, in the image of God, every man could enjoy the legislating power of the Word for his own benefit and enclose the future in promises."[17]

The concern for the protection of private property expressed in the scholastic tradition of the modern age is reflected in the theory of contracts that it proposes.[18] The rather individualistic concept of property found here (the Jesuit Gregory of Valencia referred to "the right to love one's possessions") was translated into a rather liberal concept of contract. If man were not master of the legislative power of the Word and, therefore, free to enter into the contracts of his choice, he could not be considered the true master of his property, which would be in contradiction with his divine destiny. "Man would not be the true and perfect owner of his possessions," Oñate explained, "if he could not alienate them when he wants, to the person he wants and in the way he wants, and if he could not enter into contracts when he wants and in the way he wants."[19] Through his voluntary actions, man can exercise his mastery (*dominium*) over things. It is this *dominium* that forms the basis and foundation of contract law, according to the words of the Dominican friar of Salamanca Domingo de Soto, author of the first treatise *De iustitia et iure*. Moreover, the close link between property and contracts is expressed by Luis de Molina who, after dealing with the law of property, began an in-depth discussion on the modes of transfer of the different forms of *dominium*. He added that he would articulate his treatment of contracts in two stages, first by presenting the general theory of contracts, and then by focusing on the different types of special contracts. We can therefore see a systematization of the doctrine of contracts within private law which is itself conceived in an overarching logic. This systematization is particularly well reflected in Leonardus Lessius' *De iustitia et iure*, whose treatment of special contracts is preceded by a chapter on contracts in general.

"Auto-nomy" and Contract as Private Law

The abstraction of the contractual bond leads to an analysis of agreements as a particular law binding on contracting parties who are conceived in the image of legislators. In the world of laws governing human behaviour, scholastic theologians therefore hold an important place for individual initiative. Through his words, man is able to subject his future actions to laws that are the combined product of his will and that of the co-contractor. Drawing on a Roman metaphor, theologian-jurists agreed to qualify the contract as "private law" or "particular law" (*lex privata*). More specifically, the agreement is "a private law that the person who makes a promise imposes on himself," to use the words of the Jesuit Juan de Lugo, author of a major treatise *De iustitia et iure* largely inspired by Lessius' work of the same name.[20] For the scholastic theologians, a contract is therefore the perfect expression of "auto-nomy," in the etymological sense of this term (from the Greek *autos*, "oneself," and *nomos*, "law"). The validity of this "agreement-law" depends first of all on the free will of the contracting parties, thus on the absence of deceit, error, or coercion, and on the decision of the contracting parties to continue to respect their undertaking—as Lessius clearly described. It is a law which, in the hierarchy of norms, is of course inferior to that promulgated in the common interest by civil or ecclesiastical authorities. Faithful to the Aristotelian idea of man as a political animal, the scholastics see man in relation to the community that welcomes him into its midst. They are not libertarians or advocates of the kind of individual autonomy that ignores the interests of the common good. The authorities are entitled to limit freedom of contract by making it subject to forms determined by law. Therefore, in order to protect the ecclesiastical patrimony against the avarice of certain clerics, strict formalities must be respected when a member of the clergy wishes to alienate ecclesiastical property. Moreover, given the absolute primacy of natural law, the contract as "private law" must honour the principles derived from natural law. This reference to natural law is not abstract: it concerns above all the respect of good faith (*bona fides*) and fairness (*aequitas*) in transactions.

The development by scholastic theologians of the metaphor of contract as a "private law," subject to the dictates of both the will of the contracting parties, the common good, and the principles of natural law, had such an impact that it has remained the cornerstone of contract law in the continental legal tradition via the works of French natural lawyers (those jurists of the seventeenth and eighteenth centuries who took natural law as the basis of their analyses of law). One only needs to look at the famous article 1134 of the original 1804 version of the Napoleonic Civil Code, clearly inspired by the natural lawyers, according to which "legally formed agreements take the place of law for those who have made them. They can only be revoked by mutual consent, or for the reasons authorized by law. They must be carried out in good faith."[21] Often considered as the expression of a bourgeois individualism characteristic of the French spirit of the early nineteenth century, it is in fact hard not to see in this article 1134 a text which is faithful to the heritage of the previous centuries, which had been based on canon law and natural law.[22] Then there is the following article, which in the original version of the Civil Code extends the contractual obligation "to all the consequences which equity, usage or law give to the obligation according to its nature." In the scholastic tradition, this reference to equity is omnipresent. As such, after praising the emergence of freedom of contract, Oñate explained in the same passage of his treatise that natural law compelled contracting parties to honour the duties imposed on them by natural equity.[23] For Oñate, who fell within the canonical and scholastic tradition, this natural fairness had two fundamental principles, namely the respect of the golden rule ("do unto others as you would have them do unto you") and that of justice in contracts ("do not enrich yourself at the expense of others"). A vestige of this appeal to contractual morality can still be found in the *Traité des obligations* (*Treatise on Obligations*) (1761) by the great French judge and jurist Robert-Joseph Pothier, who simply repeated the words of the scholastic theologians in explaining that the fairness that must apply in contracts does not allow "one of the parties to profit and enrich himself at the expense of the other." In the same way, Pothier borrowed the principle of good faith from the canonists and scholastic theologians, affirming that "in one's conscience, one must consider as contrary to this good faith everything that deviates in the slightest way from the most exact and scrupulous sincerity."[24] Through

Pothier and other natural lawyers, the scholastics' doctrine of contracts was therefore found in the Napoleonic Civil Code of 1804.

Today, the compatibility of the values of freedom and fairness is no longer obvious, at least in theory. Created in a context where citizens have positive law as their sole official legal guide, the new French Civil Code, introduced in 2016, has not retained article 1135 in its original place, namely just after the principle of the agreement as a private law ("*convention-loi*"). However, more than two centuries after Napoleon's codification of civil law, the separation of contract law from its jusnaturalist origins is not yet entirely complete. The former article 1135, now article 1194, remains useful in practice. It gives judges the power to take into consideration "the consequences which fairness, usage or the law give to an obligation according to its nature." To a certain extent, then, even today's doctrine of contract in France remains faithful to its scholastic underpinnings. As Jacques Krynen, a French legal historian, recently observed, "we must take measure of the fact that the legalistic system has not entirely abandoned the use of equity."[25] Moreover, the reference to equity also remains in most civil codes around the world that were inspired by the original version of the Napoleonic codification. For example, until a major law reform in 2022, articles 1134 and 1135 of the Belgian Civil Code still corresponded to their erstwhile model. On this point, it is worth recalling the analysis of the Belgian legal historian Dirk Heirbaut, who considered that the Belgians have continued to be Napoleon's most loyal subjects. We could even go further and say that Belgian contract law remained faithful to its scholastic legacy.

Legal Foundations of Contractual Obligation

Contrary to what one might think, scholastic theologians such as Leonardus Lessius did not consider the contractual bond in purely moral terms. While recognizing the moral character of the obligation to respect one's undertakings, the theologians also affirmed the legal and binding character of a contractual obligation in the strict sense. It is not only by virtue of honesty and truth that a Christian debtor is obliged to keep his promises. He is bound by an obligation of justice. To quote Lessius: "a promise creates a legal debt. This promise gives the other party the right to demand that it be fulfilled."[26] Domingo de Soto affirmed that a promise establishes a bond of trust that is not only a moral debt based on respect for the truth, but also on commutative justice. With remarkable subtlety, Lessius and his colleagues addressed the question of how a legal obligation can arise from human will. We cannot dwell here on the extensive analysis that medieval and modern scholastics have made of the effective force of human promises, notably in the context of the professions of religious vows, as Alain Boureau has shown.[27] Let us simply summarize the common view at the turn of the seventeenth century that three elements are required for a promise to become binding:

(1) the intention to enter into a legal obligation; (2) the externalization of this intention in the form of an offer; (3) acceptance thereof by the party to which this offer is made.

In the first instance, the promisor must have the intention to bind himself legally (*animus obligandi*). As Lugo explains, like a law that is not based on the actual will of the authorities, an agreement without the intention of obligation cannot give rise to a contract in the strict sense of the term.[28] As obvious as this argument may seem, it has given rise to intense debate about the differences between the mere expression of an intention and a promise in the strict sense of the word. Drawing on these discussions, Pothier gave the example of a father promising his son, a law student, a holiday trip as long as he "made good use of his time" during his studies.[29] According to Pothier, the father only intended to stimulate his son's enthusiasm, without committing himself in any way. His promise, which was only intended to encourage his son to use his time wisely in school, was only "an imperfect obligation."

The second element considered necessary for the creation of an actual contractual obligation is the externalization of the promise (*promissio externa*). Whereas God and the angels are able to discern the intentions of men, men themselves cannot guess the thoughts of each other. In practice, in the market, the externalization of the intention to bind oneself through an agreement was therefore always necessary. However, the question that occupied theologians was whether man was already bound by a purely internal promise, in his conscience. If I say to myself that I will undertake to sell my property to such and such a person, am I obliged to respect this inner promise? Lessius believed that the transfer of rights, including contractual claims, could not be effectuated by intention alone. In his view, language cannot be regarded as a pure instrument to externalize complete commitments that are already within someone internally. On the contrary, language provides symbols that create the obligation at the very moment it is expressed. Linguistic signs have a pragmatic value: they are not mere carriers of meaning, but acts; they make the obligation they signify effective: "It is more likely that, from the perspective of natural law, a purely internal promise and a gift are insufficient and incapable of creating an obligation.... The reason for this is that a promise and a gift are symbols which, in a way, act; these signs make the very thing they symbolise effective."[30]

The promise is the result of a deliberate and expressed intention, which is transformed into a real offer and only waits for the party to which it was made to accept it, in order to generate a contractual obligation in the legal sense of the term, with binding force in the external forum as well as in the forum of conscience. The meeting of offer and acceptance has been the subject of controversial analysis among theologian-jurists. While Lessius eventually convinced common opinion of the necessity of attaching acceptance to the offer in order for a unilateral promise to become binding, the Roman legal tradition also contained arguments to the contrary. Roman law provided examples of simple promises, not accepted, which nevertheless legally bound the party making them, like the *pollicitationes civitati*, unilateral offers made in particular by candidates for honorary offices, promising to build such or such public building. From the binding force of these promises before the Roman courts, theologians like Molina deduced the existence of a natural obligation from unilateral promises or *pollicitationes* alone. On the other hand, Lessius interpreted this Roman casuistry as pertaining solely to the refusal, by Roman law, to give the party making a promise the possibility of changing their mind and retracting their promise. While the result was the same, Molina's and Lessius' reasoning was different. Lessius refused to recognize the establishment of a natural obligation on the basis of a unilateral offer. He put forward a vision of the contract that could be described as "relational." Both offer and acceptance are necessary for the conclusion of a contract. Lessius took the rights of the recipient of the offer seriously, and the latter could refuse, while giving the party making the offer the opportunity to retract it until it was accepted. Lessius envisaged the emergence of the contractual obligation as the fruit of the coming together, actively and intentionally, of the two contracting parties, co-creators of an agreement that resembled a private law: "From each unilateral offer there arises a kind of conditional obligation whose binding force is suspended until the moment when it is either accepted or retracted; positive law may prevent retraction."[31]

The theory of offer and acceptance put forward by Lessius as the source and foundation of contractual obligation was accepted by other Jesuits and the majority of the natural lawyers. "Each contract comes into existence by the meeting of the offer and the acceptance," explained Oñate, "just as a physical object is born of the entirety of the matter and the form, and the man of the composition of the soul and the body."[32] This doctrine found its way into Pothier's treatise on obligations, which duly observed, in words reminiscent of Lessius', that "a *pollicitatio* according to the terms of pure natural law does not produce any obligation in the strict sense, and the party who has made this promise can withdraw from it, as long as it has not been accepted by the party to whom it was made; for there can be no obligation without a right acquired by the party to whom it is contracted against the party obliged."[33] The doctrine of offer and acceptance, put forward by Pothier, was taken up again in the Napoleonic codification and remains one of the great foundations of the generic concept of contract in continental legal traditions. Whenever offer and acceptance meet, a legal obligation is created for the party making the promise, so that the agreement must be respected.

Trust beyond Differences of (Religious) Faith

The universal scope of the obligation generated by a promise made and accepted is of crucial importance in the evolution of Western legal thought. However, it would be wrong to see this as a purely doctrinal development. While Lessius helped define a generic concept of the contractual bond, he was also aware of its economic necessity. In order to advise merchants, he regularly frequented the Antwerp exchange (*bursa*), where agreements were made between Anglicans, Catholics, Lutherans, and Calvinists. Founded in 1531 by the aldermen of Antwerp on the banks of the river Scheldt, the Antwerp exchange aimed to attract merchants from all over the world "regardless of their nation, language or city of origin," according to the words on the famous engraving by the Flemish painter Pieter van der Borcht (see picture on the front cover). In this pluralistic context, the binding force of the promise must be guaranteed beyond cultural, linguistic, and religious differences.

Whereas, in medieval times, the market was still "the work of good Christians united by a common faith,"[34] the societal upheavals brought about by the Protestant Reformation fundamentally changed the situation. They prompted a revision of the ancient doctrines concerning the legal status of heretics and the binding force of contract. According to received wisdom, which medieval canonists justified on the basis of Roman imperial constitutions, heretics could not enjoy the same rights as Catholics. The canon *Cum secundum leges*, from the *Liber Sextus* of Boniface VIII, took away the *dominium* from condemned heretics, including the right to the execution of claims. The adage *pacta sunt servanda* in its medieval interpretation therefore started to reveal its limitations. As heretics were excluded from the community of the faithful, their credibility and credit were destroyed. Whoever did not profess *Fides* in the sense of "true belief in the Catholic faith" could not enjoy any *fides* in the sense of "trust." Their access to the market was therefore denied.

At a time when European society was going through one of the most deadly crises in its history, and when hundreds of thousands of citizens lost their lives as a result of wars opposing different interpretations of the Christian faith, a contract law that could be maintained across religious divides needed to be devised. In the common interest, trade had to be allowed to take place, despite the fragmentation of the political and legal space at the dawn of the modern age. On both sides of the confessional divide, nature and natural law became the conceptual devices preferred by those who attempted to develop a safe, stable normative framework that could transcend political and religious divides. While this reconciliation project has been linked above all to the name of the Delft theologian Hugo Grotius, author of the great work *De iure belli ac pacis* (*On War and Peace*, 1625), the contribution of the Jesuits should not be overlooked—as described by Robert Feenstra, who demonstrated how Grotius' work drew on scholastic theology, in particular the theology of the Oracle of the Low Countries.

In his treatise *De iustitia et iure*, Leonardus Lessius defended the stability of rights acquired by creditors declared heretical. By insisting on the universal scope of the binding force of promises according to natural law, he denied the existence, in both human and divine positive law, of contrary provisions that would infringe the rights of heretical creditors.[35] According to Lessius, the Bible, the source of positive divine law, did not contain any recommendation on heretics losing their claims. Of course, he acknowledges the existence of provisions allowing civil disobedience before authorities that have been excommunicated by the Church, but the provisions of criminal law must be interpreted restrictively. More precisely, it was necessary, in Lessius' view, to distinguish between the domain of private debts and that of political loyalty. In the interests of peace and economic prosperity, contract law should not be affected by religious or political considerations. *Pax servetur, pacta custodiantur*: "Peace should be preserved, pacts should be respected."

4

Usury and the Debt Market

Money is fertile seed containing virtual profits made by your industry.

—Leonardus Lessius

A cursory reading of the section in *On Justice and Law* devoted to contracts quickly reveals that Lessius was highly familiar with the commercial and financial practices of his day.[1] The terms of commercial dealings between Antwerp, Florence, Naples, or Milan, the countless legal tricks to avoid the ban on interest-bearing loans—including sale on credit with immediate repurchase at a lower price (*mohatra*)—the organization of the wool trade between Flanders and Spain, the exchange fairs in Frankfurt and Besançon, annuities with a repurchase clause: it all comes under the spotlight. This impression is confirmed by Franciscus Zypaeus (Frans Van den Zype), a jurist and churchman living at the same time as Lessius. In his *Notitia iuris belgici* (*Knowledge of Belgian Law*, 1635), he referred directly to Lessius for an in-depth discussion of the exchange practices at the Antwerp Bourse.[2] "A major expert in theological doctrine, Lessius went from the lecture hall in Louvain to the Antwerp market," Zypaeus noted, "specifically to converse with the most experienced merchants there, to address the question of the equity of exchange with a sound knowledge of the practice." In his *Bibliothèque belge* (*The Belgian Library*) of 1623, a work consisting of biographical notes on the coryphaei of Belgian history, the jurist and historian Valerius Andreas noted that Lessius was a highly sought-after consultant to the elites of his day.[3] Thanks to his expertise, Lessius was called upon to give advice on the legitimacy of various transactions in a wide range of markets, from the money exchange market to the grain market and the negotiable debt market.

Money, Markets, and Merit. Wim Decock, Oxford University Press. © Oxford University Press (2025).
DOI: 10.1093/9780197827345.003.0005

Between Principles and Practices

It is the latter market, the debt market, that will be the focus of our attention in this chapter. These negotiable debts were referred to in Latin, alternatively, by terms such as *credita, debita, iura, chirographa, assignationes, librantiae,* and *nomina*. In Lessius' treatment of this subject, the words most frequently used are *chirographa*, "bond letters," and *iura*, "rights," whereas Molina primarily referred to *debitum*, "debt," and *ius creditoris*, "claim."[4] Bond letters physically represent debts. Usually, they sell at a price lower than the value of the debt itself. This reduction in price is technically referred to as a "discount." Molina also highlighted the fact that the question whether discounting debt was in accordance with the principle of commutative justice related to both debts not yet due (which are not expected to be paid immediately) and due debts (which must therefore be paid immediately). In other words, the practices analysed by Lessius and Molina ranged from speculative purchases in the bond market and bill of exchange market to the collection of due debts by factoring agents and discount loans granted by bankers to merchants. The question then arises as to whether the speculator, factoring agent, or banker can "discount" the debt by paying less than its nominal value, an operation which involves buying the debt for a reduced price, that is, below the amount stated on the paper—in technical terms, buying "below par."

Indirectly, the discount amounts to the collection of an interest rate, since at the maturity date of the debt, the buyer expects to receive the nominal value of the purchased debt. "As an example," Lessius explained, "consider a debt of 100 gold guilders with payment due in one year that is purchased, today, for 96 or 97."[5] The difference between the 96 or 97 guilders paid now and the 100 guilders received later can be thought of as the present price of money, that is, an interest rate of 3 or 4 per cent. That is the reason why the discount is regarded as a pretext to compensate for the collection of interest. This suspicion is more intense in cases where the debt is purchased at only a fraction of its nominal value, such as at 30, 40, or 50 per cent below par. "Bond letters and debt certificates, can they be sold at half price," Lessius wondered, "especially if payment is uncertain or difficult to obtain?" Think of the obstacles to be overcome to collect the debt, in the event of the insolvency of the debtor or his unwillingness to respect the agreed terms.

These are some concrete cases of conscience that take us right to the heart of financial activity in the early seventeenth century. They allow us to transcend the often-sterile discussions on the "prohibition of usury" in the scholastic tradition and its timid but overrated turnaround by Charles Dumoulin and John Calvin. Retracing the full extent of these debates would require complete volumes, as Laurence Fontaine, a French historian, has noted, someone who nevertheless had the courage and merit to provide an excellent summary.[6] It is enough to reiterate that, in theory, any interest charged by virtue of the loan, even if it was not abusive or excessive, fell under the usury prohibition. As such, historically speaking, it is more accurate to refer to an "interest prohibition." The loan contract (*mutuum*) was inevitably associated with the words of the Gospel, according to which money should be lent without expecting to get anything in return (Luke 6:35). This passage from the Gospel of Luke was the theological basis for the pontifical decrees which, at the turn of the twelfth and thirteenth centuries, made the general prohibition of lending at interest more stringent. Previously, the prohibition of lending at interest mainly related to members of the clergy, as witnessed by the first Church councils.

In practice, however, the scholastic theologians increasingly accepted techniques that made it possible to circumvent the adverse effects of the general prohibition of lending at interest. Contracts of partnership (*societas*), exchange (*cambium*), and annuity (*census*) were widely accepted as instruments of credit and profitable investment. In this way, the medieval and modern scholastics provided ample alternatives to *mutuum*, the interest-bearing loan in the strict sense of the term.[7] Moreover, at the very start of the sixteenth century, scholastic theologians succeeded in undermining all the traditional arguments in favour of the sterility of money. For example, in Konrad Summenhart's analysis of the interest-bearing loan contract in his *Treatise on Contracts* (ca. 1500), the latter was only against usury in the case of interest-bearing loans to those in need.[8]

John Maynard Keynes saw in this combination of the prohibition of lending at interest and the legitimization of interest in commercial companies and investment contracts a precursor of his theory that the rate of interest in the strict sense of the term should be distinguished from the "marginal efficiency of capital"—an anachronistic reading of the sources that was criticized.[9] We can have some sympathy for Keynes who was indignant at the prevailing preconceived notions on the scholastic doctrine of usury. In his *General Theory of Employment, Interest and Money* from 1936, he wrote that "I was brought up to believe that the attitude of the Medieval Church to the rate of interest was inherently absurd, and that the subtle discussions aimed at distinguishing the return on money-loans from the return to active investment were merely Jesuitical attempts to find a practical escape from a foolish theory. But I now read these discussions as an honest intellectual effort to keep separate what the classical theory has inextricably confused together, namely, the rate of interest and the marginal efficiency of capital."[10] In a commercial context, modern scholastics have indeed questioned the very basis of the prohibition of interest, passed down from Aristotle, for whom money cannot generate more money. Bernard Dempsey revealed that Lessius was one of the most ardent proponents of this dynamic conception of money as possessing fertility when employed by the merchant as his tool of work. Sylvain Piron's research has even shown that Peter of John Olivi, in the thirteenth century, already fully recognized the fertility of money in the context of mercantile exchanges at Narbonne.[11] At the turn of the thirteenth and fourteenth centuries, however, there was strong resistance to this modern conception of the fertility of money. The *Question on Usury*, disputed in Paris in 1330 by the Augustinian theologian Gerard of Siena, provides a good example of this more rigorous attitude.[12]

Despite this resistance, it can be seen in practice that there was generally a high degree of compatibility between the normative framework developed by Christian moralists and the realities of credit markets in the medieval period.[13] In addition, the methods of interpretation developed by the scholastics to bend the strict law to considerations of justice or expediency are similar to those of modern jurists. This is not surprising in the context of medieval and modern universities, where accepting a plurality of meanings was an integral part of the interpretive culture.[14] Similarly, circumvention as the art of reconciling the letter of the law with the spirit of the law was not necessarily considered hypocritical, either by Jewish exegetes or by Christian scholastics.[15] Moreover, we can observe parallels with present-day Islamic finance, which accommodates the realities of global capitalism while remaining true to the prohibition of *riba* ("interest"). The concept of "tolerance of ambiguity," used by the Islamologist Thomas Bauer to decipher premodern Muslim culture, can easily be transposed onto the economic morality of the scholastics.[16] In this regard, it is more useful to focus on the effects that the prohibition of lending at interest may have had on the progress of legal and economic analysis than to concentrate on its apparent effects of holding back the countries that remained true to the Catholic faith—a popular assumption that does not necessarily stand up to empirical evidence.[17]

With Joel Kaye, we can observe that the prohibition of usury prompted the scholastics to take into consideration the reality of market practices and become veritable experts on the functioning of the market.[18] This observation applies all the more to Lessius and his counterparts Molina and Lugo, which is why, in his *History of Economic Analysis*, Joseph Schumpeter particularly appreciated the empirical sensitivity of their analyses: "This realistic character of the work of the late scholastics should be particularly emphasized. They did not simply speculate. They did all the fact-finding that it was possible for them to do in an age without statistical services. Their generalizations invariably grew out of discussions of factual patterns and were copiously illustrated by practical examples. Lessius described the practice of the Antwerp exchange (*bursa*). Molina sallied forth from his study to interview businessmen about their methods."[19] The empirical reality of the debt market that Lessius faced was marked by the invention of new financing techniques and the high negotiability of bills of exchange, bond letters, and other claims. Indeed, Antwerp was regarded as the epicentre of a veritable revolution in financial techniques during the sixteenth century.[20]

Discounting and the Spectre of Usury

In the context of the increasing circulation of negotiable debt claims, a banking innovation saw the light of day in Antwerp in the second half of the sixteenth century: the modern practice of discounting bond letters, which was directly referred to by Lessius. An imperial ordinance of 1540 mentioned the arrival of merchant-financiers in Antwerp who, in times of scarce liquidity, bought bond letters in cash, on condition that they obtained a reduction in the nominal value of the letter.[21] Originally, only bond letters that were already due (*ex post*) were bought, but it was only a short step from there to the purchase of bonds that had not reached maturity yet (*ex ante*). An accounting manual published in Antwerp around 1560 gives examples of the discounting of different types of debt claims. These were often bills of exchange or credits that aristocrats or wealthy merchants had granted to the public authorities by order of the prince. Given the absence of municipal banks in the Southern Netherlands, these forced loans were a standard method for the prince to replenish the state coffers.[22] The public sale of debt claims at the Antwerp exchange (*bursa*) allowed merchants to exchange credit certificates for hard cash.

The practice of discounting represents a major step in the history of banking. However, at the time, it raised suspicions. Some conservative scholastics saw the purchase of debt claims as a purchase of the money itself, not a right (*ius*) to future money, so that the transaction was an implicit interest-bearing loan. Suspicions were heightened by the fact that, if the prohibition of interest were being circumvented, the loan contract might be replaced by the sale of a new bond letter, issued specifically for this purpose—a real possibility that was anticipated by Lessius.[23] Could this practice of discounting, so widespread and even publicly organized, be considered a disguised form of lending at interest? Was the difference between the amount of money paid by the buyer below par and the nominal value of the letter a form of "cloaked" usury? Lessius proposed resolving these problems on two levels: first, he raised the question of usury on a purely theoretical and abstract level; he then evaluated the practice by taking into consideration the specific circumstances that influence the debt market.

The answers he provided are interesting for at least three reasons. Firstly, purchasing debts gives rise to a discussion at the intersection of the two doctrines that underpin scholastic reflections on the market, namely those of usury and the just price. Secondly, resolving this problem shows us very clearly the importance of the language of law as an instrument for solving cases of conscience. Finally, and above all, the degree of approval for the purchase of bond letters at a price less than the nominal value is a good indication of the breakdown or, on the contrary, the tenacity of the old doctrine of usury in the early seventeenth century.

The Moral Relevance of Legal Qualifications

As we have already highlighted, the legal analysis of economic phenomena played a crucial role for the scholastics. To find out whether the purchase of a bond letter at a price lower than its nominal value is lawful, even if there will be no difficulty in obtaining payment, it would be decisive for Lessius to precisely define the legal character of this transaction. More concretely, he had to determine whether such a purchase is really a contract of purchase and sale (*emptio*) (as suggested by the fact that a study of this case can be found in a chapter on the purchase contract), or rather a kind of disguised and implicit interest-bearing loan (*mutuum implicitum*).

By definition, usury means the charging of interest directly in the context of a loan. While current economic analysis tends to consciously set aside legal qualifications in order to focus on a substantive analysis of market phenomena, the importance of this legal categorization for scholastic theologians cannot be underestimated. In their view, if there is no loan, explicit or implicit, there can be no question of usury. Lessius insisted on this point.[24]

The struggle for the legal categorization of discounting debts was most clearly illustrated by Lessius in his presentation of a typical argument of the common opinion against the practice of discounting debt: "A person who owes 100 guilders, who pays less than the amount due (e.g., 96) on account of the anticipation of payment, commits usury. Implicitly he lends 96 until the due date, to receive 100 in exchange, since by that time the debt of 100 guilders has become due. Yet, this is precisely the same thing as buying a chirograph worth 100 guilders for 96."[25] This is a tedious argument, to which the following objection was immediately raised: "Most of this syllogism is correct, provided that the debtor pays less precisely because of the anticipation of the due date. He does not practice usury, however, if he pays less not as the payer of a debt, but as the buyer of another individual's right. When such a right is offered for sale, the lower price is simply its estimated value. Nowhere in a civil community would it be possible to sell it for a higher price. Hence the crucial importance of the title or contractual form through which a transaction is made."

There are at least two reasons to suspect that there is a *mutuum implicitum* behind the purchase of debts at a reduced price: *primo*, it is an exchange of present money for future money; *secundo*, the difference only seems to be generated by an interval of time, which is an undeniable sign of usury, since in Aristotle's writings and up to medieval scholasticism, money is theoretically considered to be sterile, and does not produce any fruit on account of the passage of time.

In the Aristotelian conception, money is only a means of exchange. Consequently, any use of this instrument that does not correspond to its ultimate purpose violates nature.[26] For example, a debt of 1,000 guilders to be paid in a year is equivalent to 1,000 guilders to be paid in the present, since time itself does not create value and money does not produce money. Therefore, when someone only pays 950 guilders for a bond letter that contains the right to reimbursement of 1,000 guilders in the future, the course of nature is obstructed and one is guilty of an implicit interest-bearing loan. Furthermore, for medieval jurists and theologians, money is a gift from God to man, a gift that should not disadvantage one to the benefit of the other. Therefore, one must lend money out of mercy or charity, and in the form of a *mutuum*, to all those who need it, and without expecting compensation or interest (Luke 6:35). An excellent synthesis of the medieval concept of lending money can be found in the *Collectio contractuum* (1255) by the Bolognese jurist Rolandinus de Passageriis. In the introduction to his work on drafting contracts, the "father of notaries" warns his future colleagues not to forget that "the lending of money is instituted by divine Providence for a pious and just cause. Those to whom the Lord has entrusted temporal wealth should use it to support their needy brethren through loans and other acts of mercy. However, the usurers have turned the holy and pious cause of lending into the unholy cause of their own death and damnation, since they commit theft by selling time in the form of a covenant of some kind as if it were their own. In truth, time is a gift from God and the passage of time is the common property of all animals and men, rich or poor."[27]

Justice, Balance, and the Justification of Interest

The work of the jurist Rolandinus reflects rather traditional concepts of usury and time that were profoundly reshaped by the subsequent scholastic tradition. A surprising contribution to this reform was the redefinition of *mutuum* as an act of commutative justice following the revival of Aristotle's *Nicomachean Ethics* in the thirteenth century. The imbuing of scholastic morality with Aristotelian concepts was already apparent in the first half of the century, in the *Summa aurea* (1215–1229) of the theologian William of Auxerre. He explicitly identified the virtue of justice as the foundation of economic ethics.[28] The uptake of Aristotelian ideas was accelerated by the circulation of a complete Latin version of the *Nicomachean Ethics* from 1247 on, thanks to the translation by Robert Grosseteste, to which the Dominican William de Moerbeke subsequently made critical revisions. It lastingly introduced the principle of commutative justice into the domain of contract law, a principle according to which a loan must respect a balance (*aequalitas*) in terms of the obligations of the contracting parties. In the second half of the thirteenth century, the *Secunda secundae* of Thomas Aquinas' *Summa Theologica* stated that the charging of interest by a lender is inconsistent with the principle of commutative justice, since it implies an imbalance (*inaequalitas*).[29]

While it enshrined the biblical prohibition of interest-bearing loans in natural law, the notion of balance at the same time opened the door to interest being demanded to ensure that the balance was not violated in certain cases. This was the basis for the idea of "extrinsic titles." These titles (*tituli*)—also called "causes" (*causae*) or "reasons" (*rationes*), according to the legal terminology of the day—justify, in specific cases, the charging of interest for specific reasons that are related to the context and not to the loan contract itself. As such, Thomas Aquinas accepted that the lender negotiates a rate of interest as a way to compensate himself if he suffers concrete losses as a result of giving a loan, a title which in the fourteenth century was referred to as *damnum emergens*. Similarly, linking the prohibition of interest-bearing loans to commutative justice allowed Aquinas to envisage the contractual logic being abandoned in the event that the contracting parties wished not to frame their relationship in juridical terms, for instance because they were relatives or good friends. In effect, concluding a loan contract does not prevent the lender from obtaining interest which the borrower freely pays the lender in recognition of the good that the latter has done for him. While this obligation is not legally binding, and the creditor cannot therefore claim it in court, it arises from a strictly moral duty to show gratitude to one's benefactors.[30] On this Aristotelian and Thomistic basis, the scholastics managed to progressively create extrinsic titles justifying the charging of interest in practice on grounds other than the loan contract itself.

Debts as Saleable Goods and the Supreme Value of Cash

We will see in chapter 7, devoted to *subprime loans*, that Lessius freely used the theory of extrinsic titles to legitimise the concrete practices of discounting debt claims, claims which, in reality, are almost always subject to specific circumstances if only because payment is often uncertain. Let us return for the moment to the more theoretical question of whether the purchase of bond letters at less than their nominal value, and which do not represent any risk, must be qualified as a disguised loan. Again, this legal qualification mattered, because of the strict link between the interest prohibition and the contract of loan (*mutuum*).

The reasoning that Lessius pushed to its ultimate limits was that a bond letter, that is, a right to future money, is a commodity like any other. From this conception it follows that a right to future money is the subject of an authentic purchase contract (*emptio*), not a loan at interest (*mutuum*). Consequently, like any goods, a debt claim can be given a price, that is, a just price, which in essence is the result of a common estimation resulting from the circumstances of the market: "When such rights are offered for sale as goods, experience shows that by common opinion they are considered of lesser value than present money. Because cash offers various possibilities that these rights do not. Therefore, it is lawful to buy them cheaper. This conclusion is correct since the just price of any saleable item is the price set by the common estimation. If, therefore, in relation to other goods, the just price is defined as the common estimation, why not apply this reasoning to the case of bond letters?"[31]

Liquidity Preference

Lessius' insistence on its being a sale contract is a legal interpretation of the practice of discounting letters of debt that seeks to shield it from the suspicions of usury surrounding loan contracts. Lessius borrowed it from the medieval canonical tradition, where it is present *in nucleo* in authors such as Innocent IV, Peter of John Olivi, and Abbas Panormitanus. It was accepted by Martín de Azpilcueta, who asserted in his *Manual for Confessors* that the practice of buying non-due debts below par was a purchase contract and not a loan, in this case the purchase of a right to recover money when the debt became due, and not of cash.[32] A similar opinion could be found among the jurists of Louvain in the second half of the sixteenth century. For example, Johannes Wamesius noted that a debt claim was "a thing in commerce" (*res in commercio*) and was therefore capable of being owned, purchased, bequeathed, donated, or pledged.[33]

Drawing on this legal tradition, Lessius insisted that bond letters represented a right to future money, not money as such. Consequently, they were in the safe and sane realm of buying and selling, not in the dangerous waters of implicit lending at interest. Following the same reasoning, modern canonists and scholastic theologians have gradually removed suspicion vis-à-vis the practices of selling annuities and bills of exchange. By qualifying them as purchase contracts, they put an end to the interpretation that annuities and exchange rates involved the disguised collection of interest. Therefore, refuting Henry of Ghent's analysis of the annuity contract (*census*) as a *mutuum purum* in the thirteenth century, Lessius asserted that "the opinion that here [in the practice of annuities] there is no question of goods, but of money or annual pensions, is not true, since the actual and immediate object which is bought and sold via this contract is neither money nor an annual pension, but a right to claim an annual pension. Nevertheless, this right is very different from the object itself."[34]

To legitimize this rejection of medieval scholastic doctrine, Lessius referred less to the developments of legal doctrine than to the habitual dealings among merchants, which gained the power of a customary norm. In fact, Lessius even went as far as directly and explicitly criticizing the Aristotelian notion of money as a sterile and unsaleable object. He defended himself against the idea that money cannot be the object of a sale, arguing on the contrary that money can indeed be sold as a good, due to a lack of it or the difficulties and risks associated with collecting it.[35] In considering the exchange contract, Lessius formulated his interpretation of money as a veritable merchandise: "[An exchange contract] can be reduced to a contract of purchase and sale. . . . Such an analysis best approximates the customs of merchants. Merchants regard the absent money as a good and they buy and sell it for present money, as if the present money were its price. In effect, money is not only the price and measure of other goods. It may also itself be a saleable item for the following reasons: (1) its lesser or better-quality material; (2) its convenience of storage, transportation, and payment; and (3) its physical absence."[36]

A good is traded in a specific market with its own characteristics and mechanisms. The same applies to the money market, which, according to Lessius, falls under a specific economic law: "absent money is worth less than present money" (*pecunia absens minus valet quam pecunia praesens*). This is a precursor of the modern economic concept, developed above all by Keynes, of "liquidity preference." It is by virtue of having formulated this rule that Lessius is considered, along with other scholastics such as Azpilcueta, as a precursor of the theorists of money such as Keynes or Eugen von Böhm-Bawerk.[37] Lessius even managed to explain the economic logic underpinning the preference for liquidity: like Olivi before him,[38] he underlined the fact that present money offers merchants advantages, conveniences, and options that absent money does not: "Money physically at a great distance from the place where the contract is concluded is valued less than present money. Therefore, it is lawful to exchange present money for absent money for profit. The hypothesis is correct for two reasons: (1) by its very nature, absent money does not offer the same options and conveniences as present money; (2) by its very nature, absent money cannot be made present without taking on expenses and risks. Hence other goods are also cheaper absent than present."[39]

Interest and the Common Good

The idea that cash, and therefore present money, offers various advantages and facilities that debt claims do not, is ubiquitous in Leonardus Lessius' economic analyses (we will return to this in chapter 8 on the "salvation of the economy"). It is due to their enormous potential that liquidities are in such high demand, Lessius explains, that it should be permissible for merchants to agree on a price for depriving themselves of their money (*carentia pecuniae*). The practice of establishing a price of money by common estimation should even be considered conducive to fostering the common good (*bonum commune*), Lessius argued, since "many people need cash, while people willing to give credit for free are not easy to find."[40] The strength of this reasoning has been acknowledged by various scholars of Lessius' economic doctrines.[41]

Individuals with funds do not want to lend money for nothing in return, "because of the capital risk and the difficulty of getting their money back," Lessius explained, and "because they do not want to miss out on the convenience of doing business in different ways, especially through the standard exchange practices." There is then the risk that predatory lenders will set the price of money as they see fit, taking only their private interest into account. To avoid these abuses, it is better to organize a market where the price of money is set by mutual agreement between all participants. Besides the fact that reason and the common good show that fixing the price of money on the basis of a common estimation would be opportune, we must realize, explains Lessius, that this practice already exists and that its legality can be considered likely (*probabilis*). Indeed, every day, traders and bankers gather at the Antwerp exchange (*bursa*) to determine the price of money, taking into consideration various factors: "This seems to be the common practice at the Antwerp exchange. Traders meet here every day to establish the price of "going without their money" (*carentia pecuniae*), a price that traders and financiers can demand to compensate for the fact that they are going without their money during the period the loan is granted, and for the fact that they are not allowed to claim this money before the due date. They set the price themselves or through agents, taking into consideration the abundance or scarcity of money and the number of exchanges, deals, and any opportunities to make a profit with present money."[42] Applied to the concrete case of the purchase of debt claims below par, the logic of the money market implies that this practice is lawful. The price of money set by common estimation in the market is nothing more than the interest rate when money is lent or, conversely, the discount rate when bond letters are purchased. By the nature of things, in the "market for absent money," the current value of a debt claim is calculated not on the basis of its nominal value, but below par, precisely because of the preference for liquidity, regardless of the risks that all negotiable claims represent in everyday reality. This empirically substantiated logic of the preference for liquidity is moreover confirmed, Lessius reassured, by a standard rule of the highest authority: in effect, we find in Justinian's Digest a maxim according to which "it is of lesser value to have a legal claim than to have the thing itself." This same rule is invoked by all the canonists mentioned above, and in particular by Azpilcueta when he confirmed in his *Manual for Confessors* that it is "just to purchase debts more cheaply which mature in two, three, ten years, or even more, than those which are due today."[43]

As familiar as this market logic may seem to us today, it was no less concerning to moralists and jurists at the dawn of the modern age. By recognizing money as a commodity and the discount rate as the price of that commodity, Lessius and his contemporaries risked undermining the whole doctrine of usury, by replacing it with the doctrine of just price. From now on, to avoid the "ghost of usury", someone could in principle agree on a contract of sale with a bond letter instead of a loan contract, a circumvention which, moreover, Lessius was fully aware of: "In this way, more than one usurious profit could be mitigated. A usurer may claim that he is not willing to conclude a loan, but rather to purchase a right to, say, 100 or 200 gold guilders, an obligation that anyone can impose on himself."[44] Moreover, because the bond letters were sold publicly, the debtor could redeem his own debt before the due date, and even below par, provided that he himself (by showing himself to be a bad payer) did not cause the seller to want to dispose of his debt claims. This possibility was also anticipated by Johannes Wamesius in his consultation on the sale of debt claims. He specified that in the case where the person drawing a bill of exchange came to buy his own debt on the market, it was a redemption (*redemptio*) rather than a purchase, thereby triggering the perfectly legitimate discharge of the debt, even before the due date of the bill of exchange.[45]

An Unconvincing Step Backwards

Regardless of the canonical tradition from which Lessius drew, it was likely the explosive potential of the simple logic of the market which, in the end, unnerved him. Following an extensive and convincing presentation, he suddenly raised the alarm and explained that, in reality, buying debt claims below par, solely and exclusively on account of speculation over time, is unacceptable according to common opinion. The theologians Gabriel Biel, Silvestro Mazzolini da Prierio, Juan de Medina, and Domingo de Soto were cited to back up this argument, before Lessius made the surprising announcement that he supported this opinion, since it was more habitual and certain. Nevertheless, beside the fact that he supported this conservative view with the traditional argument of implicit usury, we should be wary of this sudden U-turn.

Lessius lacked strong arguments to demonstrate that it was unjust to buy a debt claim below par. What is more, he admitted that the reasoning *a contrario* of those who portrayed the purchase of bond letters below par as usurious was not at all convincing. Such individuals argued that, according to the logic of the market, it would be unlawful to buy the right to 100 guilders at 100 guilders, an incorrect reasoning, Lessius believed, since the just price includes a margin which means that the highest price can in effect be 100 guilders. Even more significant of his discrediting of this common opinion is the fact that, in his refutation of the practice of bond letters, Lessius ultimately confirmed the core of the argument of those who considered the discount as the just price for the loss of opportunity incurred by the entrepreneur who relinquished his cash: "Bond letters are valued below par either on account of the risks or difficulties involved in obtaining repayment, or because he who gives up present money deprives himself of an option or convenience which the letter does not give him."[46] Difficulties and risks are considered, from a strictly theoretical perspective, as elements extrinsic to the contract for the purchase of a debt claim. We could therefore infer that, in theory, these external factors confirm that the bond letters cannot be valued less in themselves, or by virtue of the main agreement itself. The argument of the absence of options and conveniences that cash gives, on the contrary, is undeniably a decisive factor for the intrinsically minor value of bond letters compared to present money. Moreover, the concept of a debt without risk, or *debitum liquidum*, seems entirely hypothetical. In fact, every debt claim inherently comes with doubts regarding its soundness. In view of this, it is not surprising that Alejandro Chafuen ranked Lessius among the unconditional advocates of the purchase of debt claims below par.[47] Even if Lessius officially and brusquely subscribed to the contrary opinion, one cannot help thinking that this approval is only a concession to the strength of traditional thought and the censorial power of his Jesuit order. We might also wonder about the list of authorities that Lessius produced to substantiate the market logic argument. Even if they had adopted the idea that debt claims can be purchased at a lower price, neither Martín de Azpilcueta nor Johannes Wamesius, for example, took the reasoning as far as Leonardus Lessius.

A final—but still important—qualification of Lessius' apparent reversal is based on the philosophical context at the turn of the seventeenth century. Apart from the question of how to solve moral cases in theory, the need arose, in confessional practice, for a system of moral thought that made it possible to decide on the means of action in a context of moral doubt and uncertainty. In practice, this ingenious system of efficiently resolving cases of conscience was known among the scholastics as "probabilism."[48] In principle, the aim of probabilism was to distinguish between "probable" and "improbable" opinions concerning the lawful or unlawful character of certain actions. In a nutshell, an opinion was considered "probable" (*probabilis*) as soon as it was supported either by a solid argument of reason, or by a leading authority. The major turning point in probabilism was that from 1577 onwards an action was considered justifiable as soon as it was based on a probable opinion *and that alone*. This new concept, apparently simple but in reality revolutionary, was first formulated by a Dominican friar of the School of Salamanca, Bartolomé de Medina. It was subsequently adopted by most Jesuits, including Lessius. Probabilism marked a fundamental break with the so-called probabiliorist thinking, which was also found in Salamanca, for instance with Domingo de Soto. While probabiliorism required that in cases of practical doubt concerning the lawfulness of an action, one should always follow the most probable opinion, probabilism required simply that one stick to a *merely* probable opinion. In other words, probabilism made it possible to take an action as soon as there was at least one probable opinion, based either on reason or on authority, that is, defended by more authorities or more rational arguments. Whether this probable opinion was less or more certain was beside the point.[49] In this context, we can understand Lessius' interest in building a solid argument and in offering the logical arguments necessary to justify the opposite opinion to conservative thought. In accordance with probabilism, Lessius' reasoning allowed a merchant to buy discounted bond letters, since there was a probable opinion legitimizing this practice, namely the opinion developed on reasonable grounds by Lessius, even though the common opinion was more probable and more certain. Lessius characterized his view of the justification of the price of money as probable, while agreeing with the opposite view so as not to risk being dismissed as too radical.[50]

Opportunity Costs, Risk, and the Price of Debt Claims

Up until now, the analysis of the problem of buying debt claims below par has been purely theoretical, ignoring the reality of the market where debt claims always come with risks. In actual business dealings, no debt claim is as secure as cash. The importance of Lessius' response to the theoretical question, however, was to make the pre-eminence of the logic of the market salient: he merely paid lip service to the traditional doctrine of usury. This was all the more so when Lessius considered, in practice, the question of the lawfulness of the purchase of bond letters below par, that is, in everyday life where there are specific situations that offer the possibility that, on the basis of extrinsic titles, one can purchase a right to future money for less than its nominal value. According to scholastic doctrine, usury consisted in stipulating interest by virtue of an explicit or implicit loan, but not in demanding compensation by virtue of other titles, extrinsic to the principal contract and arising from concomitant circumstances.[51]

Among the extrinsic titles generally accepted by Lessius' contemporaries were direct loss (*damnum emergens*) and opportunity cost (*lucrum cessans*). Direct loss implies that the buyer is entitled to compensation in the form of a discount, since by giving up his money he risks having to find other money himself at interest when he incurs a loss; for example, if his house collapses, he is obliged to take out a loan himself to start the reconstruction works. The opportunity cost is a compensation for the fact that by giving up his cash, the entrepreneur deprives himself of a tool to make a profit. Indeed, even if we assert that time does not create value, in an indirect way it gives the prudent merchant opportunities to make profits by investing his money. In this respect, according to Lessius, it is completely logical that merchants who give up their tool of work should demand compensation for it: "The money you lend to others is worth more to you than its intrinsic value, insofar as you can make a profit from it by virtue of your industry (*per industriam*). Money is fertile seed containing virtual profits made by your industry. Therefore, it is lawful to claim a price higher than the intrinsic value of the money."[52]

Nevertheless, according to the traditional concept of the use of extrinsic titles, the lender was still required to specify the price of his opportunity cost in each case, via an agreement accompanying the main contract. He then had to demonstrate *ex post* that he had indeed lost out on this or that opportunity. Lessius' merit is that he broadened and generalized the concept of "opportunity cost" to the point that, in whatever circumstance, entrepreneurs and cash bankers could invoke it, even if they had other resources with which to make a profit. John Noonan enthusiastically referred to an "unprecedented" view: "With Lessius, *lucrum cessans* is thus a title available to almost all lenders, not only businessmen and investors, but potential businessmen and investors; it is chargeable though the lenders have cash reserves for irrational reasons; and the value of the lender's labor need not be taken from the value of his capital in calculating the interest. This is a broad, inclusive, and unprecedented position."[53]

Besides the fact that the buyer of a debt claim deprives himself of his cash, and deserves to be compensated for that reason, there is never any guarantee that he will be able to recover the debt at the due date. This circumstance gave rise, especially in the works of Molina, Lessius, and Lugo, to the introduction and acceptance of an additional extrinsic title, the "capital risk" (*periculum sortis*)[54]—we will return to this in chapter 6. The point here is that the general approval of a whole series of extrinsic titles touching on the intimacy of the daily reality of the debt market must necessarily lead to a reversal of the traditional doctrine on usury.

Since the opportunity cost did not have to be negotiated by individual contracting parties, Lessius suggested that a general, objective price should be established in a market where money is exchanged. Therefore, in the context of discussions on the *mutuum* contract, the new extrinsic title mentioned above emerges: the deprivation of money, or the "lack of money," during the time of the loan (*carentia pecuniae*). The fact that the individual who gives up his present money for a certain period of time loses the convenience and possibility of doing business must be compensated by a price, according to Lessius: "In the same way that a price can be given to other goods and obligations, it is possible to determine the price of the obligation to go without one's money for a given period of time. Money is the tool of the merchant and, in general, to go without one's work tool is calculable in money. Why, then, should merchants not be able to determine the price of their foregone money by way of a common consensus, especially since the common good so demands it?"[55]

In this way, Lessius undermined the very basis of the prohibition of interest-bearing loans, since here is an element which in truth is not external, but intrinsic to the loan contract, that is, the transfer of money for a given period of time. The time dimension is indeed inherent to the legal definition of the loan. Let us recall that Lessius judged that the recognition of the title *carentia pecuniae* was required by the common good: going without cash simply requires that every day the market establishes a price of money to be safeguarded in all *mutuum* contracts. The scarcity of liquidity is largely due to the fact that no-one spontaneously wants to part with their available money, since it affords the opportunity to undertake profit-making activities.

In fact, under the extrinsic title *carentia pecuniae*, Lessius tended to agglomerate all the existing and at least partially accepted titles until then to reduce them to a single universal title which, in truth, moves from the exterior to the interior of the concept of *mutuum*. In the name of the common good, he defended the practice of setting the price of money on the Antwerp exchange. He was fully aware of the fact that if there was no consideration for the financial needs of the population, and if credit remained "non-institutionalised,"[56] credit was only made even more expensive, and the risk of truly usurious practices increased. But then, one might ask, what remained of the scholastic doctrine of the prohibition of interest? "This custom practised among merchants on the Antwerp exchange," Lessius replied, "does not appear to be reprehensible, as long as the rate instituted by the imperial constitution of Charles V is not exceeded."[57] For Lessius, the prohibition of interest was practically transformed into a prohibition of usury in the modern sense of the term, a prohibition that only targets abusive interest rates that exceed the legal rate set by the authorities.

5
Information and Speculation

Is industry a crime?
Is diligence reprehensible?
Or foresight to be blamed?

—Ambrose of Milan

Leonardus Lessius' analysis of the debt market reveals the extent to which the doctrine of usury, in his view, is shattered by the logic of the market. At the same time, it opens the way to an insightful examination of another major subject in scholastic economic thought: that of speculation based on private information. Still largely suspect in the eyes of great Church Fathers such as Ambrose, Bishop of Milan at the end of the fourth century, speculative activities gained in esteem among Thomas Aquinas and his commentators at the dawn of the modern age. Intended to have been uttered by a merchant so that Ambrose of Milan could illustrate dubious morality, the words quoted above[1] can indeed be read as references to a range of moral values (industry, diligence, foresight) that serve as a basis for Lessius and other scholastics to offer a startling justification of commercial and financial speculation at the time of early modernity. The origin of their reflections on this question remains, however, an old textbook case: that of the Merchant of Rhodes, a wheat merchant who, coming from the port of Alexandria, wants to sell his merchandise at a high price to the inhabitants of the island of Rhodes, where a shortage has prompted prices to rise, whereas with the information at his disposal, he knows there will be a drop in prices following the imminent arrival of his competitors. Can he morally take advantage of the information at his disposal to sell at the current price without informing the people of Rhodes? This chapter invites us to delve into Lessius' masterly discussion of this case, from which we can glean the importance he attaches to economic calculus, while exploring its limits.

Money, Markets, and Merit. Wim Decock, Oxford University Press. © Oxford University Press (2025).
DOI: 10.1093/9780197827345.003.0006

An Old Case for a New World

Before its revival at the dawn of the modern age, the case of the Merchant of Rhodes was extensively discussed by Stoic philosophers (third–second centuries BC), including Diogenes of Babylon, Antipater of Tarsus, and Cicero.[2] They all presented the case of the Merchant of Rhodes as follows. Having been informed of the arrival of other wheat traders bound for Rhodes, a merchant voyaging from Alexandria hesitates to sell his cargo at the high price he finds in Rhodes, where the population is stricken by famine. Should he remain silent, or is he morally obliged to share his information about the imminent arrival of other large shipments, which will bring the price down? The Stoics do not all have the same opinion as to the answer to be given to the doubts troubling the merchant. Diogenes of Babylon claimed that the merchant is entitled to look after his own interests, as long as he respects the laws. On the other hand, his pupil Antipater reminds the merchant that men are naturally part of the same community, and are therefore obliged to take an interest in the welfare of others. Antipater castigates his master for defending the fact that the merchant can keep his private information secret and demand the prevailing price on the market in Rhodes. He is backed up by Cicero, who believes that by not sharing his information, the merchant is engaging in fraudulent practices identical to those of someone who sells his house without revealing its hidden defects. In the fourth century, Ambrose endorsed Cicero's viewpoint, and opposed the art of commerce to divine wisdom, going so far as to identify speculation with theft.

Although the medieval scholastics were aware of Cicero and Ambrose's uncompromising opinions, they contrasted them with two examples from the biblical tradition and ancient Greek philosophy respectively. Firstly, there was the case of the patriarch Joseph, in the book of Genesis. To protect his people from a period of famine, he bought up vast stocks of wheat during the seven years of abundance and then sold them at a high price when the famine came. Secondly, the scholastics cited the example of Thales of Miletus, recounted in the first book of Aristotle's *Politics*. Drawing on his knowledge of astronomy, Thales speculated on an abundant olive harvest and rented all the olive presses in advance at a good price. In addition to these two examples, medieval and modern scholastics drew on the authority of Thomas Aquinas. In his *Summa Theologica*, Aquinas introduced a distinction between the case of hidden defects and that of the Merchant of Rhodes. While he considered that hidden defects must in principle be disclosed, he believed that such a duty does not exist in the case of private knowledge regarding future market developments. Certainly, the merchant who shares his information or lowers the price according to his knowledge demonstrates more virtuous conduct, but justice does not oblige him to do so.

More than three centuries later, in the first edition of *De iustitia et iure*, Lessius revived Thomas Aquinas' insights, to remove the Merchant of Rhodes' scruples once and for all. In Lessius' view, there is nothing stopping the merchant from defending his own interests by not revealing his private information. But the way he formulated this case of conscience is noticeably different from the stories passionately recounted by Cicero and Ambrose. In the way he presented the case of the Merchant of Rhodes, Lessius deviated from the ancient tradition. He omitted the details that made the resolution of the case so dramatic in the Stoic and Patristic tradition. In the chapter on purchase contracts in *De iustitia et iure*, there is no mention of famine, nor of shipments of wheat or other food. The concrete details of Cicero's version of the story make way, in Lessius and other modern scholastics, to a question as neutral as it is possible to be: "When I know that the price of a commodity is about to fall, can I nevertheless sell it at the current price?"[3] Besides the fact that the question is now posed in abstract terms, its relation to conscious speculative strategies becomes all the more explicit as Lessius added the question of whether the merchant can sell *more* goods on account of his private knowledge. We will return in this chapter to the answers he gives to these questions, but not without first drawing attention to the context in which the revival of the case of the Merchant of Rhodes takes place. While, in Lessius' treatise, the way the case is formulated has been significantly altered, so has the historical context of the early seventeenth century, which was marked by profound upheavals in the circulation of information.

The Acceleration of Information

In 1605, when Lessius published the first edition of his treatise, the first printed newspapers, the "gazettes," appeared at the same time under the stewardship of the Strasbourg-based printer Johann Carolus. The gazettes made information more accessible to a wider group of merchants. From the end of the 1610s, printing houses specializing in "news" were set up in Amsterdam and Antwerp, with the Low Countries rapidly playing a pioneering role in this new industry.[4] During the course of the seventeenth century, at least forty-three gazettes were in print in the northern and southern Netherlands by competing printers, who tended to set up shop not far from the marketplaces. As Arthur der Weduwen noted, the printing presses of Van Hilten, Lieshout, and Meininga were located at the corner of the Amsterdam Stock Exchange or near the Pont Neuf. Since the stock exchange was usually only open for an hour, just before noon, traders would rush to these gazettes before and after, in order to finetune their strategies. In *De Spaansche Brabander* (1617), a masterpiece of Dutch literature, Gerbrand Adriaensz Bredero depicted a certain Andries, a "man [who was] always the first to know everything," because he went "to the Pont Neuf in the early morning" to "take the news in its nest before it flies away."[5]

The new presses only accelerated the flow of information, already driven forward by improvements to both public and private postal networks in the sixteenth century.[6] It was a veritable "communication revolution" at the dawn of the modern age, driven by individuals who continue to enjoy renown in our day. The Taxis family built a fortune thanks to its monopoly on the distribution of information within the Habsburg empire. The headquarters of their postal empire was set up in Brussels in 1501, near the Grand Sablon. The splendid funeral chapel of the Thurn and Taxis family in the Church of Notre-Dame du Sablon, remodelled by Lamoral-Claude-François de la Tour-Tassis at the end of the seventeenth century, remains a privileged witness to the close ties between the Thurn and Taxis family and this city in the heart of Europe. The "backbone" of the postal network of the Taxis started from Brussels, connecting the cities of the Netherlands to Augsburg, Innsbruck, Trento, Venice, Rome, and Milan.[7] Between Brussels and Paris, the Thurn and Taxis family ensured the relaying of news within forty-four hours. From 1541 on, they operated a daily connection between Brussels and Antwerp. The Thurn and Taxis family quickly realized that their postal network could serve the interests not only of the Habsburg princes, but also of merchants, bankers, and private individuals of whatever background, including the clergy. We cannot rule out that Jesuits such as Lessius knew members of the Thurn and Taxis family or their staff intimately.

In the commercial metropolises, the acceleration of information heightened the rivalries between traders, all eager to be abreast of the latest political and economic goings-on and frantically searching for any privileged information that would allow them to make a profit. This thirst for information is ubiquitous in the *Confusión de confusiones* (1688), a unique work detailing the activities of the Amsterdam Stock Exchange. Through interesting and humorous dialogues between an investor, a philosopher, and a merchant, its author José de la Vega, a Jewish trader, intellectual, and patron, revealed the rules of the game of financial speculation.[8] The use of information played a major role in this regard. For example, the investor explained that "the cunning shareholder does his best to have correspondents in India who can keep him informed, through other circuits of informers in England, Aleppo, or elsewhere, about the desired peace in India, about the good situation of the firms of the India Company, its transactions in Japan, Persia, or China, and their usefulness, about the number of ships returning to the fatherland, their cargoes, and the quantity of spices they have on board."[9] And the experienced investor added that the cautious speculator is well advised not to rely too much on the information he receives in this way, primarily because some actors have an interest in spreading false information. Regardless of the risks associated with the circulation of news, whether true or false, business circles were nonetheless eager for information. The growing supply of printed newspapers met this pressing demand. It was accompanied by the rise of books instructing readers on how to use the new media. In one of the first Dutch-language manuals of its kind, published in the middle of the eighteenth century, the author considered that "no one involved in worldly affairs can ignore the utility of 'currents' or newspapers."[10]

Competition, Just Price, and Common Estimation

In a world witnessing the acceleration of information, where the prudent and efficient management of a network of correspondents represents the very art of commerce, a return to the pure and simple condemnation of speculative activities as found in Ambrose is inconceivable in the eyes of the scholastic theologians. In a context of heightened rivalry, the trader cannot be expected to compromise his own dealings "by behaving like a professor," to use the words of Francisco de Vitoria.[11] It would be absurd, according to the founder of the School of Salamanca, that the merchant who is better informed than the others should be penalized. "The fact that I know the future," explained Vitoria, "is part of my art." Like most scholastics of the modern age, he wanted to have this exercising of the art of commerce recognized, with the merchant authorized to make a profit based on his privileged information. Similarly, Luis de Molina considered that the profits made by the Merchant of Rhodes "are the result of his industry, skill, and good luck."[12] Anyone entering the world of business engages in a competition, even a struggle, a *certamen* according to the word used by scholastics such as Conrad Summenhart and John Mair.[13] Information is an indispensable and legitimate weapon in this competition.

To keep ahead in such an environment, the race for good information is an essential component of the merchant's profession. Indeed, it allows the merchant to anticipate market evolutions, exploit price differences, and enjoy good business. A well-informed merchant endeavours to buy goods cheaply to sell them more expensively. Unless the just price of a commodity has been fixed by public authorities, it "does not reside in an indivisible point," to quote a common maxim of scholastic economic thought since at least Duns Scotus in the thirteenth century. On the contrary, it allows a margin, a "latitude" (*latitudo*), which offers opportunities for arbitrage and speculation. This price, which the scholastics designated with different expressions such as "the vulgar price," "the current price," or "the natural price," is separate, on account of its margins and its fluctuations, from a "legal price," set for its part, through a legislative act, by the public authorities. According to Lessius, the latitude of the current price is explained by the fact that the vulgar price reflects the value judgements of the *vulgus*, that is, a multitude of individuals who are not at all of the same opinion.[14] The current price is established without interference from the public authorities, which is why it is also called the "natural price," after Bellarmine or Molina.[15]

The vulgar price is established on the basis of what the scholastics call a "common estimation" (*aestimatio communis*), that is, the evaluation, by the community of actors in the market, of the circumstances or factors that determine the price. For Lessius, the same factors must be taken into consideration by the authorities when setting prices through law. He listed the following factors: "Some pertain to the goods themselves, their abundance, scarcity, necessity, and utility; others pertain to the sellers, including the labour, expense, and risk involved in acquiring, transporting, and storing the goods. In addition, there is the mode of sale (*modus vendendi*), i.e., whether sellers sell on their own initiative or at the request of buyers. Other factors relate to the buyers, whether there are many of them or not many, and the abundance or scarcity of money."[16] Although an in-depth examination of the scholastic doctrine of the just price is not our objective here, various elements nevertheless deserve our attention. In addition to the reference to the balance of power between supply and demand as a factor determining price, the empirical observation that the mode of sale profoundly affects the mechanism of setting prices is a common thread running through Lessius' work. In the words of an adage often invoked by modern scholastics, "spontaneous goods lose a third of their value."[17] Lessius refers in this context to the authority of Cajetan, the first major commentator on Thomas Aquinas at the dawn of the modern age (see here p. 22). Indeed, Cajetan analysed at length the impact of the mode of sale (*modus vendendi*) on prices.[18] Sellers who spontaneously offer their goods drive down their price, a phenomenon frequently observed on market days, according to Lessius, and especially at the end of the market, when buyers and liquidity are scarcer. A similar observation relates to public sales. In particular, debt claims, which are often auctioned off at a fraction of their nominal value, provide a concrete example of the impact of the mode of sale—we will return to this later in chapter 6 on *subprime loans*. At the same time, Lessius observes that auctions are also likely to result in the opposite phenomenon, namely a considerable rise in prices, among other things when buyers start to bid higher. At an auction, Lessius explained, "the price of goods is accidental and uncertain. [Goods] are frequently sold for less than the price the merchants paid because of the small number of buyers and their lack of interest. But they are also often sold at a higher price, because of the large number of buyers or their enthusiasm."[19] Moreover, if the price of goods put up for auction is subject to chance, so are the merchant's profits. Lessius continued: "In the first case, it is a matter of misfortune for the merchant, in the other a matter of good fortune. The just price of a market is the price that can be obtained according to the mode of sale and without any fraud. This is the standard practice of pious and experienced men."

The Condition of Merchants

For Lessius, it was clear that markets function according to their own logic. The primary task of the merchant is to decipher this logic in order to limit risks and seize opportunities. This is the random condition unique to his profession: sometimes he wins, sometimes he loses, depending on his fortune and how good his calculation of the potential risks and benefits was.[20] Therefore, an adequate understanding of the factors of labour, costs and risks is required in calculating the just price. As Lessius made clear, the common estimation takes these factors into account, but only to the extent of the costs ordinarily incurred by merchants in acquiring, transporting, and storing certain goods. "I am not talking about costs that are the result of misfortune or carelessness,"[21] he explained. Although the expenses ordinarily incurred by merchants must be reflected in the just price, there is no room for compensating extraordinary costs: "In setting the price, ordinary labour and costs have already been taken into account. If some merchants are incurring more costs, that's their misfortune. The common price cannot be raised as a result. Conversely, the common price should not fall when there are no costs at all. This is the merchant condition, the *conditio mercatorum*: they can earn profits by incurring smaller costs, while they can lose money by incurring enormous and extraordinary costs."[22]

Lessius offers here a remarkable analysis of the simple, but uncompromising, logic that underlies the world of business: if you want to make a profit, you have to make sure that you reduce your costs below the average. This truth is the *conditio mercatorum.* The more the merchant can reduce his costs, the more generous his margins. On the other hand, it would be imprudent to interpret Lessius' analysis according to models in vogue since the start of the rivalries between Marxists and capitalists in the twentieth century. Lessius defended neither a "utility theory of value," which reduces economic value to its utility for buyers, nor, on the contrary, a "production cost theory," which assumes that economic value must correspond to the producer's costs.[23] Lessius' thought corresponded with mainstream thought in scholasticism in the modern age, which recognized the primacy of the fundamentals of supply and demand without forgetting that the just price must reflect a pecuniary reward for the costs ordinarily incurred by a merchant who is neither imprudent nor afflicted with misfortune.

The virtues of prudence and "occupation"

By analysing the circumstances which determine the setting of a just price, the merchant can therefore seek to increase his margins. If he manages to sell the same good with less costs than those automatically envisaged in the vulgar price or the legal price, he is assured of a profit. In addition, the more he is able to reduce risks, especially by diligently seeking out accurate information, the more he knows how to control chance and attract good luck. Instead of curbing his commercial spirit, the just price allows the merchant to pursue his dealings rationally while respecting a moral framework, especially since the latitude of the just price allows him to speculate on price differences for the same good, but in different places (arbitrage). The prudent merchant is able to anticipate profits by using the doctrine of just price as a compass that indicates the right path to deserved profit.

On the other hand, Lessius urged merchants to remain prudent. He conceived of a mercantile morality that encourages, even obliges, market participants to fully exercise the cardinal virtue of "prudence" (*prudentia*), which is analysed in the first book of *On Justice and Law*. His treatise opened with an explanation of the etymological origins of the virtue of "prudence" or "foresight" which is essential to success in daily life: "It would seem that the word "prudence" derives from "seeing far" (*porro videre*), according to Isidore in his *Etymologies*, book 10, chapter 15. The prudent individual is therefore characterized as 'far-seeing,' he is perceptive and sees the contingencies of what is uncertain."[24] Following Thomas Aquinas, Lessius explained that prudence includes the abilities related to memory, intelligence, docility, wisdom, reason, foresight, circumspection, and careful attention. The prudent man tries to master the vicissitudes of the future by using his understanding of the present moment and his past experiences. Negligence, like fraud, is the opposite of exercising prudence. And while "solicitude for temporal things" should not be exaggerated, "prudence of the flesh" is part of the authentic prudent management of life insofar as the individual continues to acknowledge the primacy of the spiritual life.[25] There is then a topos of Christian spirituality concerning the merits of work, the dangers of idleness, and the moral necessity of "busy-ness" or "occupation"[26]: "The Lord does not want all the things necessary for man's life to fall down to him automatically, without effort and solicitude. This would give him the opportunity for idle inactivity—the origin of the greatest of evils, quite rightly called 'the devil's pillow.' The Lord wants man to apply himself to work and to demonstrate solicitude, so that, occupied in this exercise (*occupatus exercitio*), he stays away from the pleasures and other sins that are the fruit of idleness."[27]

As such, public authorities, legislators, judges, military personnel, economic administrators, and all individuals must exercise prudence—political, legislative, civil, military, economic, and personal prudence respectively.[28] Specifically, the merchant must be "occupied" in the goings-on of the market, working to reduce his costs compared to the average, and staying ahead of his competitors in terms of his knowledge of market developments. Keeping abreast of opportunities for arbitrage and speculation is part of the necessary solicitude of the prudent merchant.

Public Truths and Private Truths

In addition, the just price allows the prudent merchant to capitalize on his qualities of perceptiveness, foresight, and insight. The just price is like a benchmark that allows him to orient his activities. If it is established on the basis of the public estimation of the circumstances determining the price, the merchant can speculate on the more truthful nature of his personal estimation, different and perhaps better, of these same circumstances. If a given merchant's personal estimation suggests that the common estimation ignores certain circumstances that may influence the market price, there is nothing to prevent him from making a good deal. Similarly, the fact that the just price is based on an average of costs that are higher than the expenses actually incurred by a given merchant does not prevent the merchant from making a profit. On the contrary, the objectivity with which the just price is imposed creates margins, both literally and figuratively, for prudent merchants whose private knowledge has no impact on the common estimation. This is the core of Lessius' defence of the Merchant of Rhodes, who refuses to share his information in order to sell at the current price: "Even if the seller knows that the price will soon fall, and the buyer does not know this, he can sell his goods at the current price. . . . The reason is that a good can be sold at the price established by the common estimation as long as that estimation applies. The just price is the price determined by the order of the prince or by the common estimation. The private knowledge of the seller does not change the common opinion and estimation."[29] As such, the speculative activities of the patriarch Joseph recounted in the book of Genesis serve as a precedent: "Likewise, the private knowledge of the buyer does not change it. Otherwise, the buyer would not be able to buy at the current price if he knew that the price would soon rise. But this is false, as shown by the example of Joseph (Genesis 41). Aware that unprecedented scarcity was coming, he bought up all the wheat in Egypt at the current price."

Private knowledge (*scientia privata*) is not included in the common estimation, which reflects the assessment of price-determining factors by the majority of market participants. In the real world, the factors determining this market price depend on the estimation made by the community of intelligent and experienced men, and this estimation may well prove to be wrong and false. However, collective ignorance does not prevent the common estimation from serving as a basic criterion for knowing what the just price is, insisted Lessius.[30] Here, as elsewhere in his analysis of the case of the Merchant of Rhodes, he took specific inspiration from the Augustinian friar Pedro de Aragón, of Salamanca. In his own treatise *On Justice and Law* (1590), Aragón explained that the just price depends solely on the knowledge *or* ignorance of the public.

More broadly, by insisting on the futility of private knowledge and the primacy of public truth, Lessius and Aragón were the heirs to an epistemological conception of truth that referred to the community, not to the individual or to God. A parallel can be drawn with scholastic reflections on the information and knowledge that matter in court judgements. In principle, the judge is not supposed to take his private knowledge into account, or even the innocence of the accused, because only the public evidence should guide his decision. According to a famous adage, *Iudex secundum allegata non secundum conscientiam iudicat*, the judge must render judgement on the basis of proof and evidence.[31] The judge is not supposed to take into consideration his "conscience," in the double etymological sense, of his moral convictions and his private knowledge. In the view of the Salamancan theologian Domingo de Soto, this principle derived its legitimacy from the need to respect collective truth in the interest of the "tranquillity of the republic".[32] Public knowledge, however erroneous, must override the private knowledge of the judge in the interest of maintaining order. In this way, Soto anticipated the famous adage, echoed by many contemporary jurisdictions, that it is not enough to do justice; more important, justice must be seen to be done.

In Praise of Imperfection

Like court judgements, prices do not reflect the knowledge of the individual or of God, but the truth as it appears publicly to the community of men. Only God has the knowledge of the price that perfectly reflects the true condition of things. According to Juan de Lugo, a Jesuit theologian, "we men do not know in a precise and determined way . . . the correct mathematical value of a thing (*valor iustus mathematicus rei*)."[33] Lugo's words resonated with the renowned liberal economist Friedrich Hayek. In the lecture he gave in September 1974 on the occasion of receiving his "Sveriges Riksbank Prize in Economic Sciences in Memory of Alfred Nobel," he spoke of the impossibility for individuals to know all the parameters that determine the equilibrium price of all goods and services. Referring to the scholastics, whom he regarded as "remarkable anticipators of modern economics," he urged his fellow economists to be modest rather than to cultivate the illusion of one day finding the perfect mathematical model that will allow the calculation of a single equilibrium price: "Indeed, the chief point was already seen by those remarkable anticipators of modern economics, the Spanish schoolmen of the sixteenth century, who emphasized that what they called *pretium mathematicum*, the mathematical price, depended on so many particular circumstances that it could never be known to man but was known only to God. I sometimes wish that our mathematical economists would take this to heart."[34] In the absence of a mathematical model that perfectly corresponds to the real world, merchants must find their orientation thanks to the estimation, fallible of course, of the community of men. The most advanced mathematical models would not change anything, in Hayek's view. And for good reason: in the divine world, characterized by complete transparency and perfect knowledge of all information, there is no room for speculation. The epistemological imperfection and the dispersal of information in the world of business are the conditions of possibility of the permanent competition between merchants. If, thanks to his extraordinary talent and continual efforts to keep abreast through all possible networks and media, a given individual has other information that allows him to have better knowledge than that which is at the basis of the common estimation, he can go ahead and profit from his superior knowledge. In a divine world, this race for profits would become utterly impossible.

Private Interests, Useful Lies, and Charity

If the divine world is characterized by perfect transparency and total knowledge, thereby excluding any possibility of arbitrage and speculation, it is also supposed to be harmonious, far from the conflicts of interests of the earthly realm. Since the reality of the merchant condition is rather different, scholastic theologians have, at the same time, considered the question of whether there are limits to the spirit of speculation. Can the merchant pursue his interests, without disclosing any information to the people of Rhodes, if the buyer suffers losses by buying at the current price? Should he be concerned about the interest of his counterparty? Is he obliged to reveal his information if he is expressly asked about what he knows? Does he risk failing in his Christian duty of charity by considering only the law of just price? These are questions that Lessius asked in following the scholastic tradition, and in particular by taking inspiration from the opinions of Pedro de Aragón.

Aragón maintained that the Merchant of Rhodes not only had the right to remain silent about his private information. He went further by giving the merchant the right to lie if the buyer asked him questions about his private information.[35] Although lying is generally prohibited, an exception is made in the world of business, to the extent that exercising the function may justify it. In this specific case, it is a "dutiful lie," a noble lie told out of duty (*mendacium officiosum*). For example, Lessius noted that "no-one is obliged to reveal the truth to another person when it is a matter of preserving a significant advantage and if the knowledge of the truth could lead the other person to prevent the advantage or to benefit from it himself. This lie is not to be considered as a pernicious lie, but as a lie told out of duty (*mendacium officiosum*)."[36] From a historical perspective, it would be rash to think that if Lessius accepted white lies, this could reflect lax ethics. While Augustine is responsible for the strict prohibition of lying, denying that a noble lie even exists, the notions of tricks, white lies, and useful simulations have indeed played a role in the long tradition of ancient and Christian philosophy, as Alberto Bondolfi has demonstrated.[37] Justifiably drawing on the authority of Pedro de Aragón, Lessius drew on this tradition to propose (albeit with some reluctance) the following response: "If he is asked whether he expects ships or a large quantity of goods to arrive, and if he says he does not know, I believe that in that case he is not obliged to pay back his profits. He is not obliged to reveal the truth if he will incur so much disadvantage. Moreover, some believe that he is not even obliged to do so if he explicitly denied that these ships or goods were on their way. This is a dutiful lie, which serves to avoid causing losses for oneself."[38]

Like Aragón, Lessius applied an analogy common in the scholastic tradition, comparing the situation of merchants to that of two rival beggars. If one of them is already at the door of a rich man asking for alms, he can chase the other beggar away, claiming that there is nothing left for him. Both beggars have the same right to alms, but if one suffers because the other exercises his right, the loss should be considered accidental. Nevertheless, Lessius specified that the poor beggar, or even the merchant, must have a real interest in defending his position if he wanted to tell a dutiful lie, on pain of incurring liability. At the same time, Lessius warned against a lack of prudence in business dealings. Market participants must find out about the reliability of their partners. If the buyer should have known better than to rely on the information given by a seller, he only has himself to blame if he suffers losses due to the dutiful lie of the other party. Naivety comes at a cost.

In the context of business dealings, it should be expected that a counterparty will seek to defend his interest at all costs. This emerges from another case analysed by Lessius, where he defended the merchant's right to conceal private information, even to lie, since according to Lessius this is part of mercantile habits and customs: "In the following case, the merchant is not obliged to give back his profits. When asked about the price of wheat in a certain province, he claims that prices are lower there and that there is an abundant supply of wheat, his aim being to discourage his competitors from transporting their supplies there, because this would lower the value of his own stocks. Following mercantile practice, the truth is not revealed in such cases, to avoid losses."[39] The assumption that charity is practiced in business is naive. There can be no presumption of donation between merchants. Unless they know each other very well, are friends, or belong to the same family, merchants do not give each other gifts. Lessius therefore specified on several occasions that "there is no presumption of gifts between strangers, unless there are clear signs of a wish to the contrary."[40] Moreover, even if the merchant wishes to be charitable, he is not obliged to disadvantage himself in order to prevent his partner from suffering losses. According to a popular adage among modern scholastics, "charity begins at home."[41] A healthy practice of charity is not incompatible with an individual defending his own interests. Of course, this is a situation where both parties are exposed to losses. Lessius was less explicit than other scholastics in asserting that charity did not prevent the Merchant of Rhodes from making pure profits while the buyer suffered losses.[42] He limited himself to saying that the conduct of the Merchant of Rhodes "can sometimes be detrimental to charity, especially if you sell a significant amount of goods to a person who will suffer serious losses, even to the point of losing his status and his fortune."[43]

Nevertheless, Lessius seemed to indicate that in less extreme cases, charity was in general not incompatible with speculative activities. He referred to Thomas Aquinas' assertion that any other conduct is gratuitous and unnecessary, thereby falling under the term "supererogation," that is, that which is not strictly necessary to demonstrate good Christian conduct. As such, we can assume that Lessius would have followed John Mair's view that charity does not stop the Merchant of Rhodes from preferring to make a profit himself rather than promote the interests of others or avoid the moderate losses of another merchant. "I would be imprudent not to make a profit when it comes along," explained Mair, who transposed the case of the Merchant of Rhodes to northern regions: he described a wheat merchant arriving in London from Normandy, and a Burgundy wine merchant speculating on higher prices in Paris. Mair highlighted the fact that these merchants even had an obligation to look after their own interests and those of their families first. Even if this involved making a profit at the expense of the other contracting party, one's own interest must be defended, in Mair's view. Therefore, Mair distanced himself from Summenhart, who in his *Opus septipertitum de contractibus* had condemned the merchant who is prepared to make a profit without worrying about the losses actually suffered by the other party as a result of the transaction.[44]

Nevertheless, Mair, like Summenhart and Lessius, was considering transactions between professionals. When it came to individuals who have no experience or knowledge of how the market works, such as peasants or widows, they were unanimous in saying that the seller must reveal all his information and prevent the weaker party from suffering harm. Instead of punishing the naivety and the lack of prudence of imprudent professionals, it is a question here of protecting buyers against the consequences of their honest simplicity (*simplicitas*). A European jurist of the twenty-first century would quickly recognize in this distinction the distant origins of the "consumer," who enjoys higher protection in his transactions with professional sellers.

Insider Information and Insider Trading

Up until now, the information that allows the Merchant of Rhodes to enrich himself comes from his intelligent and personal reading of the evolution of the factors determining the market price. But what about his private use of information that is supposed to be publicly available, such as a change in the legal price of wheat decreed by the government? Can the wheat merchant who is aware, through his network or his personal contacts with government officials, of an impending fall in the legal price, anticipate this change by selling more stock before the government measure is made public? Faced with this question, which had already been widely discussed by medieval jurists, Luis de Molina differentiated between information that could be kept confidential, on the one hand, and knowledge that had to be shared publicly, on the other. Information relating to changes in the legal price fell into the latter category, in his opinion. Consequently, he condemned the merchant eager to enrich himself thanks to his privileged information regarding an economic measure decreed by the government but not yet made public: "If you take advantage of your knowledge of a law that has not yet been promulgated to enrich yourself at the expense of others, you are appropriating, at their expense, knowledge of a thing that should be publicly known. Therefore, you do them an injustice."[45]

While Molina's reasoning is based on the authority of the leading jurists of the sixteenth century such as Arias Piñel, it was not followed by Lessius. The latter ignored Molina's distinction between information relating to laws and information relating to market events. According to Lessius, there are at least three reasons why a merchant could use his inside information about a change in the law to sell more goods than expected. Firstly, there is no law prohibiting him from profiting from such knowledge. Secondly, contractual justice, the ultimate criterion for assessing the morality of the merchant's conduct, is unconcerned with the merchant's reasons for selling more. Thirdly, the intention behind the speculative conduct does not change the moral character of that conduct, which remains right in itself. Consequently, Lessius argued, the merchant can sell both at the current price and in larger quantities to take advantage of the fact that he is aware of an impending change in the legal price or exchange rate: "Even if I know that a decision has been made by the prince or magistrate concerning goods or currency, as long as this decision has not been promulgated it is not binding and remains without force. The previous price therefore remains applicable."[46] While Lessius allows merchants to enrich themselves on the basis of his insider information, he nevertheless prohibits the public authorities from committing insider trading. The reason is simple. Governors and public administrators are, by virtue of their office (*ex officio*), obliged to safeguard the public interest. The merchant, on the other hand, like any other citizen, is not subject to the same obligation: "The magistrate is bound by his function to make every effort to ensure that such decisions relating to changes in price do not harm anyone through other individuals. However, it does not follow that the person who takes advantage of this kind of information is responsible for the loss suffered. The latter is not obliged by his function to take to heart the interests of the citizens and prevent losses."

In Lessius' vision, the public good is of vital importance, but it is not primarily the merchant's responsibility to promote it. It is the authorities who must fulfil their duty to safeguard the public interest. The merchant, on the other hand, must first protect his own interests and play the market game skilfully. Moreover, Lessius was quick to cite the authority of the great Salamancan canonist Diego de Covarrubias, who drew an explicit parallel between the Merchant of Rhodes and the card player who finds that he has an excellent hand. It would be against the "natural law of gambling," according to Covarrubias, to prohibit this player from raising the stakes to take advantage of his good luck.[47] According to Covarrubias, this natural law of gambling also included the use of the "positive deceit" (*dolus bonus*) mentioned in Roman law. For Covarrubias, this positive deceit is synonymous with *sollertia*, an almost untranslatable word that combines notions such as ingenuity, know-how, skill, and industry. Clearly, positive deceit is part of the intelligent and industrious use of the laws of the business game.

The arguments of Lessius and Covarrubias seem to herald the assertion by Milton Friedman, that beacon of American neoliberalism in the second half of the twentieth century, that "There is one and only one social responsibility of business—to use its resources and engage in activities designed to increase its profits." In order to avoid confusion with the excesses of unfettered libertarianism, it is nevertheless important to recall Alain Supiot's[48] analysis of this famous utterance. It applies, *mutatis mutandis*, to Lessius' words. According to Supiot, taking into account the context in which it is made, Friedman's assertion should not necessarily be considered shocking. His neoliberal views started from the paradigm of a social order governed by the rule of law, guaranteed by heteronomous public authorities whose mission is to look after the public good and to preserve, in the long term, mankind, nature, and money. In this context, speculation could certainly become wild, but it must respect basic legal principles (such as the doctrine of just pricing, in Lessius' case).

6

Risk, Insurance, and Subprime Debt

The hidden reasons
that may reduce risk,
of which I alone am aware,
do not diminish the common estimation.

—Leonardus Lessius

The speculation inherent in market activity is not without risk, because economic calculus is subject to a range of errors, if only because the information gathered does not always prove reliable. For Lessius, these risks are at the very heart of the justification of the profits generated by speculative activities. While a merchant may seek to forge privileged contacts with colleagues and rub shoulders with men of power in order to keep himself continually informed, he cannot foresee or control all the factors likely to influence the evolution of the market. We only need to think of the example of Francesco di Marco Datini, the wealthy fourteenth-century merchant and benefactor whose archives are kept in the magnificent Palazzo Datini in Prato, near Florence. Some 150,000 letters (7,000 of which written by himself) testify to a frenetic letter-writing ability that allowed him to stay abreast of any event impacting his commercial empire. However, there remained countless uncertainties, ranging from doubts about the loyalty of his contacts to the political vagaries, as well as circumstances directly impacting the circulation and price of goods, such as wars, weather conditions, disease, fire, pirates, the arrival and departure of competitors' ships, and so forth.[1] In this chapter, we will first discuss Lessius' brief but characteristic analysis of insurance contracts, the unrivalled legal technique for guarding against the vagaries of business. We will then focus on how Lessius' understanding of the risks inherent in the condition of merchants (*conditio mercatorum*) led to his innovative analysis of the market for highly risky debt, also known as subprime debt. In both cases, we will witness the consequential application of the logic of speculation revealed and approved by Lessius in his analysis of the case of the Merchant of Rhodes.

Money, Markets, and Merit. Wim Decock, Oxford University Press. © Oxford University Press (2025).
DOI: 10.1093/9780197827345.003.0007

Uncertainty and Insurance

The difficulty of predicting all the vagaries of economic life, combined with the unreliability of information, underpins Lessius' analysis of the insurance market, an analysis that focuses in particular on the dubious practice of underwriting insurance contracts for losses that are believed to have already occurred. Apart from this specific case, insurance in itself was no longer considered problematic by Lessius, and therefore did not warrant too much attention. Unlike other scholastics, he did not even give his opinion on life insurance, perhaps because this had already been legitimized by Domingo de Soto and Luis de Molina.[2]

In effect, since the fifteenth century, insurance had generally been regarded without suspicion in moral terms, especially when it allowed merchants to insure their maritime voyages.[3] In the mid-sixteenth century, Soto summarized the common attitude towards insurance:[4] it was a very useful, even necessary, contract for the common good, he wrote, since it supported merchants in their commercial ventures, especially at sea. It took away worries and encouraged the risk-taking necessary for business. Soto then argued that risk can be given an economic value, the price of which can vary according to the common estimation. At the turn of the seventeenth century, Molina specified that the just price of insurance allows a certain latitude, like the just price of any other good: "This price is not indivisible; on the contrary, it manifests a margin between the lowest, medium, and highest just price. In addition to rising and falling with the value of the insured object, it varies with the level of risk to which the insurer is exposed: depending on whether the journey made by the ship carrying the cargo is longer or more difficult, whether there are pirates, etc."[5] Molina was clearly au fait with insurance practices. He referred to the estimation of insurance prices in Lisbon, Seville, and Genoa, and quoted extensively from the *Tractatus de assecurationibus*, a treatise on insurance written in 1488 by the Portuguese jurist Pedro de Santarém, a pioneer of insurance law.[6] Molina attacked the opinion (albeit a minority one in his day) of the late medieval scholastic Konrad Summenhart, according to which the legitimacy of profits made by insurers depended on their being directly involved in the management of the risk. For example, a ship's captain whose cargo is insured must be involved in this risk management. Molina, on the other hand, considered that direct involvement was not necessary for the insurer to show the effort and work necessary to justify the profits. The insurance contract was the perfect meeting place of *fortuna*, *industria*, and *dexteritas*, the latter quality including the intelligent anticipation of the future. In Molina's view, the justice of insurance contracts required above all that "the event that is the object of the insurance must be uncertain, at least as far as the knowledge (*notitia*) of both contracting parties is concerned, since they must both be simultaneously exposed to gains and losses in order for the contract to be just."[7]

It is the subjective character of certainty in relation to the insured loss that leads, already in Molina, to a nuanced reflection on the practice of so-called late insurance. For while it is obvious that his perfect knowledge of a loss that has occurred would prevent the insured party from subscribing to the policy in good conscience, in reality his knowledge of events is rarely perfect. Similarly, there is no doubt that the insurer cannot legitimately sell a policy to a merchant when he knows with certainty that the ship to be insured has already arrived at its destination. However, it often happens that a loss occurs without any of the contracting parties being aware of it. In this case, Molina approved of taking out a policy relating to an event that had already occurred, provided that the insurer and the insured party exposed themselves equally to the profits and losses: "In view of their knowledge of the event, they expose themselves equally to the gains and losses."[8]

Molina's reasoning was followed by Lessius. He fully approved of insurance taken out by merchants who were almost sure, but not entirely certain, that the insured object was already lost when the insurance was taken out. In the eyes of both Jesuits, the uncertainty regarding the reliability of the information justified the actions of the insured party. The merchant obviously hoped to get a good deal, but he always ran the risk that his information was ultimately erroneous, paying a premium for nothing. Conversely, the insurer may speculate on whether the information about the loss is false, hoping to collect a premium without actually having to compensate the insured party. "The insured party exposes himself to the risk of losing his money by paying premiums without the insurer suffering any inconvenience, for in the unlikely event that the insured object is not lost, the insurer will be able to keep the premium,"[9] Lessius explained. It was therefore a matter of fairness, in his view, to consider the possibility that the insurer may also lose the gamble, and that the insured party may therefore win if the information concerning an established claim turned out to be correct. However, Lessius qualified his assertions: in this case, the compensation claimed by the insured party must not exceed the amount he would have been willing to pay himself if he had known the facts with certainty, or at least the amount considered fair by a prudent expert.

Mercantile Customs and Late Insurance

It is likely that in analysing the case of late insurance with a certain goodwill, Molina and Lessius wished to take into consideration the customs of the mercantile community. Molina's treatise is full of references to legal works that reflected Portuguese practice of the time. In his discussion of late insurance, Molina drew on the early Portuguese case-law reports written in the last quarter of the sixteenth century by António da Gama and Alvaro Valasco.[10] While Lessius omitted explicit references to the *Consuetudines compilatae*, the official text of the customary law of the city of Antwerp from 1608, he did refer to late insurance.[11] Similar practices were observed in Burgos, Bruges, and London in the second half of the sixteenth century, prompting Guido Rossi to conclude that late insurance was a common mercantile practice at that time.[12]

The practice of late insurance seems to have been particularly well established in Antwerp. In the *Centuria consiliorum* (1584) by Elbert de Leeuw, known as Leoninus, professor of canon law and later of civil law in Louvain, there was a reference to a late insurance policy.[13] A merchant from Genoa took out insurance in Antwerp on 23 January 1540 for a cargo shipped from Chios (Greece) to Ancona (Italy), but which was lost on 13 or 14 December of the previous year. Although Leoninus left no doubt about the invalidity of such contracts from the perspective of medieval Roman law (*ius commune*), he admitted that the local custom of Antwerp tolerated the practice as long as the insured party was not deemed to have had the possibility of knowing with certainty that the risk had actually occurred. Moreover, the custom started from the principle that information is relayed at a speed of one Roman mile per hour. After this objective time frame, any insurance taken against a past risk is void.

Leoninus insisted on the conditional nature of the permission of late insurance as prescribed by custom. Without this limit, he explained, no-one would still be willing to take out marine insurance. The insurance policies would be seriously imbalanced in favour of the insured party and at the expense of the insurers, especially since the premiums that the latter could charge were moderate. As a result, insurers would have an incentive to quit their profession altogether. Approving, without restriction, insurance policies taken out for risks that have occurred would therefore end up disadvantaging the merchants themselves. They would not find anyone to insure them against future risks. In addition, even if the insured party could demonstrate that he was not aware of the loss at the time of signing the contract, this objection, based on private knowledge, was worthless.

What matters was not the time it took for the insured party, in particular, to have actual knowledge of the claims, according to Leoninus. It was enough to determine how long it usually took, in general and in similar circumstances, for someone to acquire this knowledge "according to the nature of the thing," that is, according to normal communication by sea or land.[14] For Leoninus, attempts to objectify time limits were praised because they helped combat bad faith and abusive speculation. In the case of the merchant from Genoa, the arrival of the news of the incident at Chios should have taken no more than 16, 20, or 23 days, according to the opinion of the experts consulted by the court. But the merchant did not conclude the agreement until 40 days after the loss, which, according to Leoninus, is twice the time limit for calculating the speed of information, according to custom. The insurance was therefore void.

The methods of calculating the speed of information were not unanimously accepted by the experts. Relying on the authority of the sixteenth-century Portuguese jurist Alvaro Valasco, Molina cited a mercantile custom that sought to objectify time limits, and then challenged it. According to this custom, news travelled at a minimum speed of 24 *leucas* or *parasangas* (leagues) per day by sea, and at a speed of 30 *leucas* per day by land.[15] In contrast to the objectivity imposed by custom, complicated by the different measures in use at the time, Molina argued for a fully casuistic approach.[16] What was needed was the judgement of a prudent and experienced man capable of assessing the various circumstances of the case at hand, such as particularly unfavourable weather conditions. Furthermore, Molina believed that in case of doubt, the judge should not presume the parties have knowledge. One should not conclude too quickly that the insured party or seller of the insurance was acting in bad faith.

The analyses of Leoninus, Molina, and Lessius do show the extent to which they tried, each in their own way, to reconcile practice and norms. The Jesuits appear to be even more forgiving than Leoninus. Leoninus envisaged litigation in court and tried to combat fraud by insisting on the conditional nature of the custom in Antwerp, which made it easier to prove the bad faith of insured parties. In contrast, Molina and Lessius showed the opposite inclination. Having made a fundamental distinction between situations of *scientia* and doubt, they assumed that certainty is much less frequent in practice, compared to uncertain information. In case of doubt, we should presume good faith. However, if there was absolute certainty about a future risk, insurance taken out after the fact was prohibited.

Molina and Lessius asserted that an insured party who has certain knowledge of the occurrence of a loss could no longer be insured. This would be a fraud, since he knew that the undertaking he was requesting from the insurer is impossible. Similarly, they condemned insurers willing to underwrite a policy that covered a risk they were certain did not exist. This undertaking had no value, Lessius reasoned, since the condition with which it was made ("if risk *x* occurs, I will provide compensation") was impossible. If the insurer was certain that a cargo had arrived unscathed at its destination, he could no longer insure it, since it was no longer exposed to any risk. On the other hand, Lessius accepted that an insurer may offer a policy for a risk which he was not entirely certain no longer existed. In this case, the premiums charged may vary according to the degree of risk: the greater the risk, the higher the premiums can be, which is why Lessius insisted that estimating the risk must always be based on good faith.[17]

Common Estimation, Private Information, and Speculation

In principle, therefore, uncertainty is the only basis for making a profit without compromising one's soul. Nevertheless, the existence of a market for insurance products requires some clarification as to the nature and estimation of this uncertainty. An event may be certain in the eyes of one individual, but not in the eyes of the majority of merchants who assess the circumstances of the market. In effect, Lessius considered that certain insurance products were so habitual that their degree of uncertainty and their price were determined by the common estimation, which allowed prudent individuals to envisage speculative strategies. This is a particularity that, thanks to his attentive eye for the actual functioning of the market, Lessius offered in the consideration of insurance and which had remained absent in the analysis of his predecessors.

Lessius was referring in particular to the maritime insurance taken out against the risks of shipwreck caused by a storm or by a hijacking of cargo by pirates. The obligations to compensate against these risks were sold like commodities. Their value was estimated in the public sphere based on information shared by the community of insurers and merchants. In other words, if a specific insurer did not suffer from the uncertainty that determines the collective spirit of the market—because he had been informed by a letter from a friend or because he could read the stars, Lessius explained—he could seize the opportunity to speculate on the ordinary price of an insurance policy: "This obligation is usually valued as much, because the ordinary risks are significant. The hidden reasons that may diminish risk, of which I alone am aware, do not diminish the common estimation of risk, because they are not known."[18] Clearly, Lessius' justification of speculative activities in the insurance market is reminiscent of his analysis of the Merchant of Rhodes, a prototypical case of the merchant's speculative calculus. Lessius continued his reasoning by transposing the logic of the market for goods to the insurance market: "Goods can be sold at the price that experts generally give them, although this estimation is based on a supposed scarcity from the outside which however is not real in view of the multitude of goods that are hidden or about to arrive. Similarly, this obligation may be sold at the price set by the common estimation of the experts, although this estimation depends upon the common opinion as to the risks which you know, here and now, are likely to occur."

Lessius' arguments were immediately followed by a series of questions that offer a glimpse into his understanding of the concrete realities of the insurance market: are "fictitious" insurance policies, where the goods to be insured do not exist or are of lesser value than the policy suggests, legitimate? How does insurance underwritten by several insurers at the same time work when each insurer is only responsible for a part of the goods? In his response to the first question, Lessius noted that, in practice, insurers had little interest in the actual value of the objects insured. They were only interested in their estimation and therefore in the premiums. Lessius pointed out that this kind of fictitious insurance is like a gamble, but reminded insurers of their obligation to compensate the insured party for the full amount in the event of a loss, even if the goods had been overvalued. The second question allowed Lessius to give free rein to his accountant's mindset—an eminently Jesuit mindset, according to the observations of Paolo Quattrone.[19] If half of a cargo is lost and several insurers are each obliged to cover part of the risk, it is advisable to proceed as follows when calculating the respective compensation. First, it is necessary to estimate whether the liability of each insurer was related to specific parts of the cargo. If this is the case, only the insurers whose own parts are affected have to intervene. On the other hand, if the liability has been divided in an abstract way, as a percentage, all insurers are required to indemnify in proportion to their share: "If the cargo is estimated at 8,000 gold pieces and there are four insurers who have each undertaken to insure one quarter, i.e., for an estimation of 2,000, then it follows that in the event of a loss of half of the goods, they are each obliged to contribute 1,000; if the loss involves a quarter of the cargo, 500, and so on."[20]

Risk and the Subprime Market

The consequential application of market logic is not only evident in Lessius' assessment of insurance. He provided an even more telling application by analysing the buying and selling of letters of debt. In transactions of this type, risk management once again plays a key role. Johannes Wamesius summed up this challenge when explaining that there were numerous risks attached to debts, "because of the instability of the destiny of men and the frequency of bankruptcies, especially among merchants."[21] There were therefore a variety of questions raised by the market for debt claims, which went beyond the sole problem of usury. Subprime debt in particular gave rise to an in-depth reflection on speculation and risk management. In the first instance, Lessius asked whether it was lawful for someone to buy a debt claim at a low price which was considered *subprime* by common estimation, when that individual was certain of obtaining almost full repayment of the debt claim. Moreover, we can ask the question the other way around: can a seller of a subprime debt get rid of that debt at the price set by the common estimation, without telling potential buyers about the risks associated with the dubious status of the debt claim sold? This is a "very frequent case between merchants,"[22] explained Lessius, as ever aware of the realities of the market.

Before looking further at Lessius' approach to these questions, it is worth recalling one of the conclusions of chapter 4, "Usury and the Market," namely that Lessius' pragmatic attitude meant that he recognized a whole range of "extrinsic titles" that justified the sale or purchase of debt claims at a price that varied substantially from their nominal value. The title "capital risk" (*periculum sortis*) played a fundamental role in assessing the practices of the market for debt claims. Still prohibited by Summenhart, Soto, and Azpilcueta, this title enjoyed unprecedented approval in Molina, Lugo and

Lessius.[23] Molina believed that no-one can deny that it is legitimate to accept a price for the risk involved in lending money, especially because it may be difficult or impossible to get back what one has loaned.

"The higher or more likely this risk is, the more the thing decreases in value,"[24] he explained. In contrast to more conservative opinions, the Jesuits considered that this title not only justifies the compensation for the difficulties of subsequently recovering the money loaned (due, e.g., to the distances to be travelled, court costs, etc.), but also the actual fear of not getting paid back, given that loans are made to strangers or unreliable individuals.

In one of the practical cases submitted to him during his lifetime, Lessius mentioned "capital risk" as a very important title that justified interest being charged in situations "where the status of the counterparty is not sufficiently transparent, or even suspect in some way."[25] In the context of an increasingly international and anonymous market, this opened the door to an almost universal acceptance of an interest rate based solely on the title *periculum sortis*. Unsurprisingly, Lessius was an enthusiastic advocate for this title: "The fact that I am incurring such a risk is capable of pecuniary estimation, so I can demand the price. For example: I lend money to a man who is not well known, to a bankrupt individual or a man of dubious reputation; or I am afraid of having major problems in recovering the capital. . . . For it is perfectly just to demand the price for what is capable of pecuniary estimation."[26] Moreover, Lessius also adopted the controversial analogy made by Juan de Medina, a sixteenth-century Spanish theologian, between the lender who is wary of his debtor and the landlord who wants to protect himself against the risk of a tenant who does not respect the premises. If the landlord has the right to raise the price of his lease to protect himself from this risk, why not accept that the lender charges the price of his concern? For Soto, the two cases were not comparable because the landlord did not transfer the right of ownership to the tenant, whereas a loan is in fact characterized by the transfer of this right. But Lessius did not accept this objection, since, fundamentally, the obligations of the borrower and the tenant were the same, just as the risks to which the lender and the landlord were exposed are the same: the object or money lent must be returned intact—this is exactly the risk taken by the landlord and the lender. In addition, there is the argument that the lender may require the debtor to provide a security interest or other collateral to protect against the risk of non-repayment. If the creditor waives this possibility, and therefore acts as the personal guarantor of the obligation contracted by the debtor, he may claim the price. Nevertheless, Lessius made it clear that the creditor could not oblige the debtor to accept him as guarantor, since the debtor must have the possibility to solicit another guarantor.

For debt claims, it is always possible to justify the discount through the title "capital risk." Since, to quote Lugo, "where can we find a debt without risks these days, a debt which, in terms of security, would be identical to present money?"[27] By virtue of the capital risk, Lessius accepted that the price of debt claims may even fall to less than half their nominal value: "Sometimes it is indeed right to buy bond letters for less than half their nominal value, especially if repayment is so difficult to obtain or uncertain that by virtue of this concomitant circumstance their price is prudently estimated to be so low."[28] But Lessius went further. He was adamant that debt claims could be purchased below par, even if they were only due a few months after issuance, and that there was no risk of non-payment.[29] In justifying his opinion, Lessius revealed his deepest thoughts. First, he openly admitted to following Cajetan's opinion on this matter. He subsequently mentioned his sympathy for the practices of the "community of merchants" (*communitas mercatorum*) of the Antwerp exchange (*bursa*). He reiterated his defence of the new title "lack of money," even in the case of those who were not specifically inconvenienced by being deprived of liquidity: "What is to prevent them from estimating, in order to avoid major inconvenience, the price of the lack of money for the duration of one, two, three, four, five months or even a year, even if some are not inconvenienced by this foregone money? It is enough that the majority suffers for a common estimation to be made of the price of this inconvenience."[30] This common estimation, which is the result of the market, is binding on everyone, regardless of the particular situation. What weight should we then give to these words of Lessius when he affirmed that he "did not readily dare to apply this reasoning in practice," explaining "that he found no other author who supported it?"[31] Especially since he noted, immediately after this unlikely U-turn, that, "he would nevertheless not want to oblige someone to pay money back after the fait accompli."

Common Estimation, Private Industry, and Speculation

What about when a buyer will definitely not encounter difficulties in collecting a debt, because of his privileged information, or because he knows the debtor in person or can exert pressure on him through his network? Is it lawful for this buyer-speculator to purchase a debt at half price? The intent of the title "capital risk" is certainly not met in his particular case.

And yet, Molina and Lessius allowed this buyer to make a profit. Here is the case and its solution as proposed by Molina: "A debt has little value in the eyes of the creditor, for example because it is owed by the king and there is little hope of recovering it, and a certain individual nevertheless hopes to recover it on account of his industry (*industria*) or the favour he enjoys with the king or his ministers. In this case, the contract is valid and fair by its nature, entailing no obligation of repayment, as long as the buyer gives the price of the debt that corresponds to its real value in the eyes of the seller. Whether the buyer will easily recover the debt and make a large profit is irrelevant."[32] As an argument, Molina explained that the price did not depend on the buyer's personal estimation. The estimation of the price may possibly take into account the particularities of the seller's situation (which is in accordance with a principle of scholastic economic thought that Odd Inge Langholm has referred to as "the double rule of just pricing"[33]), because the seller may wish to compensate himself for the losses he personally incurred; on the other hand, he could not take into account the personal situation of the buyer, or otherwise the latter would be punished for having built up a good network of contacts and for fully putting his industry to work: "The price of a thing bought is not the value it has to the buyer. It is clearly not determined by his industry or the favour he enjoys with an individual. On the contrary, the price of something is its value in and of itself and the value it has for the seller."

Lessius pushed this argument even further, using the market argument as he developed it in his analysis of the case of the Merchant of Rhodes. In contrast to Molina, Lessius no longer envisaged the transaction between a single seller and a single buyer. He generalized the case by situating it in an abstract market, governed by its own mechanism of evaluation of the economic value of the debt claims, regardless of the situation of two contracting parties. According to Lessius, the price of subprime debt claims is determined by the common estimation in a market where there are a large number of potential buyers of subprime debt. If, therefore, common opinion deems that certain claims are doubtful, their price will fall, regardless of the private knowledge of certain individuals. This mechanism is further reinforced by the modality of the sale (*modus vendendi*) of the debt claims, most often organized in the context of an auction: "When these debt claims are put on sale, their price does not depend on the convenience of any particular person or group. The price comes from the public estimation that is established when the civilian community gathers as a whole at the market for an auction."[34] The market produces an objective and standardized price for all those participating in its activity. If a given entrepreneur, through his network of contacts or his commercial acumen, will not have any difficulties obtaining full reimbursement in due time, the market price does not cease to be the reference point. Again, for Lessius, it was the condition typical of merchants that came into play here: sometimes you win, sometimes you lose, due to price fluctuations. The merchant must try to master the market game and exploit its opportunities, using his prudence and industry. In practice, it is thanks to his zeal, his vision and his efforts to establish a network of reliable contacts that he can speculate on the purchase of debt claims that seem too risky in the eyes of others.

Here, as in the case of the Merchant of Rhodes and the sale of insurance, Lessius believed that the merchant must be allowed to make a profit from his private information about the true value of the debt claims. Referring to an opinion described as "probable," Johannes Malderus, bishop of Antwerp from 1611 to 1633, a contemporary and epigone of Lessius, explained: "The industry (*industria*) which makes it possible for the merchant to ensure payment must be considered as part of the advantages which his good fortune reserves for him."[35] Even more than Lessius, however, Malderus emphasized the particular way (*modus vendendi*) in which subprime debt is sold, namely by auction. It was generally accepted that the setting of the just price has its own, more flexible, rules in an auction (compare Cajetan's reflections on this subject—see chapter 5, p. 75). Outside of this specific context, Malderus prohibited the speculative purchase of subprime debt, fearing usurious practices and the outright identification of bond letters with commodities.

For his part, Lessius warned against speculation that risked harming the interests of the most vulnerable individuals. Here, as in his discussion of the case of the Merchant of Rhodes, he invoked the moral responsibility of professional merchants: they should not abuse their expertise in the face of simple and honest people (*simplices*). He evoked the specific case of soldiers paid by the Ottoman emperor in the form of bond letters and forced, by penury, to sell them at auction. The merchant who, thanks to his privileged contacts, was certain to recover the sums due could only make large profits on the backs of these poor soldiers by violating the principles of charity (*charitas*). Similarly, Lessius castigated the officials who made it difficult, if not impossible, to pay the bond letters. By their fraudulent behaviour, they tried to force the holders of the bond letters to sell them at auction and then buy them themselves at a lower price.

The Sale of Subprime Debt and the Limits of Speculation

The hunt for fraud is also at the heart of scholastic analyses of the sale of subprime debt, especially when potential buyers are not informed of the insolvency of the debtor. Although occurring frequently, as Lessius admitted, he stressed the unquestionably illicit character of these practices. Apart from the fact that they are a direct contradiction of the principles of charity, especially when weaker parties are likely to incur significant losses, they also run counter to justice in the strict sense of the term.

The analogy with the case of the Merchant of Rhodes reaches its limits here, according to Lessius, because different types of information circulate on commercial and financial transactions. On the one hand, there is information relating more to the context of the transaction, such as the broader political and economic trends. On the other hand, there is information relating to the quality of the merchandise which is the subject of the transaction. Here, Lessius reapplied a distinction which was articulated very explicitly in the analysis of the case of the Merchant of Rhodes by the Franciscan theologian Antonio de Córdoba. In effect, Córdoba specified that a distinction needs to be made between knowledge (or even ignorance) of the conditions that affect whether a price is just or not, and knowledge of conditions that are fortuitous and external.[36] The solvency of the debtor is an intrinsic element of the contract on which the contracting parties must unambiguously agree, on pain of the contract being declared void. Selling subprime loans without highlighting the debtor's insolvency is like selling a right to the fruits of barren land, according to Lessius: "This practice seems to violate the rules of justice. A right to collect fruit from a barren field is of little value in itself, and cannot be sold at the same price as a right issued for a fertile field. The same applies to a right against an individual who is insolvent. This defect therefore obviously concerns an intrinsic quality. It must therefore be disclosed, on pain of nullity of the contract on the grounds of fundamental deceit."[37] The sale of subprime loans is of crucial importance, insofar as it prompted Lessius to articulate the distinction between the case of the Merchant of Rhodes—explicitly invoked by the contrary opinion—and those cases involving the sale of defective goods. In his way, the boundaries appeared of the domain where speculative reason was allowed to rule. If a creditor wanted to get rid of a toxic debt without telling the buyer, he was not only putting the virtuous circulation of money at risk—he was imperilling the very salvation of his soul.

7
Monopolies and Industry

> *Any manoeuvre, any industry carried on by merchants which has the effect that they alone sell a good or that they sell it at a certain price, is regarded as a monopoly.*
>
> Leonardus Lessius

The previous chapter leaves no doubt about Lessius' positive attitude towards the speculative logic of the market economy. Prudence, a virtue of the practical life, requires the merchant to anticipate market evolutions and to capitalize on his privileged information. The benefits he derives from this are the fruit of his "industry" (*industria*), that is, of his constant application, his zeal, and his work ethic. The ethical matrix of scholastic economic thought urges merchants to behave responsibly, but it leaves no room for naivety or carelessness. At the same time, it assumes that economic activities take place in a competitive order, which requires certain guarantees. While industry and the appetite for profit are judged favourably by Lessius, the survival of the competitive order obliged him to accept certain limits. Can the merchant not be overly industrious, taking speculation to the extreme in order to become the only one to own and sell a given commodity? What if he manages to get along so well with some of his competitors that they form a cartel? What about the merchant who works hard to gain a dominant position and block market access to his competitors? The aim of this chapter is to illustrate how Lessius and other Jesuits sought to safeguard the competitive order, while acknowledging the merits of the merchants looking to accumulate their wealth through their industry. A preliminary historiographical detour is called for, which will allow us to grasp the links, long unsuspected, between the direction that the great European project of a single market took after the Second World War and the liberal instincts of the scholastics of the modern age.

Money, Markets, and Merit. Wim Decock, Oxford University Press. © Oxford University Press (2025).
DOI: 10.1093/9780197827345.003.0008

Joseph Höffner or the Scholastic Spirit of Ordoliberalism

Modern historiography's interest in the struggle of scholastic theologians against cartels and monopolies—which, admittedly, has remained very modest—can be traced back to a book written during the Second World War by Joseph Höffner. In *Wirtschaftsethik und Monopole im fünfzehnten und sechzehnten Jahrhundert* (*Economic Ethics and Monopolies in the Fifteenth and Sixteenth Centuries*), published in 1941, Höffner outlined the competitive model put forward by the scholastic theologians of the fifteenth and sixteenth centuries. In contrast to the anti-competitive developments that had been witnessed in his country for several decades and that were skilfully exploited by the Nazi regime, Höffner delved into history in search of a counter-model.[1] At the very moment when the captains of the German industry conspired with the Führer to build factories in the Polish plains using cheap prison labour (in the summer of 1941, the "final solution" of the Jewish question was being concocted at the Wannsee conference), Höffner discreetly drew attention to the reasons why the scholastics condemned the concentration of economic power at the dawn of the modern age. Fearing the decline of contractual freedom and rejecting the economic coercion brought about by monopolies, scholastics such as Leonardus Lessius condemned cartels and other forms of monopoly in the name of the common good and natural law.

It is not often that a reader is prompted by the colophon of the book he or she is reading to take a look at the list of names that make up the editorial board of the collection in which the book was published. Often long, and replete with unknown scholars, the colophon is mostly ignored, as is the name of the collection that houses the work. In the case of Joseph Höffner's book on business ethics and monopolies in the time of the modern scholastics, however, the reader is well advised to override their bad habits. The list of editors of the "Freiburger Staatswissenschaftliche Schriften" ("Freiburg Political Science Writings") reveals a remarkable and unexpected link between the economic thought of the scholastics and the ordoliberal current that provided the ideological foundations of the post-war European economic project. Apart from the salient reference to the University of Freiburg im Breisgau in the name of the collection itself, the following names appear in this list: Walter Eucken, Franz Böhm, and Hans Grossmann-Doerth, that is, the founding fathers of the so-called Freiburg school of ordoliberalism, a school of thought that fascinated Michel Foucault in his attempt to grasp the origins of the post-war German and European liberal model. This school also had a lasting influence on the European economic constitution and its competition policy, as has been pointed out by David Gerber and Peter Nedergaard.

While our insight into the personal relationships between Höffner, Böhm, and Grossmann-Doerth is vague, the relationship between Höffner and Eucken is well known, although overlooked. Höffner's book is in fact the result of his doctoral thesis in political science, whose promoter was none other than Walter Eucken. It was under the auspices of this major economist and founding father of ordoliberalism that, on 26 January 1940, Höffner, already a doctor of theology at the Pontifical Gregorian University in Rome (an academic title that the Nazis did not want to recognize as it was issued by a foreign authority), defended his doctoral thesis at the University of Freiburg im Breisgau.[2] It was also Eucken who accompanied Höffner's post-doctoral thesis in the social sciences on the scholastic conception of human dignity in the period of Spanish colonialism.[3] Accepted by the faculty in October 1942, his post-doctoral thesis was not published until five years later. Joseph Höffner, who had hidden a Jewish girl, Esther Sara Meyerowitz, in his parish house, and a Jewish woman, Edith Nowak, in the home of his sister Helene, consciously noted in the introduction to this publication that the grave violations of human dignity in the days of Spanish imperialism had been repeated in his own time, provoking an outcry that shocked the Christian conscience. Sixteen years after his death, in 2003, Joseph Höffner, together with his sister, received the title of "Righteous among the Nations" from the Yad Vashem Memorial in Jerusalem.

Joseph Höffner is not only a hero of the resistance. Like his friends in Walter Eucken's circle, in which he remained an active member throughout his life, he was also a hero and architect of the "Wirtschaftswunder," namely the dramatic recovery of the West German economy following the devastation of the Second World War. An expert in the political economy of the scholastics and a dynamic Catholic priest, Höffner became the right-hand man of Conrad Adenauer, the leader of the Christian Democrats and the first chancellor of West Germany. Höffner also had a career in the Church, first as bishop of Münster from 1962 and then as archbishop of Cologne from 1969 until his death in 1987. The message he took with him wherever he travelled, sometimes at conferences (e.g., at the meeting of the International Union of Catholic Employers' Associations in Cologne in 1952),[4] sometimes in his publications (such as his contribution on the scholastic roots of competition law published in *ORDO*, the journal of the ordoliberals[5] in 1953), was that of a profound and historical alliance between Christian faith and economic liberalism. The Institute for Christian Social Sciences, which he founded when he was appointed professor at the University of Münster in 1951, still helps disseminate his thinking on the ethics of the liberal economy.

Market Economy and Catholicism

If the links between Catholicism and ordoliberalism seem to be surprising, it is because the contribution of Catholics like Höffner to the legitimization of liberal economics in Germany and in the post-war European Communities remained for a long time a "hidden history."[6] Nevertheless, the contours of this story become clearer as the research progresses. As noted by James Chappel, a remarkable harmony between Catholic political economy and neoliberalism emerged in the 1940s and 1950s.[7] On the other hand, while coryphaei of the Freiburg School such as Walter Eucken, Alfred Müller-Armack, and Wilhelm Röpke declared that they were Protestants, they had no problem accepting the major contribution of their Catholic colleagues to the ordoliberal project. Müller-Armack, a sociologist, economist, and Christian Democrat politician who was behind the concept of the "social market economy," recommended to his Protestant counterparts and ordoliberal friends that they draw on Catholic social doctrine to develop a new conception of society, since this doctrine was much more developed than that of the Protestants, by its own admission.[8] Röpke, a founding member of the Mont Pelerin Society, fully acknowledged the merits of the Catholic economic ethic that sought to achieve a balance between the market and solidarity. He found the emblematic expression of this in the social encyclical *Quadragesimo Anno*,[9] promulgated by Pope Pius XI in 1931 in reaction to the stock market crash of 1929. This encyclical was actually written by the famous German theologian Oswald von Nell-Breuning, a Jesuit who regarded his own writings as mere footnotes to the scholastic thought of the sixteenth and seventeenth centuries.

In January 1956, Röpke asked his friend Daniel Villey, a French economist and brother of the legal philosopher Michel Villey, to take a stand in the debate and confirm the compatibility of Catholicism and liberalism.[10] In November of the same year, Daniel Villey wrote an article entitled "L'économie du marché devant la pensée catholique" ("The Market

Economy and Catholic Thought") in the *Revue d'économie politique*.[11] In this article, Villey denounced the morality of good intentions which he considered as commonplace in the French Catholic Church. He highlighted the fact that Catholics, including bishops, were completely ignorant of market mechanisms. For example, he took aim at a pastoral letter from the Archbishop of Rouen stating that "employees who agree to work overtime must ask themselves if they are not disadvantaging their fellow workers." He rejected this sentence as a "fallacy of the fixed quantum of work," using Röpke's expression. Villey deplored an appeal by the archbishop of Toulouse asking business leaders not to lay off workers. According to Villey, it was morally acceptable for a company to try to remain profitable first. In his view, behind the movement of "social Catholicism" which was popular in France at least since the 1860s, was a glaring ignorance of the laws of economics and a resentment of modernity. Despite his admiration for the leading Catholic intellectual Emmanuel Mounier, he suspected that the philosopher was more familiar with the writings of Karl Marx than with those of Adam Smith. In the context of the start of the schism between the economic cultures of the East and the West, Villey also warned against the temptation of the central planning model, arguing that income inequality was no less pronounced in Russia than in the United States. Nevertheless, Villey asserted that economic liberalism was not inconsistent with social legislation that guaranteed a "certain redistribution" of income. Here he sounded very close to the German ordoliberals. It is not surprising, therefore, that barely a year after the publication of his article in the *Revue d'économie politique*, a German translation appeared in the journal of the ordoliberals, *ORDO*.[12]

While it is beyond the scope of this work to address the finer points of ordoliberal economic thought, or to launch a study on the relationship between Catholicism and ordoliberalism, it is nevertheless worth recalling how much scholastic thought and ordoliberalism not only converge in the central role they attribute to free competition and the fight against cartels, they also share the idea that the economic order must necessarily fall within the broader political and spiritual orders. The ordoliberals were not blind followers of capitalism, materialism without spiritual values, or individualism without consideration for the common good.[13] On the contrary, in Walter Eucken's conception, the notion of *ordo* goes back to the concept of metaphysical order introduced by Augustine and developed by Thomas Aquinas.[14] This notion embraces the idea that the economy, as a part of a whole, falls within an order that precedes and prevails over it. The economic order cannot be seen in isolation from the political, moral or legal order. There is a kind of interdependence (*Interdependenz der Ordnungen*) between these different orders which is necessary for their correct functioning.[15] As such, to prevent the market from self-destruction, it must be framed by moral norms and by a strong state that sets the rules and ensures that they are respected, in particular by tackling concentrations of economic power. The main purpose of competition law is therefore to protect the economic freedom of market participants; it is not primarily aimed at increasing growth or efficiency, as Franz Böhm observed.[16]

In contrast to so-called classical liberalism, ordoliberals therefore consistently advocated for well-targeted public intervention in the market.[17] This explains the strong emphasis on the notion of "politics of order" (*Ordnungspolitik*) in the ordoliberal philosophy, which manifests itself in the crucial role of law in regulating the market. The state is called upon to guarantee respect for legal principles that are considered prerequisites for the correct functioning of the market, such as private property, freedom of contract, and civil responsibility. These are the constituent parts of the "society based on private law" (*Privatrechtsgesellschaft*) which (again according to Böhm) the competitive market order presupposes.[18] Without private property, without freedom of contract, and without a public institution to ensure compliance with the rules, there can be no economic freedom. Is it any wonder that in the 1950s and 1960s, when the ordoliberal model was rising, the study of the scholastic roots of private law was put on the agenda in Freiburg? In 1953, the *Zeitschrift der Savigny-Stiftung für Rechtsgeschichte*, one of Germany's leading journals on legal history, published a famous article on the outstanding contribution of the scholastics to the development of European private law ("Natürliches Privatrecht und Spätscholastik") by Hans Thieme, a close colleague of Böhm's at the Freiburg Law School.[19] Thieme subsequently provided guidance for several doctoral students who continued this exploration of the scholastic roots of private law.[20]

A Small Phenomenology of Monopolistic Practices

What could the ordoliberals have discovered in modern scholasticism so valuable that they were able to draw inspiration from it in their attempt to reinforce relations between morality, law and economics in the vacuum left by the disastrous experience of the Nazi regime? What interest did Joseph

Höffner, in particular, have in delving into the voluminous works of Molina or Lessius, written in Latin, to examine their deliberations on cartels and dominant positions? It seems to us that this question can be answered rather succinctly: apart from the fact that the scholastic tradition bestowed Christian legitimacy to the German project of economic recovery, it also provided reference points for better thinking about anti-competitive phenomena. Known for providing sound definitions to concepts before commencing their arguments, the scholastics in effect tried to comprehend the various phenomena designated by the term "monopoly." Strictly speaking, the term refers to a situation where goods are sold by a single merchant or, conversely, to a situation where several sellers deal with a single buyer—a situation that is more accurately referred to as "monopsony." The Jesuits attempted to account for the much broader use of this word. In a definition that has caught the attention of historians of economic thought, Lessius stated with great clarity that "any manoeuvre, any industry carried on by merchants which has the effect that they alone sell a good or that they sell it at a certain price, is regarded as a monopoly in the broad sense by the doctors."[21] To this general definition, based on the notion of the perversion of industry and including both monopolies in the strict sense of the term and cartels, is then added a list of four specific practices which, according to Lessius, give rise to a monopoly in the broad sense of the term: "This may happen in four ways: (1) they agree on the price, *conspiring* that no-one should sell for less; (2) or they make sure that they alone sell certain goods, either (2.1) by profiting from a *privilege of the prince*, or (2.2) by simultaneously buying up all the goods by their *industry* to keep these out of circulation until their prices rise, or (2.3) by *obstructing* competitors who want to import these goods from elsewhere."

This definition of monopoly and the way it is established is remarkable in several respects. Clearly, economists and lawyers familiar with European competition law will immediately notice a foreshadowing of the founding principles of the European economic constitution, enshrined, respectively, in the famous articles 101 (agreements between undertakings) and 102 (prohibition of abuse of a dominant positions) of the "Treaty on the Functioning of the European Union." More important, however, in the context of this book, is that this definition reveals that Lessius' regard for ingenious and industrious merchants is not without limits. He appears to want to make a distinction between a good and a bad form of industry: if it becomes excessive, industry is likely to harm the community and, therefore, is liable to sanctions. Accompanied by intrigues and "machinations" (the term Lessius uses), industry becomes a scourge rather than a blessing for the general interest. Other scholastics, such as Pedro de Oñate, readily addressed monopolies in the context of their analysis of fraud in sales contracts. If competition is distorted, the market can only generate profits for a privileged caste. Competitors, consumers, and the entire community of citizens come to suffer. Hence the profoundly "anti-cartel" sentiment of modern scholastics, which was well highlighted by Joseph Höffner, Raymond de Roover, and Barry Gordon.[22]

Nevertheless, Lessius' attitude towards monopolies was not entirely negative. At the very end of the chapter on sales contracts in *De iustitia et iure*, one of the questions addressed took the form of a rhetorical question, for which the implied answer was in the negative: "Is any monopoly unfair?" Although he took the prohibition of monopoly as the starting point of his reflection, Lessius attempted to demonstrate that there are reasons to doubt that condemning dominant market positions applied equally to any form of monopoly. Clearly, following the scholastic tradition, he did not accept price cartels or barriers to market entry under any circumstances. But he acknowledged the power of the authorities to grant certain monopolistic privileges in the public interest. He also called into question the outright condemnation of dominance stemming from industry—we will return to this later. What is important to remember is that here as elsewhere, Lessius showed himself to be an original thinker and a good balancer, always concerned to measure the pros and cons in each specific case.

A Missed Reference to Roman Imperial Law

In the context of Lessius' reservations regarding outright condemnation of any form of concentration of power in the market, a Roman imperial constitution of A.D. 483 is conspicuous by its absence in *De iustitia et iure*: that of Emperor Zeno concerning the prohibition of monopolies.[23] This constitution is considered the most absolute expression of the criminalization of monopolistic activity in the Western legal tradition. It was reprised in the Code of Justinian of 533, and subsequently commentated on by the jurists from the revival of the Justinian law at the university of Bologna from the end of the eleventh century. In the twentieth century, it was still the basis for anti-monopoly ordinances in South Africa, a country whose legal tradition was lastingly marked by the Roman experience following its colonization by the Netherlands, which had created a Roman-Dutch legal system in the seventeenth century.[24]

As is often the case with Roman legal provisions handed down to us through the centuries, the Latin of the original text is not entirely transparent (in modern editions, the title of the provision has been changed to correct grammatical errors in older editions, including that of the French humanist Denis Godefroy at the end of the sixteenth century).[25] According to the common interpretation, summarized by Baldus, the great Bolognese jurist of the fourteenth century, Zeno's constitution stipulated a general prohibition of monopolies (private monopolies as well as those authorized by the prince) and then condemned two kinds of agreements: cartels concerning the price of a good and agreements between workers so that one of them would not finish the work started by another. According to the interpretation by medieval jurists, Zeno's constitution provided for severe punishment for monopolists, namely confiscation of their property and then exile, whereas participants in a cartel were only punished with a pecuniary fine.

Zeno's constitution has also given rise to less absolute interpretations. Whereas most jurists and scholastic theologians interpreted the prohibition of monopolies and cartels in the broadest possible sense, the advisors and lawyers of large companies argued for a stricter interpretation. In the modern age, interpreting this constitution became all the more important as it served as a model for the various anti-monopoly measures in the Holy Roman Empire decreed by Emperor Charles V in the 1520s.[26] Indeed, the emperor was engaged, at the behest of the estates, in a struggle against the concentration of economic power in the hands of the large German banks—the Fuggers and the Welsers—and the major import and export companies trading goods from the New World. The advice given by Konrad Peutinger, a well-known jurist of the time and advocate of the monopolists, was memorable, whereby he argued for a narrow interpretation of Zeno's constitution in order to undermine the authority of the anti-monopoly measures decreed by Charles V. According to Peutinger, Zeno had only intended to sanction monopolies affecting everyday consumer goods, such as food. He could therefore argue that the major companies involved in the global spice trade escaped the prohibition on monopolies.[27]

The reference to Zeno's constitution was conventional in almost all the texts of modern scholastics dealing with monopolies. In the *Manual for Confessors* by the Dominican friar Silvestro Mazzolini da Prierio from 1506, an emblematic work of the great Thomistic revival in Bologna at the end of the fifteenth century and a great source of inspiration for the theologians of Salamanca and Louvain, the very brief note on monopolies had two elements. On the one hand, an explanation of the Greek etymology of the term "monopoly" (composed of *monos*, "one," and *pôlion*, "sale").[28] On the other, a reference to the confiscation of goods and the exile stipulated by Zeno. A little less than a century later, in his *De iustitia et iure*, Luis de Molina opened his discussion of monopolies with an exegesis of Zeno's constitution.[29] In order to interpret this famous text of Roman law, Molina explicitly referred to the medieval legal doctrine (*ius commune*). He observed the distinction between monopolies in the strict sense of the term, punishable by the confiscation of goods followed by exile, and cartels, punishable by a pecuniary fine of forty pounds of gold for the members of a cartel. Molina also noted the more stringent fine of fifty pounds of gold imposed on administrators or judges if they neglected their duty to pursue anticompetitive practices.[30] The reference to Roman law therefore allowed Molina to underscore the criminal nature of monopolistic activity, an aspect that receives remarkably less attention in Lessius' *De iustitia et iure*.

Artificial Scarcity and Limits to Speculation

While the absence of references to Zeno's constitution, an emblem of Roman antitrust policy, is striking in Lessius' consideration of monopolies in general, the lack of references to either Roman or canon law is even more striking in the specific case of acquiring a dominant position through excessive industry. This is the third way of creating a monopoly explained in the definition given by Lessius, described as the overall purchase of all items of a single good. Lessius took the specific example of a purchase of all stocks of wheat before, during, or after the harvest. While he vaguely referred to the common view that this practice of hoarding is reprehensible, no mention is made of Justinian's Digest or the *Decretum Gratiani*, which prohibited speculative practices intended to acquire a dominant position. Nevertheless, the *Lex Julia*, a well-known Roman law on the supply of wheat, specifically targeted the conduct described by Lessius, prohibiting any individual or collective activity which would lead to artificially making the price of essential commodities expensive.[31] Another passage from the Digest extended the application of this law to other goods and unambiguously condemned all the monopolists (referred to in the text as "Dardanarians") who abused their position of strength: "Those who are accustomed to embrace every opportunity to increase the price of food are called *dardanarii*, and provision has been made by the Imperial decrees and constitutions for the repression of their avarice. It is provided as follows in the Decrees: 'moreover, you should take care that there are no *dardanarii* of any kind of goods, and that they do not adopt measures for storing away merchandise which they have purchased, or, that the more wealthy of them may not be unwilling to dispose of their goods at reasonable prices in expectation of an unproductive season, so that the price of food may not be raised.'"[32]

This condemnation of hoarding practices, based on the authority of Roman law, is reflected in all subsequent legislation against merchants hoarding goods in order to artificially increase their price. The prohibition of monopolies and cartels in the ordinance of King Francis I of 20 June 1539 provides a good example.[33] Similar prohibitions are attested to in the Low Countries. In a perpetual edict of 4 October 1540, Emperor Charles V forbade merchants from buying all goods of the same kind simultaneously in order to keep them and then sell them at excessive prices.[34] Considered extremely detrimental to the common good, this practice was punished by confiscation of the goods and other arbitrary penalties. It was not just symbolic legislation. The prohibition of artificial scarcity was fully recognized by the leading lawyers of the day, including Joos de Damhouder. In his treatise *Praxis rerum criminalium* (*Practice of Criminal Matters*) from 1554, which circulated throughout Europe, he offered a detailed overview of monopolistic practices while asserting the application of the penalties provided for by Roman imperial law and the edict of Charles V.[35] Various cases illustrate the actual prosecution of the crime of artificial scarcity. In 1565, after it was revealed that the families Fourmestraux, De Lobel, Mahieu, and Van der Leure in Lille had colluded to monopolize wheat in Antwerp and Amsterdam, they were forced to sell their stocks. In the same year, another attempt to monopolize wheat by the leading Antwerp merchant Pauwel van Dale was exposed when the granary of his warehouse collapsed under the weight of the wheat stocks.[36] In the following decades, various legislative initiatives reiterated the prohibition of artificial scarcity.

In medieval Christian Europe, the Digest was given additional weight by the canon *Quicumque*, an equally well known provision of canon law found in Gratian's *Decretum* of 1140[37] (in reality, the provision was of Carolingian origin[38]). It condemned anyone engaging in speculative activities with the aim of creating artificial shortages of wheat or wine. If the aim of the speculator was to make a profit to satisfy his greed, he was in fact only making a "dishonest gain" (*turpe lucrum*) which he was obliged to pay back. In his commentary on this famous provision, the twelfth-century canonist Huguccio made an important distinction between speculative profits motivated solely by greed and profits made in order to provide a living for oneself and one's family. In the latter case the profits were considered untarnished. In the first half of the thirteenth century, Bishop Lawrence of Spain, another canon lawyer, stated that speculative activities intended to create artificial scarcity (*caristia*) were motivated by avarice. At the same time, the canonist Sinibaldo de Fieschi—the future Pope Innocent IV—argued that monopolistic practices could sometimes be legitimate if they were undertaken in the public interest. In the modern age, the tradition of medieval canon law was beautifully summarized in Martín de Azpilcueta's *Manual for Confessors*: "He who, with the intention of creating a shortage, buys oil, wheat or wine in such immoderate quantities at the time of the harvest that he can sell them for more money afterwards, commits a mortal sin. This is the meaning of the canon *Quicumque*. I said 'with the intention of creating a shortage,' because it is not a sin to act in such a way to feed one's family, even if they are no longer in need or if the surplus is sold at the current price. In the same way, someone who looks after the interests of the community (*respublica*), such as Joseph, or those of the needy poor; or someone who wants to prevent goods from leaving the country or being squandered, or for any other morally acceptable end, according to the interpretation of Innocent,[39] does not commit a sin."

Azpilcueta's assertions expressed with remarkable clarity the difficulty of drawing a line between morally acceptable and unacceptable speculative activities. For scholastics like Azpilcueta and Lessius, who accepted the speculative conduct of the Merchant of Rhodes, the question arose with all the more vigour because they fully approved of the industrious pursuit of profit. Since the limits to industry are very difficult to draw, Azpilcueta proposed adopting a subjective criterion. The moral judgement made on a speculative activity depends, ultimately, on the intention of the individual who has created a situation of scarcity. Hoarding goods for the purpose of protecting the interests of the family and the republic is legitimate. For Azpilcueta, the case of the patriarch Joseph, who reserved large stocks of grain to sell them at a high price when the famine came, falls under this category. On the other hand, any speculative action motivated by greed alone is prohibited. But it is clear that a casuistic approach is called for. The morality of the intention is a criterion that can be more easily adopted in the confessional, where the search for truth is not hindered by the rules of proof, than in the civil courts. Nevertheless, even in the confessional, the criterion of intention leaves the door wide open to abuse. How to disprove a penitent who claims to have monopolized grain in order to look after the interests of his family? Subjective motivations cannot be perceived from the outside. To put forward the criterion of intention is to place the final moral judgement in the hands of God.

Between Apology and Punishment of Excessive Industry

The dilemma faced by Azpilcueta is also central to Lessius' analysis of artificial scarcity through excessive industry. If Lessius did not reject all dominant positions outright, and if he omitted references to texts of Roman and canon law condemning monopolies, it was undoubtedly because he wanted to create room for a more nuanced approach to the practices of artificial scarcity. Contrary to common opinion, Lessius found it difficult to categorically disapprove of the ultra-speculative practices of individuals who hoarded goods to keep them out of circulation and raise their prices. The case of artificial scarcity generated by industry prompted Lessius, keen to remunerate the latter, to define the limits of his "meritocratic philosophy." With his characteristic ingenuity and respect for individual rights, he noted that the process of acquiring a dominant position through industry did not in itself violate so-called commutative justice, which guarantees equality in commercial exchanges. Unless the merchant resorted to fraudulent methods, it is assumed that he acquired his dominant position through multiple transactions which, in themselves, respected the just price. Moreover, the property right acquired on the monopolized goods is the same as the property right on any other good. This right includes the right to enjoy and dispose of the good in the most absolute sense. In other words, the merchant would in principle even have the right to destroy goods over which he has, in fact, complete control.

His respect for freedom of contract, private property, and commercial industry obliged Lessius to be more specific than previous authorities in his assessment of artificial scarcity practices. He was fundamentally convinced that, if there are any at all, the reasons for prohibiting such market abuse practices cannot be found in the individual relationship between market participants. The so-called particular justice does not prevent someone from gaining control of a market by pursuing a dominant position, through his industry and through legitimate transactions. Moreover, commutative justice does not give citizens the right to demand the sale of goods taken out of circulation by a merchant. Only a contract freely entered into by the seller and the buyer allows a legitimate sale. Nevertheless, the prudent merchant may have good reasons for not putting his goods up for sale. Even the community, Lessius explained, does not essentially have the right to ensure that prices do not rise when a good is scarce on the market. By explicit analogy with his solution of the case of the Merchant of Rhodes, Lessius reminds us that the market price depends on publicly available information. If, therefore, the majority of citizens and merchants are unaware that a monopolist is concealing a large quantity of goods, even if his granary overlooks the market place, the price remains high. Since it is not perceived as such by the majority of market participants, the objective reality is not reflected in the market price, which is nevertheless fair: "The republic has no right in the strict sense of the word to claim that the price must not increase if the supply of available goods in the city is high, but concealed and unknown. This is the logical continuation of *dubitatio* 5 (on the Merchant of Rhodes)]. The price depends on the common estimation. Otherwise, the individuals who in good faith sold at a high price when the just price was high would be liable to subsequently pay it back. This price is not even unjust to the person or persons who conceal the goods, for they have obtained this price without engaging in unjust activity."[40] The rigour of Lessius' analysis is remarkable. Once he has defined the just price, Lessius uncompromisingly draws the logical conclusions. As was the case with the Merchant of Rhodes, Lessius opposed the more stringent analysis of Juan de Medina. According to Medina, who cited Zeno's constitution as well as the canon *Quicumque*, the professional speculator cannot take advantage of situations of scarcity to sell his goods at a higher price, even if the scarcity has been artificially created by other market participants.[41] From the viewpoint of market justice, Lessius could not accept such a rigorous position. Taking inspiration instead from the *De iustitia et iure* of his colleague and friend Luis de Molina, he adopted a more permissive stand towards speculators. For Molina, industrial monopolists were simply exercising their right to buy goods at market price and then sell them at a higher price.[42]

Despite all these arguments that illustrate their goodwill towards industry, Molina and Lessius cannot be considered as lax moral advisors or as defenders of a market unregulated by political forces. On the contrary, they admitted that excessive cases of artificial scarcity are rightly prosecuted by the public authorities on account of their negative effects on the common good. Molina cited and accepted the legitimacy of the anti-monopoly ordinances of Portugal and Spain, which sanctioned the practices of monopolizing wheat. Regardless of his apology for industrial monopolists on the grounds of commutative justice (the standard criterion for assessing whether there is a balance in transactions between individuals), Lessius acknowledged the importance of imposing limits on excessive industry in the public interest (*utilitas publica*).

It was therefore necessary to add a public law dimension to this assessment of dominant positions. In the words of the scholastics, "particular justice" had to be complemented by "general" or "legal justice" (*iustitia legalis*). Just as he conceived of property rights in fairly strong terms without denying the power of public authorities to limit the exercise of these rights in the public interest, Lessius could accept restrictions on mercantile industry by laws protecting the common good. As such, he recalled that, in the general interest, many crimes have been prosecuted by the public authorities which, from a narrower legal perspective, were not subject to criticism. Since protecting the common good is legitimate, even necessary, Lessius could only conclude that the general principle of prohibiting monopolies applied even to those which were the fruit of industry.

Public Utility and Legal Monopolies

In concluding his reasoning, Lessius followed the common scholastic opinion that the general interest required a prohibition of dominant positions resulting from excessive industry. Private property, freedom of contract, and commercial zeal must yield to the rules of public law. The fundamental prohibition of monopolies was thus reinforced in the scholastic tradition. The limits imposed on industry and individual freedom served to protect "common freedom" (*communis libertas*). This is the term used by Cajetan, the former master general of the Order of Preachers and source of inspiration for the School of Salamanca, in his *Summula peccatorum* (*Little Summa of Sins*) of 1523.[43] Nevertheless, it should be remembered that in the name of the precedence of public utility, the scholastics were also unanimous in accepting the existence of special cases where monopolies could exceptionally be tolerated by the public authorities, provided that the latter were truly concerned with promoting the general interest, in particular by stimulating industry. While insisting on the prohibition of monopolies in principle, the scholastics opened the door to exceptions that were often very real in practice.

In Luis de Molina's defence of legal monopolies, the monopoly of the Portuguese crown over trade with India, reinstated by King Philip III at the end of the sixteenth century, played a predominant role. Molina, who had made a career as a professor of theology in various universities throughout Portugal, explains that the rise in royal revenues through this monopoly was beneficial to his subjects. The monopoly over trade with India allowed the king to finance his military campaigns without having to raise additional taxes.[44] Indeed, it appears that until the Twelve Years' Truce (the brief cessation of hostilities between 1609 and 1621 in the War of Independence between Spain and the Netherlands), a large part of the revenues from the monopoly of the spice trade with India was immediately reinvested in the struggle against the Dutch.[45] It is probably no coincidence that, in an analysis echoing Molina's positions, Lessius admitted that one of the legitimate reasons for establishing a legal monopoly was to replenish public funds. The granting of monopoly privileges to the highest bidder was therefore a popular alternative to levying taxes. Lessius specified that the monopolistic privileges granted by the prince in the domain of trade in "all goods commonly necessary for the political life of the republic" must be subject to adequate regulation.[46] If the monopoly pertained to the trade of luxury goods or entertainment, the prince could not intervene. On the other hand, for essential goods, Lessius requested that he set the price so that justice and freedom of contract were guaranteed. For the rest, Lessius remained suspicious of legal monopolies and demanded that there be good reasons for derogating from the prohibition against monopolies.

Apart from the monopoly that served to replenish the public coffers, Lessius abstractly referred to another example justifying the legitimacy of granting a monopoly privilege: the incentive to take commercial risk. When a given trade required considerable expenditure, so that no-one could carry it on profitably without public protection, at least for a certain period of time, a monopoly privilege could be granted temporarily to stimulate industry.[47] Although he omitted them in his *De iustitia et iure*, it is likely that Lessius would have considered printing privileges as good examples of this kind of monopoly. These privileges allowed a single publishing printer to reproduce and exploit a work. They spread across Europe as quickly as the printing presses did in the early sixteenth century, allowing publishing printers to recoup the large investment made in printing equipment and make a reasonable profit. Granted by the king to printers, these privileges could nevertheless be revoked at any moment and were only valid within the king's jurisdiction.[48] They put printers in a situation of constant dependence on the royal power, which could therefore ensure the loyalty and orthodoxy of the press. To give but one illustrative example, the expansion of the renowned firm of Christopher Plantin in Antwerp, thanks to the numerous monopolies for printing religious books (such as the *Antwerp Polyglot Bible*, which took four years to print) granted by the Spanish crown, went hand in hand with its intensified demonstrations of allegiance to the Catholic faith.[49]

Monopolies and the "Fruits of Industry"

While printing privileges did not, in principle, offer any protection for the authors of the works in question (the vast majority of applications were lodged with the royal chancellery without their consent), they nevertheless played an important role in the development of intellectual property rights. The examination of these particular privileges by modern scholastics offers a nice illustration. According to Molina, these privileges are not only justified by the public utility of the printer's profession. It is the very conception and composition of books that benefit to a considerable extent from these privileges. Ultimately, this contributes to the common good (*commune bonum*).[50] Also, the interests of the authors and the printers partly overlap. In a letter sent in 1609 to Jean Moretus, son-in-law and successor of Christophe Plantin, Lessius explained that the printing privilege was in the interest of both the publisher and the author. Thanks to the printing privilege, the author could indeed hope that the printer would be more inclined to take care with the publication of the book.[51] Let us recall that from the 1617 edition of Lessius' *De iustitia et iure*, published since 1609 by Plantin-Moretus, the title page of the work was composed of an engraving by Peter Paul Rubens, the great master of Baroque art (see Fig. 7.1, p. 114).[52]

Juan de Lugo's analysis of certain monopolistic privileges is highly explicit in terms of its public utility. While he accepted in principle the prohibition of monopolies, he nevertheless acknowledged the utility of the exceptions often made by the public authorities, especially with regard to printing privileges. Who would be willing to incur the enormous costs of a print run, Lugo

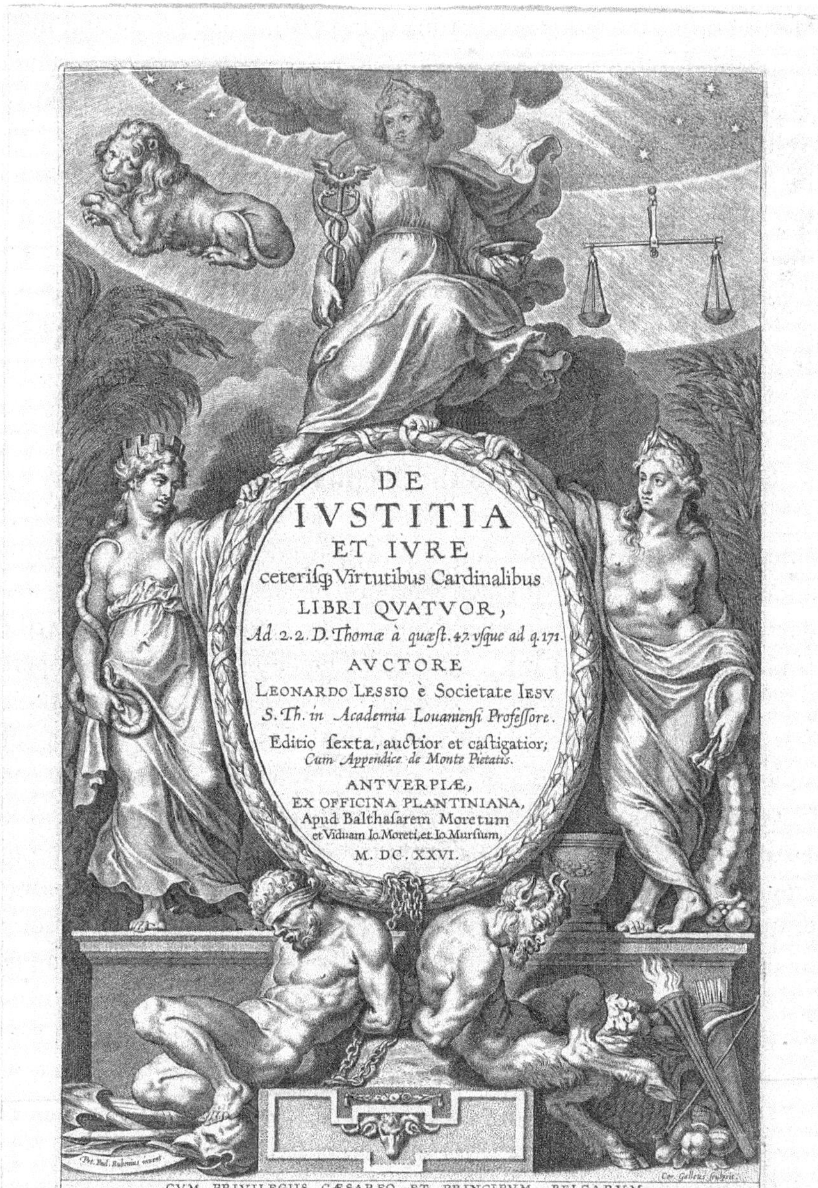

Fig. 7.1 Leonardus Lessius, *De iustitia et iure*, 1626, title page, engraving by Peter Paul Rubens (ca. 1617)

wondered, if other publishers could reproduce the same work at a lower cost? Taking inspiration from Molina and Lessius, he went even further and developed a remarkable defence of legal monopolies granted for the benefit not only of printers, but also of all creative and inventive spirits: "To support and encourage the intelligence and industry of authors and printers, they deserve to be granted this kind of monopoly for a period of ten years. Similarly, it is quite right that this power be granted to the inventors of machines or techniques useful to the republic as a reward for their inventions. These are the fruits of their industry (*fructus industriae*). It would be inappropriate for competitors to enjoy equal benefit from the attentive vigilance of the authors/inventors, and at their expense."[53]

As such, in Lugo's *De iustitia et iure*, we can glimpse a scholastic legitimization of not only printing monopolies, but also of copyrights and patents, by virtue of their capacity to stimulate industry. Strangely, this premature interest in intellectual rights by scholastic theologians escaped the perceptive eye of modern writers such as Joseph Höffner.[54] Nevertheless, at about the same time as Juan de Lugo, Pedro de Oñate also justified the public recognition of a right to intellectual property because it allowed creative people to exclusively exploit, at least for a time, the fruits of their talents and industry. According to Oñate, the authors and inventors "exercise as their own right by refusing to share their personal expertise, for they are like their private property (*privata bona sua*)."[55] Once again, this highlights the meritocratic leanings of scholastic economic thought in the seventeenth century. At the heart of their analysis, there was no longer a general prohibition of monopolies based on a venerable text of Roman law, as had been the case in the medieval legal and theological traditions. The crux of the analysis of monopolies by modern scholastic theologians was a reasoned reflection on the virtues and vices of hard work (*industria*). Protecting this "industry" required both the prohibition of monopolies as a matter of principle and the granting of statutory monopolies in exceptional circumstances.

8
The Salvation of the Economy

Bono publico nati sumus
("we are born for the public good").

—Leonardus Lessius

The preceding pages have revealed the important role of the "public good" as an argument in Leonardus Lessius' economic thought. In the name of the general interest, he sometimes condemned and sometimes favoured certain monopolistic practices. His scrutiny was clearly not limited to individual transactions, as he was aware of the general dynamics of the economy. Far from devoting his thoughts exclusively to the salvation of individual economic agents, he was mindful of the salvation of the economy as a whole. Lessius' recognition of the importance of the public good was not opposed to his liberal and meritocratic instincts. On the contrary, as this chapter will illustrate, for Lessius the common good is served above all by the virtuous circulation of money. Leaders wishing to serve the public good must acknowledge its economic foundations. In particular, the salvation of the economy depends on a system of credit adapted to the needs of all sectors of society. As a matter of fact, his concern for the public good prompted Lessius to defend some of the most controversial innovations in the credit market. In the name of public interest and the salvation of the economy, Lessius legitimized Mounts of Piety, public credit institutions based on pawnbroking, as well as "triple contracts," commercial investment vehicles often suspected of being disguised interest-bearing loans.

Credit and Piety

Anticipating the economic policy of the Archdukes Albert and Isabella of Austria (rulers of the Southern Netherlands from 1598 to 1621 who were eager to revive the economy after decades of war), Lessius defended the establishment of a Mount of Piety in Brussels. This is obvious from the

Money, Markets, and Merit. Wim Decock, Oxford University Press. © Oxford University Press (2025).
DOI: 10.1093/9780197827345.003.0009

first edition of his *De iustitia et iure* in 1605. The Mounts of Piety (*montes pietatis*), also called "Mounts of Charity," were loan institutions supported by the public authorities. They have been the subject of various studies.[1] The foundation of the Mounts of Piety in Italy in the late fifteenth century was part of an attempt to establish a Christian alternative to the Lombard usurers and Jewish bankers. Similar considerations played a role in the establishment of the first Mounts of Piety in the Southern Netherlands in the early seventeenth century. Through these institutions, Lessius, as well as the Archdukes, wished to put in place a credit system accessible to all, and in particular to the poorest individuals, while combating usurious practices and increasing the supply of investment instruments for rentiers and capitalists.

The capital of the Mounts of Piety was in fact constituted by a combination of pious donations and sales of annuities offering an interest rate of around 6.25 per cent. The "mountain of money" thus accumulated (the word "mount" refers to the verse in Psalm 67 that evokes the image of a mountain of God bearing benefits[2]) was loaned to the customers of the Mount of Piety at an interest rate of between 12 and 15 per cent. By charging a moderate interest rate that was much lower than the rates usually charged by Lombard or Jewish bankers, which could reach 30–40 per cent, the Mounts of Piety made credit available for the poorest people while offering the possibility of an ethical investment to capital investors. They pursued a charitable purpose without undermining, and even stimulating the functioning of the economy.

The close links between credit, piety and charity are illustrated through the following event. On 4 May 1515, on the occasion of the tenth session of the Fifth Lateran Council, Pope Leo X urged Christians to donate their wealth to the Mounts of Piety, emphasizing the pious nature of this financial practice, which allowed them to acquire indulgences. However ambiguous such an exhortation may seem to the modern individual (a more or less conscious heir to the Protestant critique of traditional ecclesiology and the practice of indulgences, in particular), it illustrates the perfect synthesis between the salvation of the economy and the economy of salvation in Roman Catholic theology at the dawn of the modern age: the Christian fosters his spiritual salvation by contributing to economic prosperity, just as he fosters the salvation of the economy by being concerned about the salvation of his soul. Ethical investment is both a guarantee of spiritual bliss and material prosperity. In the face of the Protestant threat, Catholics in modern times have continued to assert this idea. By virtue of the Papal Bull of 3 March

1552, Pope Paul III granted a plenary indulgence to all those who ensured the financial stability of the Mount of Piety in Rome. The following year, the churches of Rome organized collections specifically to replenish the coffers of the Mount of Piety in Rome, which had been founded in 1539 under the aegis of Pope Paul III, at the request of the Franciscans and with the financial help of a congregation of benefactors. Throughout the century, the Mount of Piety in Rome benefited from the moral support of the pontiffs.

The Franciscans and the Origins of Mounts of Piety

It is no coincidence that Franciscans fought for the establishment of a Mount of Piety in the capital of the Counter-Reformation. As shown by the Franciscan historian Herbert Holzapfel in his seminal work on the origins of the Mounts of Piety,[3] it was the Friars Minor who, in the second half of the fifteenth century, initiated these simultaneously charitable and financial institutions.

The first Mount, the "Monte dei poveri" in Perugia, was founded in 1462 under pressure from Franciscans who were critical of the lending privileges granted by the city to Jewish bankers. One of them was Fortunato Coppoli, a jurist and former judge of the municipality of Perugia who entered the Franciscan order under unusual circumstances, immediately after getting married. Coppoli is said to have helped set up a dozen Italian Mounts, but he was not the only Franciscan friar to expend inexhaustible energy in establishing Christian institutions of finance. His contemporary Bernardino da Feltre, also a lawyer by training, is the Franciscan whose name is undoubtedly most linked to the success of the Mounts of Piety. The establishment of around thirty Mounts of Piety is attributed to his tireless preaching, and his justification of the Mounts had both an immediate and lasting impact, still recalled by Lessius in the early seventeenth century.

Particularly fervent, Franciscan jurists such as Fortunato Coppoli and Bernardino da Feltre clearly wanted to provide an untainted Christian alternative to the Lombard bankers, whose practices were denounced as usurious. The followers of St. Francis defended the idea that pawnbroking at interest is acceptable in a Christian society as long as it serves the public good, a conceptthat would be re-used by Lessius, as we shall see. This gave rise to the legitimization of a kind of Christian-style capitalism by the Franciscans, and subsequently by certain Jesuits (a subject revisited several times byGiacomo Todeschini[4]). The anti-Semitic character of this initiative has not been lost on researchers. The historian Myriam Greilsammer has shown that even usurers of Christian origin, especially the Lombards, were regarded as "metaphorical Jews"[5] and therefore rejected.

The Mount of Piety in Brussels: A Controversial Establishment

At the turn of the sixteenth and seventeenth centuries, Lombard moneylenders in the Southern Netherlands were subject to ever-increasing opprobrium on account of their trade. Following a period of relative tolerance towards their banking activity, which was always subject to the goodwill of the sovereign who could withdraw their banking privilege at any moment, the idea that a public alternative should replace the abusive practices of the Lombards started to gain ground. This was to become concrete when Archdukes Albert and Isabella came to power in 1598. Without going so far as to completely abolish the Lombard banks, the Archdukes strongly favoured setting up public credit institutions, after the model of the Italian Mounts of Piety.

The person appointed by the Archdukes to realize this project was Wenceslas Cobergher, a painter and architect from Antwerp. Following a long artistic sojourn in Italy, Cobergher had returned to his native country to become the favourite architect and engineer of the Archdukes from 1605 on. With the support of the archbishops of Mechelen and Cambrai, in January 1618 Albert and Isabella appointed him as general superintendent for the establishment of Mounts of Piety. In September 1618, the first Belgian Mount opened in Brussels, designed according to Cobergher's plans. Under his leadership, a further fourteen Mounts of Piety were set up in the major cities of the Southern Netherlands.[6] Ferdinand of Bavaria, prince-bishop of Liège and archbishop of Cologne, adopted the model of the Mounts for the Principality of Liège from 1622 on, with the explicit approval of the Jesuits and the Conventual Franciscans.[7]

There was considerable support on the part of religious orders for the Christian public finance project. Continuing the apologetic effort launched by the Franciscans at the end of the fifteenth century, the Jesuits played a key role in the controversy surrounding the establishment of the Mount of Piety in Brussels in 1618. The Mount was attacked by the city, because it did not appreciate the tax privileges and immunities granted to Cobergher, his family, and the staff of the Mount. But the resistance put up by the Lombard moneylenders through the intermediary of Jean de Lillers, their lawyer and spokesman, was even more vociferous.

As soon as the Mount opened, Lillers sought the advice of fourteen theologians and canonists from the universities of Louvain and Douai to argue that the banking activities developed by the Mounts of Piety were unlawful. Among these experts was Jacobus Jansonius, professor of exegesis at Louvain and teacher of Cornelius Jansenius (who gave his name to Jansenism), who was a fierce opponent of Lessius in the polemic of grace versus free will. The hostility between the two men was not limited to questions of dogmatic theology. Their views on political economy were just as divergent. Whereas Lessius approved of the interest rate charged by the Mounts of Piety, the more stringent Jansonius emphasized the absolute prohibition on interest-bearing loans. At the start of 1619, the publication of a notice condemning the Mounts prompted Lessius and three other Jesuits to draft a reply in defence of the Mount in Brussels. This affirmative opinion received a counter-reply from Jansonius, who, for the occasion, had managed to rally to his cause a professor of public law, Antonio Perez.

In addition, Lillers lodged a complaint with the Privy Council against the establishment of the Mount of Piety in Brussels, which prompted the intervention of the ecclesiastical authorities. Johannes Malderus and Mathieu Van den Hove, the bishops of Antwerp and Mechelen, reiterated their support for the Mount in a notice of 16 November 1619. In the meantime, Lillers had been condemned by the Council of Brabant to five and a half years in prison and to perpetual exile, but via Jansonius he continued to discredit the Mount in Brussels, in particular before the apostolic nuncio. However, the nuncio decided not to intervene on account of his good relations with the Archduchess Isabella. After being pardoned in 1624, Lillers found refuge in Paris, thanks to the financial support of the Lombards. There, he sought the advice of theologians at the Sorbonne and devoted himself to writing various works against the new institutions of Christian finance, including *Le Panthéon usuraire* and *La Cassandre des monts-de-piété belges*, to which the supporters of the Mounts of Piety responded just as fiercely.

Among these was Jean Boucher, a French theologian at the University of Paris, a follower of the Catholic League, and author of a subversive work against King Henry III that was recently proven to have been inspired by the scholastic theologians.[8] Boucher was faithful to this same tradition in his work on *L'usure ensevelie ou défence des monts-de-piété de nouveau erigez aux Païs-Bas pour exterminer l'usure*, published in Tournai in 1628, a city where the author had taken refuge following the coronation of Henri IV in 1594. In his defence of the Mounts of Piety, dedicated to the Archduchess Isabella, there are certain references to Lessius. As a matter of fact, in the fifth edition of his *De iustitia et iure*, published in 1621, Lessius had taken the opportunity to explain in great detail his moral support for the Mounts of Piety.

Lessius and the Public Utility of the Mounts

At the time of the controversy surrounding the Mount in Brussels in 1620, Wenceslas Cobergher invited Lessius to reiterate his opinion in an extended version of his now famous treatise *De iustitia et iure*, by including an "Appendix on the Mount of Piety." This was the occasion for Lessius to set out his viewpoint while refuting the criticisms that Jansonius and his allies had thrown at him in 1619. Without exploring all the twists and turns of Lessius' thought put forward in this long appendix, we will limit ourselves to illustrating the weight of the argument of public utility in this apologia. Firmly anchored in reality, the appendix opened with a specific reference to the general socio-economic policy of the governors of the Southern Netherlands, under which the Mount of Piety initiative in Brussels fell: relief for the poor and the eradication of usury. In it, Archduke Albert is presented as a responsible prince concerned with the welfare of his people: "Albert of Austria, the eminent Prince of the Netherlands, saw at the beginning of his reign that his people were crushed by usury. In order to relieve his people, he took the following measures, insofar as circumstances allowed. First, he obliged the recognized usurers not to charge rates higher than 22 percent, whereas previously they had charged 33 percent. . . . Then, to further relieve his people, he was advised to establish a Mount of Piety."[9] Lessius then explained that the project for a public credit institution involving pawnbroking required funds that the Archduke could not raise for free. Hence, it was inevitable that a basic capital fund was built up by selling annuities (*census*) with an annual return of 6.25 per cent, financed through the interest payments by the clients of the Mount. Lessius specified that the ecclesiastical authorities had given their blessing in advance. They had also reiterated their moral support in the notice of 16 November 1619 against the accusations of Jean de Lillers. Malderus and Van den Hove welcomed the project of "the industrious Cobergher" for the acquisition of buildings and the raising of funds by the sale of annuities "as being useful to public affairs, convenient for the poor and destitute, and recommended by piety."[10] As such, the main argument of the prelates to legitimize the institution of a charitable bank depended on its public utility. It cannot be ruled out that they were inspired by the argument developed in this sense by Lessius a few years earlier, for in the first edition of his *De iustitia et iure*, in 1605, there is a striking exhortation to imitate the Italian model of the Mounts of Piety on account of their public utility: "It is necessary to work hard and to do everything possible so that such Mounts are set up throughout our cities—after the suppression of the usurers, who gorge on the resources of the people everywhere by dominating the market. In many ways, this would be extremely useful for the republic."[11] As a direct or indirect source of inspiration for the policy pursued by the Archdukes and approved by the religious authorities, Lessius undoubtedly helped pave the way for the creation of the Mounts of Piety in the Netherlands. Aware of the innovative character of the Mounts in this region, he did not omit to mention their long history throughout Christendom. "For more than one hundred and sixty years," he insisted at the very start of his argument, "the devout faithful in various parts of the Christian world have made large sums of money available to lend to the poor—sums commonly referred to as 'Mounts of Piety.'"[12]

Lessius demonstrated his knowledge not only of the historical origins of the Mounts, but also of the arguments put forward by the Franciscans. Using a familiar technique, Lessius contrasted the public utility of the Mounts with the purely private interest pursued by the Lombard usurers.[13] The practice of usury, which leads people to ruin, would disappear with the abolition of private banks. According to Lessius' initial estimates, it was possible for people to borrow at lower rates, 6–10 per cent. Replacing the Lombard banks with the Mounts of Piety would also advance public utility, since it would put an end to the export of capital by usurers outside the country. This was a rather patriotic argument, already successfully used by the Franciscans involved in the justification of the first Mounts. Lessius was criticized by Laurence Beyerlinck, a theologian from Antwerp, for borrowing this argument from the Franciscans without criticism: "If Lessius is referring to people who until recently, with the permission of the prince, held banks in our regions, then he is mistaken in alleging that these people are exporting capital abroad. Practice actually shows the opposite."[14] Although Lessius may have too readily embraced the protectionist argument used by the Italian Franciscans, he remained critical regarding the possible abuses of public pawnbroking institutions. He explicitly stipulated that the Mounts of Piety must respect certain conditions. For example, in the event of payment default, the pawned item would be put up for sale, but the remaining balance—after deducting the loan fees and the loan amount—had to be returned to the client. So as not to succumb to the same selfish temptations as the Lombards, the Mounts must not get rich with the sale of the pawned items.

In addition, the loans granted by the Mounts had to actually support the needs of the poor, although this condition was nevertheless open to interpretation. The notion of "poverty," it should be remembered, was at least flexible in the Ancien Régime. A nobleman unable to live up to the requirements of his rank could be qualified as "poor," as could a merchant unable to carry on his activities due to a lack of funds. In his study into the practice of Mounts of Piety in the Netherlands, Paul Soetaert concluded that "despite their charitable appearance [they] never functioned as charitable institutions."[15] Even the Archduchess Isabella turned to the Mount of Piety in Brussels to finance military expenses after the end of the Twelve-Years' Truce, and the non-repayment of her "royal debt" brought the Mount to the brink of bankruptcy.

Interest between Compensation and Fairness

More than anything else, what troubled people about the operation of the Mounts was the obligation for borrowers to pay a monthly fee as a contribution to the costs of the institution. Paying the salaries of the Mount's staff, renting the building, doing the accounting, and paying the investors' annuities required considerable funds, to which the borrowers had to contribute. Easily assimilated to interest, the justification of these sums paid by the borrower was at the crux of the debate. It was the Dominican friars in particular, and especially Cajetan, the Master of the Order between 1508 and 1518, who was opposed to the payment of the sums for fear of violating the prohibition on lending at interest. Yet, the Franciscans and Jesuits drew on all their intellectual capital to demonstrate the legitimacy of the interest collected by the Mounts of Piety.

To justify the interest payments, the Franciscans Fortunato Coppoli and Bernardino da Feltre, jurists by training, put forward a rather original legal analysis of the practice of pawnbroking granted by the Mounts. They analyzed the Mounts' lending practices in terms of a set of four contracts, each individually legitimate: a loan, a pledge, a mandate, and a contract for hire. The sum paid by the client to the Mount was considered the price of a contract for hire of work (*locatio conductio*), not of a loan. It was just the salary paid to the Mount's staff, not interest due by virtue of a loan. If it wanted to respect fairness, the Mount had to provide a compensation mechanism for its staff. In a notice by Bernardino de' Bustis, another jurist who became a Franciscan, we read that the industrious work (*industria*) and goodwill of the staff of the Mounts vis-à-vis the poor deserve pecuniary as well as symbolic recognition: "A carpenter or a cheap porter has the right to recognition, in the form of money, on the part of the one to whom they have lent money, even if the borrower was not poor and they were not motivated by charity. Then how could it be that the very onerous obligation incurred by the individual, highly industrious and abounding in goodwill towards the poor, should not be recognized by the Mount, which is governed by piety and fairness?"[16] Although Lessius did not exactly copy and paste the idea of the Mount as the result of a "fourfold contract," his reasoning in support of these institutions nonetheless rested on a combination of references to fairness and specific legal categories.

Above all, Lessius made use of the legal principle that an individual who spontaneously manages the affairs of another without the latter's prior consent can claim compensation for the costs usefully incurred in doing so. Dating back to Roman law, this case is known as "management of business" (*negotiorum gestio*). It implies that the manager of the business (*negotiorum gestor*) may claim compensation from the beneficiary for useful expenses. According to Lessius, the relationship between the Mounts of Piety and their clients finds its legal expression precisely in the category of management of business, since the Mount manages the affairs of others. Consequently, the clients of the Mount owe it compensation for useful expenses: "Whoever manages someone else's business can always claim compensation, especially if he acts on public authority. The director of the Mount who accepts money against payment of annuities in order to lend this money to someone in the community who so requests it, this director manages the business of others, that is, of the whole community. He is considered to act with the latter's approval, for he does not accept money for his own benefit, but in the interest of the whole community (*in commodum totius communitatis*), especially of those who need money in that community. The community must therefore compensate him so that he can pay the annual annuities."[17]

The sum paid to the Mounts by the borrowers is thus, in reality, only an indemnification for the commitments made by the *negotiorum gestor* to the benefit of the community. The construction and maintenance of the building, the salaries of the staff, the annuities to be paid to the investors—all are costs usefully incurred by the Mount in the public interest, and in particular for the benefit of needy clients. It is therefore appropriate that clients make a contribution in this regard, paying monthly sums in proportion to the capital borrowed, so that the activities undertaken to provide this service do not prejudice the Mount: "Fairness never demands that one lend at one's own expense. One can therefore claim as much as is necessary to avoid losses, which in concrete terms means the rent of the building, the salaries of the staff, accounting costs, and so forth. There is no more convenient way to claim this compensation than to ask for an individual contribution based on the amount of the loan."[18] No-one is obliged to lend out at his own expense: this was a familiar principle among canonists and theologians at the dawn of the modern age. In the absence of an actual textual basis in Roman or canon law, this rule was seen as an expression of a superior principle of fairness—an abstract argument, but one that was very popular among the defenders of the Mounts of Piety.

Fairness played a crucial role in the justification of the Mounts for another reason. In order to justify the interest paid to the Mounts, theologians and canonists made ample reference to the well-known maxim according to which "he who bears the burdens of something must reap the benefits of it, and, conversely, he who reaps the benefits of something must bear the burdens of it." Incorporated in the famous rules of Pope Boniface VIII from 1298, this adage was considered to be the expression of a supreme principle of fairness, and was among the three basic axioms to be memorized by students in studying cases of conscience taught by Lessius.[19] While the maxim was often applied to resolve private law cases,[20] it also lent itself to considerations of public interest, as the debate on the Mounts of Piety illustrates here. Pope Leo X referred to the maxim in his Papal Bull of 1515. A century later, Lessius referred to it in his apologia for the Mounts, with various formulations: "The fees are made for the grace and the benefit of those who will solicit the help of the Mounts, in particular so that they will not be obliged to borrow money from usurers and suffer an even greater prejudice. If someone wishes to take advantage of the benefits offered by the Mount, they can enter into an agreement to contribute to the costs. For it is only fair that he who wishes to benefit from a thing should also contribute to whatever is necessary for its preservation."[21]

From Charitable Credit to Commercial Credit

Achieving a balance between burdens and pleasures, costs and benefits, obligations and debt claims: this is actually the supreme criterion at the core of Lessius' analysis of new banking activities in the early modern Low Countries.[22] Once convinced of the public utility of a given financial practice, he attempts to demonstrate at all costs that the transactions which the practice involves respect the balance required by justice and fairness. In this way, an interesting parallel can be drawn between his approval of the establishment of the Mounts of Piety in Brussels, and his defence, just as remarkable, of the so-called triple contract.

A conceptual fiction put forward by jurists and moralists anxious to justify its use, the "triple contract" relates to the practice of granting commercial credit in return for an interest rate. A lender safely invests in a business with the expectation of a fixed annual profit, while the entrepreneur is free to reap the remaining profits. From a legal perspective, the agreement between investor and entrepreneur can be analysed, in retrospect, as a combination of three contracts: a partnership or commercial undertaking (*societas*), an insurance policy (*assecuratio*) and a sales contract (*emptio*). The contracting parties enter into a partnership insofar as they pool something (capital and industry respectively) for a common project. In addition, there is insurance, since the entrepreneur guarantees the investor's capital for a price, for example 10 per cent of the capital invested. Conversely, the entrepreneur buys all the potential profits, for example at an amount corresponding to 15 per cent of the invested capital. The result for the lender is a secure investment with a 5 per cent margin. Consequently, in some regions, this type of contract was also referred to as a "5 percent contract."

Whereas the Mounts of Piety were primarily charitable (at least in theory), the triple contract takes us into the world of business and investment. As in the case of the Mounts, the phenomenon was not new, but it was becoming more prevalent in the Southern Netherlands at the time of Lessius. While the apologia of the Italian Mounts by the Franciscans anticipated Lessius' discourse on the Mount of Piety in Brussels, it is the memorable defence of the investment practices of German bankers by Johann Eck from Ingolstadt in the early sixteenth century which was the precursor to Lessius' approval of the triple contract a century later. In 1515, at a meeting in Bologna convened by the Fuggers, a grand banking family from Augsburg, Eck put forward a striking argument in favour of the triple contract (also called the "German contract"), thereby contributing to the moral justification of the commercial and financial practices of his hosts.[23] Is it any wonder that Johann Eck, an apologist for protocapitalism, was one of the main targets of Martin Luther's famously scathing criticism?

Usury, Leonine Partnerships, and Freedom of Contract

Like any form of financing involving a charge, the triple contract was viewed with suspicion in a society which had inherited the prohibition of lending at interest, handed down from the Bible and reinforced by Aristotelian philosophy. The fixed margin of the lender, as well as the monthly amount received by the Mounts, could easily be regarded as a disguised form of interest, "cloaked" usury, the result of an "implicit loan." Hence the unrelenting resistance to triple contracts as well as to the Mounts.

Despite Eck's apologia, the Jesuit Peter Canisius, a native of Nijmegen and author of a catechism that soon became highly popular, reignited the controversy in the 1560s with his scathing sermons against the usurious banking practices in Augsburg. At the same time, Domingo de Soto's *De iustitia et iure*, the first treatise of its kind to include a notable critique of the de facto circumvention of the prohibition on lending at interest, began to spread in Europe. Soto was opposed to the practice of triple contracts and expressed serious reservations about the actual functioning of the Mounts of Piety. Moreover, Pope Sixtus V's Papal Bull *Detestabilis avaritia*, promulgated in 1586, appeared to endorse this return to a more uncompromising attitude towards the current market practices. Various theologians and canonists, including Lessius, opposed this Papal Bull, which was regarded as inapplicable in entire regions of Europe, owing to its lack of popular acceptance.[24] At the end of the sixteenth century, the triple contract could therefore count on the moral support of most Jesuits, such as Molina and Lessius, who saw it as an instrument for promoting commercial activities that offered investment opportunities for the wealthier classes. At the very least, the triple contract could be considered a lesser evil which avoided genuinely usurious practices.

Apart from the suspicions of "cloaked" usury, the triple contract also raised concerns on account of the imbalance it appeared to create between the investor and the entrepreneur in terms of their exposure to risk. On account of the capital guarantee, the investor seemed to be protected from all loss, and was moreover guaranteed of receiving annual dividends. According to the traditional view, inspired by Aristotle and reprised by medieval jurists, a partnership resembled a kind of friendship, a fraternity, where losses and profits were shared. This "principle of sharing the profits and losses" was, in the words of the jurists of the time, the "nature" of the contract. Still very much a part of Islamic finance (the PLS-principle), this sharing implied that profits as well as losses were to be distributed among all partners, preferably in equal shares, unless otherwise agreed. The prototype of an invalid partnership was the so-called Leonine partnership, already present in Roman law, where one of the parties received all the profits without being exposed to any losses. While, economically speaking, suspicions of "cloaked" usury were justified insofar as the fixed margin could be considered a functional equivalent of an interest rate, theologians such as Eck and Lessius stressed the importance of legal categories in the normative analysis of business. As such, technically speaking, the margin that accrues to the investor does not originate in a loan contract: from a legal perspective, it is the result of three contracts combined, each legitimate in itself.

Whereas the opponents recognized the legitimacy of these three contracts on condition that they be concluded successively between the partners and third parties (e.g., between the investor and a professional insurer), Eck and Lessius did not object to the three contracts being concluded directly between the entrepreneur and the investor. Freedom of contract allows the lender to make his consent to the partnership contract conditional, meaning that he can demand that the contractor provide him with insurance, rather than entering into an insurance contract with a third party. As long as the price of this additional obligation is paid, the agreement is legitimate. Conversely, the entrepreneur may consent on condition that an agreement is reached on the purchase of potential and future profits. He pays the price, and in this way the investor's obligation to settle for a smaller margin has been compensated. Everything can be negotiated, as long as the freedom and balance of the obligations are safeguarded:

"Concluding these different contracts simultaneously or successively does not change the justice of the agreements, as long as the equality and freedom of the two partners are respected."[25]

Freedom of contract, so important in the eyes of Eck and Lessius, played an even more important role in their rebuttal of the argument that the principle of sharing profits and losses is violated. Drawing on the arguments of

Konrad Summenhart, author of a seven-volume treatise on contract law, Eck demonstrated that the validity of a partnership does not depend on the sharing of risks and benefits. While the principle of sharing profits and losses may be considered laudable, and a natural element of the partnership contract, Eck wished to distinguish between the "natural" and the "substantial" elements of a contract. He explains, by way of analogy, that it is natural for someone to laugh, but that there can also be individuals without any sense of humour. In the same way, it is natural for partners to each be exposed to the risks of their business, but a partnership can exist without this being the case. The substance, and therefore the validity, of a partnership contract depends on the contributions made by the partners pursuing a common interest. As the sharing of risks and benefits is not part of this substance, it can be subject to specific negotiations and agreements.

Comparative Cost-Benefit Analysis

What concerned Lessius more than anything else in agreements in general and triple contracts in particular was the balance between burdens and pleasures, costs and benefits, duties and rights,. To assess this balance in the triple contract, he made a comparative analysis of the costs and benefits of each partner. It goes without saying that the traditional way of looking at money and capital investment favoured a presumption of imbalance in the obligations, at the expense of the entrepreneur. The question was whether the lender, like a kind of parasite, was not getting rich while sleeping, without any worries and leaving the work and effort to the individual who borrowed the money. This was the spectre of usury, so well articulated in a fifteenth-century sermon by the Franciscan Bernardine of Siena: "This profit, that is, usury, does not come to the lender by virtue of his industry or labour, nor by virtue of his intelligence, concern, or reward for anything else that would make the profit just and fair."[26] To combat these received ideas, Lessius highlighted the costs, inconvenience, and worries to which the lender was subject, while minimizing the more visible efforts of the entrepreneur in a triple contract.

In Lessius' view, the partners in a triple contract each commit to three types of costs. Let us start with the entrepreneur. The latter will first have to implement the project by making the capital bear fruit through his work and his industry. He must then cover the capital risk. Finally, he pays fixed dividends to the investor each year. According to Lessius, the burden of these different commitments should not be overestimated. As regards insurance, it is highly relative: if the project fails, the entrepreneur will not be able to repay the capital in any case; if, on the other hand, the project is successful, he will be delighted to keep his promise for fear of losing his credibility among other merchants. Similarly, the obligation to pay dividends is not too onerous, as day-to-day experience shows that the profits made by entrepreneurs easily reach twice the margin promised to investors. In addition, alternative methods of financing commercial projects, such as the sale of annuities, are no less expensive. And as regards the first cost, the industry applied, the fact of having more money due to outside investment benefits the entrepreneur. He would have wanted to implement his project in any case, and being able to manage more money and flaunt more wealth will only enhance his reputation. His credibility is boosted: "The work and the obligation to spend money for the undertaking are not valued highly by the merchants who accept the money. With the same effort, they spend their money and the investor's money. Moreover, this enhances their credibility and makes them more illustrious, as they benefit from all the power offered by cash. This allows them to buy more cheaply, partly because they are more credible and partly because they are able to buy as many goods as possible with cash."[27]

Lessius almost managed to make it seem as though the costs incurred by the entrepreneur are, in fact, profits. Compared to those of the entrepreneur, the costs to the investor are real. Firstly, he risks his capital. This may appear to be a fictive cost insofar as the capital guarantee is one of the essential features of a triple contract but, as Lessius pointed out rather accurately, the insurance promised by the merchant is not very reliable. Investors are more than happy to pay a higher premium for a more secure guarantee or for the additional security of a pledge or mortgage. There is a second cost that should not be underestimated: by investing in the partner's project, the lender foregoes the benefits and options offered by cash.[28] For example, he will no longer be able to seize opportunities arising in the market. This opportunity cost is a heavy burden in an environment where, according to day-to-day experience and the admissions of merchants, the profits that an industrious individual can make are as high as 10–12 per cent. For the same reason, the third obligation incumbent on the investor represents a significant cost: by entering into a sales agreement for future profits for a modest price, the industrious lender deprives himself of a potentially higher margin. As Lessius explained in his treatment of the loan contract, "the money you lend to others is worth more to you than its intrinsic value insofar as you can make a profit from it by virtue of your industry. Money is the fertile seed containing virtual profits made by your industry."[29] Lessius therefore managed to invert the traditional image of the borrower saddled with obligations and the profiteering, parasitic lender. Intimately linked to his discourse on the fruitful nature of money (which Lessius defended against the view that money is sterile, put forward in the Aristotelian tradition), his justification of the triple contract rested on rejecting the accusation that such a contract would lead to an imbalance between the partners' obligations. But Lessius went further: not only is the triple contract not a violation of the precepts of justicein contracts, it is also beneficial to the civil community as a whole.

The Public Utility of the Triple Contract

Like the Mounts of Piety, commercial loans with capital guarantees and fixed dividends are therefore beneficial to the economy as a whole, in Lessius' view. Despite strong resistance, including from Bishop Malderus of Antwerp, who had supported the establishment of the Mount of Piety in Brussels, but remained critical of the triple contract, Lessius never abandoned this viewpoint. He warned the political elites against taking a position which he regarded as disconnected from reality, and therefore highly detrimental to the interests of society. In contrast to the Synod of Antwerp, which resolved in 1610 to condemn triple contracts, Lessius pleaded for a general acceptance of this common practice, whose utility for the community he continually emphasized. Firstly, triple contracts offer a safe and sound way for lenders—including widows, orphans, and religious institutions—to invest their money without risk or peril to their souls. The offering of investment instruments must be sufficiently broad and diversified, in Lessius' view, so that people do not start squandering their wealth or growing it by illicit means. He invited sceptics to consider what would happen to rentiers if they did not have the triple contracts or the purchase of the annuities by the Mounts to ensure relatively guaranteed profits. They would then resort to truly usurious practices, clandestinely charging exorbitant interest rates, creating monopolies, stealing, and so forth. This would not be advantageous, either for the prosperity of the country or for the salvation of souls.

If the instrument of the triple contract were to disappear as a result of civil and ecclesiastical interventions, the common good would suffer considerably. Lessius proved to be a shrewd analyst of the interconnection between the various credit markets: "It is clear that the triple contract is advantageous for the prince and the republic. If this type of contract is prohibited, merchants will no longer be able to supply money to the prince except under pernicious conditions. They will be obliged to raise funds in another way, through bills of exchange, which are priced at 12, 14, 18 percent or more on an annual basis. Consequently, referring to these bills of exchange and to compensate themselves, they will demand much higher interest rates from the prince."[30] Mindful of the economic realities, the Oracle of the Low Countries therefore proposed taking the deep links between the supply of commercial credit and the market for public debt into consideration. Given that the civil authorities relied on merchants for borrowing money, the rates at which these merchants could borrow were automatically reflected in public debt rates. If merchants could no longer raise funds through the relatively inexpensive triple contracts, they would charge higher interest rates on loans to the public authorities.

By way of conclusion, we should highlight the fact that Lessius' judgements analysed above were imbued with what Alain Wijffels, a legal historian, has termed "policy considerations." It is, according to Wijffels, "the part of a decision where the judge takes into account how the social order in the broad sense, including the political order, the economic order, public life in general . . ., might be affected by the principle established by his decision."[31] In the Ancien Régime, these political considerations were frequently expressed through references to principles of fairness or public utility.[32] Lessius' apologia in favour of the Mounts of Piety and the triple contract were good examples. They recall his advocacy of a money market where the interest rate is set by common estimation for the sake of the common good (see chapter 4).

Leonardus Lessius fully understood the importance of assessing the consequences that the decision of a particular case may have on the general interest. Mindful of the empirical evidence, he considered the societal impact of endorsing the financial practices examined in this chapter, an impact that he believed was entirely positive. In other words, Lessius' judgements on the Mounts of Piety and triple contracts are of interest to us not only because they offer excellent examples of his lucidity as an economist and his skill as a jurist, but also because they illustrate that, rather than hindering financial innovations, arguments based on public utility and an overarching consideration of the salvation of the economy helped to provide them with definitive legitimacy.

9
The Economy of Salvation

> *In pursuing an evangelical life, we are all merchants; we acquire possession of heavenly goods by the implementation of the commandments.*
>
> Basil the Great

An advisor mindful of the realities of the market, fully open to the commercial spirit while emphasizing the need to observe the principle of justice in contractual exchange: this is the picture of Leonardus Lessius that emerges from the preceding chapters. By following the advice of this Jesuit confessor, the merchant who works hard and plays the market game skilfully, without cheating, knows that he deserves to reap the benefits. The accumulated profits are simply just recompense for the intelligence and industry applied in the exercise of his profession—the just recompense for his merit—as long as he continues to accept the risks. While Lessius' economic ethics reveal his profoundly "meritocratic" instincts, his deepest reflections on merit (*meritum*) are actually developed in a completely different context: that of the theological analysis of the relationship between the individual and his Creator. We should therefore integrate into our study of the economic and legal thought of Lessius his contribution to the theological debates on the mysteries of faith. For this, we will leave his observations on the economy in *De iustitia et iure* and turn to his works on the dogma of the Christian faith. In particular, we will focus on his thoughts on the "economy of salvation," that is, the rules of the game of the supernatural order, which determine how one can "make merit" in the eyes of God, and obtain eternal life through the interplay of good works and divine grace. To set the stage, we will briefly examine the advent of the economy of salvation in the Christian tradition before analysing its outcome in Francisco Suárez and Leonardus Lessius.

Money, Markets, and Merit. Wim Decock, Oxford University Press. © Oxford University Press (2025).
DOI: 10.1093/9780197827345.003.0010

(Un)binding Heaven and Earth

At first glance, it is not obvious that eminently theological subjects such as the salvation of the soul are intimately connected with commerce, industry, and contract law. This was nevertheless the case in the Judeo-Christian tradition for centuries. At least since the Protestant revolution of the sixteenth century, the modern individual has become accustomed to thinking of the realities of the hereafter as profoundly distinct from an overtly earthly logic. Neither the observance of laws nor good works—prayer, fasting, charity—can guarantee us entry into paradise, we learn from Martin Luther and John Calvin. A Christian spirituality that envisages the relationship between God and man in too strict economic terms seems a contradiction, even a vulgar and repugnant idea. Such a pragmatic view of faith seems more symptomatic of decadence rather than common sense. It is worthy of a revolt, one like the protest against the dilution of the authentic faith set in motion by Martin Luther in Wittenberg in 1517. His declaration of justification by faith alone, regardless of one's works, would open the door to a new world.

In the wake of this revolution, a new conception of salvation was born, but also new concepts of the State and of law, as Harold Berman[1] has repeatedly shown with remarkable clarity. It became extremely difficult, even arduous, for the modern Western individual, the heir to this new world, to grasp the reality of the economy of salvation of the ancient and medieval periods. Nevertheless, for a while, especially in the face of the Protestant threat, this old economy of salvation was reinforced by Jesuits such as Francisco Suárez and Leonardus Lessius.

Giacomo Todeschini and Odd Inge Langholm have produced a series of excellent studies on the use of commercial vocabulary in the development of a Christian spirituality relating to the path of virtue and the attainment of salvation.[2] The assimilation of the faithful Christian to a merchant in the quotation from the *Commentary on Proverbs* by Basil the Great,[3] bishop of Caesarea until his death in 379, is just one example. This was often supplemented by a warning against the devil, who was portrayed as a bandit threatening to steal the gold coins that constituted the virtues of the good Christian. As demonstrated by Gérard Génelle, Augustine used metaphors drawn from financial life to help his audience understand the Gospel message.[4] There are indeed recurrent references to business dealings and money in Augustine's sermons: we need only think of his comparison of almsgiving with *traiecticia pecunia*, the credit granted for long-distance trade in the hope of making a considerable profit in the long run.[5] Moreover, eminent scholars such as Jean Gaudemet have highlighted the remarkable way in which the Church Fathers drew on their knowledge of Roman law to make the deepest mysteries of the Christian faith transparent.[6] One example is the central metaphor of *redemptio*, according to which Christ was sent to earth by his Father to redeem souls from the devil, at the cost of his own life. This metaphor comes from the legal cases of the redemption of prisoners and slaves in Roman law.[7]

More than ten centuries after the golden age of the Church Fathers, it was the conflation of religious, legal, and economic vocabularies, intensified by medieval canonists and scholastic theologians, that provoked Martin Luther's indignation. Luther was certainly not the only one, or the first, to be troubled by the idea that the intimate truths of the spirituality of the hereafter could be illuminated by the logic of the market. But in the long run, it was his protest movement that has been the most significant in terms of its consequences. Luther feared the juridification and institutionalization of the Christian faith, orchestrated by Rome. The privileged position claimed by the clergy in managing the economy of salvation only added to his irritation. As a mediating institution between God and man, the Church claimed power over the links between heaven and earth. It dispensed the sacraments as moments of earthly connection with the divine; it stimulated the material aspect of devotional practice, inviting the simple faithful to tangibly experience God by incorporating all their senses; it organized a market of salvation by selling rights to the remission of sins (indulgences) in exchange for cold, hard cash.[8] The confrontation with all these material aspects of a religion deemed too human pushed Luther to radicalism. In his eyes, salvation could not be bought, because God did not allow himself to be tainted, and clergymen had no right to come between the faithful and their heavenly Father. However, the Christians of the day were unlikely to be concerned by the close ties between heaven and earth that were forged under the auspices of the Roman Church. A famous passage from Christopher Columbus' account of his fourth and final voyage to the Indies provides a rather nice illustration: brandishing the virtues of gold in his letter of 7 July 1503 addressed to the king and queen of Spain, he explained, probably not without a certain irony, that treasures are made of gold, and that "he who possesses it does all he wishes to in this world, and succeeds in helping souls into paradise."[9]

Works and Salvation

The idea that gold can elevate souls to heaven was the subject of a fascinating study by Peter Brown. In *The Ransom of the Soul*, Brown explores the gradual rise, in the patristic writings of Late Antiquity, of a Christian view of the fate of the soul after death.[10] His study examines the evolution between the conception of the hereafter by Cyprian, bishop of Carthage from 248 to 258, and Julian, archbishop of Toledo between 680 and 690 (see also chapter 1, p. 21). For the sake of brevity, we will limit ourselves to a few elements of this breathtaking work that testify to a growing interpenetration of market logic and Christian spirituality. In Brown's view, the notion of life after death evolved to extend the time period between the moment of death and the divine judgement that gives access to eternal life. This extension leaves room for the elaboration of a whole economy of salvation in which links between heaven and earth, the dead and the living, and between good works and salvation appear. Cyprian still imagined death as the instant meeting of the martyr, the perfect Christian, with God, and was not interested in the vague fate of ordinary Christians. On the other hand, Julian envisaged death as the start of the journey of the soul towards heaven, advancing more or less rapidly according to the vices and virtues accumulated during one's life. According to Peter Brown, the profound difference between the world of Julian of Toledo and that of Cyprian of Carthage lay in the former's increasing attention to the fate of the soul of each individual, which depended on the precise and individual combination of sins and merits.[11]

The fact that man can, through his good works, accumulate merits that allow him to advance more rapidly on the path to heavenly bliss, is an idea that profoundly marked the course of medieval Christian Europe. Prayer, charity, and fasting, the guarantors of a good balance with, respectively, God, the other and oneself, are as much a means of bringing rich and poor together as of accumulating credit in the eyes of God. Since the rich man can atone for his sins with alms, according to the famous phrase in the Book of Proverbs (13:8: "The ransom of a man's life is his wealth"), charity is no longer just a matter of social justice, but also of divine justice. In addition to strengthening the links between the poor and the rich in this world, good works also help preserve the links between the living and the dead. For the ancient Christian communities, works of charity were not only a way of crediting one's own account with God, but also of crediting the accounts of others. As such, the practice of intercessory prayers gained in importance, giving the living the power to act on the fate of the dead. By praying for the souls of the dead, the living can atone for the sins of the latter and shorten the time between death and the blissful vision. By giving alms, Christians can not only look after their own salvation, but also redeem the souls of others. As Peter Brown notes, the enunciation of these very concrete links between those dwelling on earth and the souls of the dead reached its zenith with the majestic monastic foundations from the seventh century onwards. This is to say that, in Christian Europe, the physical landscape, the social fabric, and the actual economy were shaped by the idea of the economy of salvation.

This idea of the economy of salvation, on account of its mercenary aspect, nevertheless is a source of surprise and even discomfort for the modern individual. The concept of building up a "treasure in heaven" through good works, widespread among early Christians, has embarrassed many, including historians and exegetes confronted with the words of Jesus in the Gospel according to Matthew (19:21), "If you want to be perfect, go and sell all your possessions and give the money to the poor, and you will have treasure in heaven." In this regard, an anecdote related by Peter Brown is revealing. When Klaus Koch, a Protestant theologian, brought together various specialists in 1968 to discuss the interpretation of this passage about the treasure in heaven, the words of Matthew could not be seen as anything but a metaphor. How could the first Christians, with their haloes of perfection and authenticity in the imagination of the protagonists of the Reformation,[12] have believed that you can accumulate treasure in heaven by practising charity? "What an abominable idea for Protestants!," was how Koch put it.[13] It is not surprising, therefore, that most dictionaries and encyclopaedias of Christian theology have completely overlooked this concept. Nevertheless, it is present in the Gospels, as evidenced by Luke 12:33, where Jesus urges his disciples to provide themselves with moneybags that do not grow old, with a treasure in heaven that does not fail, where no thief approaches and no moth destroys.

Moreover, as Sylvain Piron pointed out, recourse to economic logic is far from being unique to the Judeo-Christian religion. Based on the work of Ching-lang Hou, Piron cites the example of the offertory in Taoist liturgy.[14] With this money, individuals could credit their accounts with the "Celestial Treasury." This "celestial tax" was not a payment for services rendered by the Taoist clergy, even though they were tasked with collecting it. The offertory was intended directly for the deities, so that the faithful could obtain something from the gods in exchange for their contribution.[15]

A Treasure Full of Merits

The possibility of "hoarding" merit goes to the heart of the economy of salvation as it was conceived in the early centuries. It puts Basil the Great's *Commentary on Proverbs* in a new light. There seems to be little reason to doubt that acquiring heavenly goods by implementing the commandments refers to the accumulation of treasure in heaven. What we can say is that the link Basil establishes between the industrious Christian and the merchant is direct: one who pursues an evangelical life *is* a merchant. There is nothing in Basil's Latin text that suggests a purely metaphorical understanding of the text, *as if* the charitable Christian could be compared to a merchant. A Christian life is lived on two distinct levels: that of the natural order and that of the supernatural order, and there are multiple areas of contact between the two. In either case, the devout Christian is called upon to expend his energy in acquiring goods, with the assurance that a virtuous life will be rewarded in heaven. The highly material dimension of this vision of the relationship between earthly life and the hereafter is further illustrated by an anecdote related in the *Dialogues* of Gregory the Great.[16] A Roman cobbler had the good habit of distributing part of his weekly profits to the poor every Saturday. A vision revealed to a devout Christian showed the consequences for the future of the cobbler's soul: in heaven, a house was built to welcome him.

Our knowledge of the origins of this highly pragmatic view of obtaining salvation has been greatly enriched by Gary Anderson, a biblical scholar. In his works *Sin: A History* (Yale UP, 2009) and *Charity: The Place of the Poor in the Biblical Tradition* (Yale UP, 2013), Anderson provides an impressive analysis of the biblical origins of the economic conception of both sin and merit in the Judeo-Christian tradition. He notes the shift towards an economic conception of sin understood as a "debt" in biblical texts dating from the fifth to the second centuries B.C., particularly in the Book of Daniel. In the fourth book of Daniel, King Nebuchadnezzar learns that he can redeem his sins by practising charity (Daniel 4:27). Moreover, this new notion of sin went hand in hand with a perception of good works as giving rise to "credits" which could negate sin debts. The debt constituted by sin can therefore be compensated by the credit that is the fruit of good works, in particular charity. Secondly, the merits accumulated by good works are transferred to a "treasure in heaven," an image that goes back to the Book of Tobit.[17]

Unsurprisingly, the texts of the Books of Proverbs, Daniel, and Tobit, revisited by Anderson, gave rise to much controversy in the Protestant communities of the sixteenth century.[18] Martin Luther was not the first to point out that an overtly mercenary conception of the spiritual life was not without its dangers. The first major controversy on this subject was triggered at the start of the fifth century between the monk Pelagius and Augustine. Fleeing the sack of Rome in 410, Pelagius and his followers landed in Carthage, and shocked Augustine, the local bishop, on account of their radical assertions on the role of good works in justification. Entire libraries are filled with studies examining this conflict in great detail. It is enough to recall here the extent to which Pelagius emphasized the ability of the individual to ensure his own salvation at the risk of losing sight of the necessity of divine grace. To obtain direct access to paradise, he enjoined his followers, mostly members of the Roman nobility, to give up all their wealth. Augustine saw this as a direct threat to the Christian economy of salvation, built around the less radical, regular practice of almsgiving as a way of atoning for one's sins.[19] Thereafter, all theologians suspected of overemphasizing the contribution of the individual to the process of justification faced the charge of "(semi-)Pelagianism," including Leonardus Lessius (see chapter 1, p. 24).

"On a matter which touches the deepest part of religious life, one must obviously expect to encounter different nuances according to the times and the circumstances," warned Jean Rivière in 1928 in his article on merit in the *Dictionnaire de théologie catholique* (his contribution, meant to offer a concise synthesis of the subject, was nevertheless 212 broad columns long).[20] It would be impossible to analyse the complete history of the economy of salvation here, and even more so to repeat the excellent work of Rivière. The preceding pages have had the sole objective of giving an idea, however fragmentary, of several key elements of the debates on the economy of salvation which should put Leonardus Lessius' viewpoint on this question into perspective. In his day, on account of the Protestant Reformation, debates on grace and merit had become more numerous and polemical than previously, so much so that Ignatius of Loyola, in his *Spiritual Exercises* of 1548, advised his followers to refrain as much as possible from taking part in these quarrels, except to warn against the double threat of neglecting good works and defeatism engendered by the doctrine of predestination: "We should not make it a habit of speaking much of predestination. If somehow at times it comes to be spoken of, it must be done in such a way that the people are not led into any error. They are at times misled, so that they say: "Whether I shall be saved or lost, has already been determined, and this cannot be changed whether my actions are good or bad." So they become indolent and neglect the works that are conducive to the salvation and spiritual progress of their souls."[21]

Nevertheless, the scale of the Reformation and the firm response it required from Rome put paid to Ignatius' good advice. Faced with the dual threat of Protestantism and conflicting currents within the Catholic tradition, the Council of Trent (1545–1563) reaffirmed the value of good works before God, while combating the negative stance towards the concept of merit in evangelical Christianity promoted by the Protestants.[22] Consequently, the possibility of thinking of the relationship between the individual and his creator in contractual terms was put forward more than ever thereafter, in particular by the Jesuits. Peerless examples of this can be found in the works of Francisco Suárez and Pedro de Oñate, as we shall see. More prudent, Lessius sought a balance in formulating this problem, but his fight to safeguard the economy of salvation was no less determined.

Súarez: Metaphysician and Jurist

While we have already referred to Pedro de Oñate's exceptional mastery of legal technique, the reputation of Francisco Suárez, a member of the School of Salamanca, is often associated with his metaphysical disputes or his philosophy of law. However, his legal skills, even in practice, were just as impressive as those of an Oñate or a Lessius. Suárez's conviction, expressed in the prologue to his *De legibus et Deo legislatore* (*Treatise on the Laws and God the Legislator*, 1612), that no-one can claim to be a good theologian without a good knowledge of the law speaks volumes. References to Roman and canon law are scattered throughout his arguments on all sorts of issues. Although he did not author an autonomous treatise on contract law, he brought his original thinking to bear on the most diverse problems. It is within his vast work on ecclesiastical penal law, *De censuris* (1603), that he delivered one of the most remarkable arguments for legal security in contracts.[23] Moreover, his awareness of the rights of the defence and the finer points of criminal procedure prompted him to question not only the alleged inability of excommunicated individuals to enforce their contractual rights, but also the appropriateness of *excommunicatio latae sententiae*, that is, direct exclusion from the Church, inflicted automatically, without trial or the intervention of a judge. Concerned with respect for individual liberty, Suárez's *Treatise on Laws* contains passages in which he reveals himself to be a fine exegete of Roman law and a worthy advocate of interpreting penal laws that could limit freedom of contract restrictively, which he considered a kind of natural right worthy of the highest protection.

While Suárez's original ideas on the theoretical foundations of law deserve more attention, this is all the more so for his resolutions of practical cases, which have gone virtually unnoticed despite their republication in 1948.[24] They show that Suárez was completely at ease practising canon law, advising on the most technical aspects of the law of benefices, wills, marriage, and religious persons. He even ventured into resolving practical cases relating to bills of exchange, contracts of sale, and contracts for leasing services. Once again, the law of contracts is at the heart of the debates in a unique place in the immense work of Suarez, where we do not expect to find such profound juridical reflection, namely in his six small theological works (*opuscula*) dealing with the problem of God's justice and the merits of individuals seeking to obtain salvation. Among these "minor works" (nevertheless reaching 600 pages in the eleventh volume of the complete works of Suárez published by Charles Berton in Paris in 1858), two deserve a particular mention. In the fourth opuscule on the freedom of the divine will, Suárez asks whether God's freedom can be tainted by the obligation to reward the spiritual merits of individuals, a duty originally conceived as a "debt" contracted by God to man on account of his promises. The other *opusculum* which catches our eye is the sixth, which directly concerns the question of divine justice, namely the rewards of God for the merits of individuals and, conversely, the divine sanctions inflicted for our sins. We will also occasionally turn to the fifth minor work, which addresses the so-called mortified merits, a concept that refers to good works whose redemptive value has been annulled as a result of sin, but which is reborn with the sacrament of penance.

A Debtor God

The simple fact that asking the question of the applicability of the precepts of justice to God seems suspect does not escape the great Suárez. Since the relationship between a creditor and his debtor in most cases involves a balance of power in favour of the former, the very suggestion of God being indebted to mankind can easily prompt indignation. How can God, the supreme being, be reduced to a mere debtor of man on account of the latter's merits? At first glance, such an idea appears to bear witness to human pride and arrogance. Suárez highlighted this indignation at the start of his fourth opuscule, recalling at the same time that the Christian tradition clearly refers to the notion of a debtor God.[25] In particular, he evoked the famous passage from a work of Cyprian on almsgiving, where God is constituted as a debtor to man on account of the latter's charitable works. As we have seen, the context of this assertion is not trivial. This assertion was part of one of the first attempts, in the mid-third century, to put in place an economy of salvation that would encourage Christians to share their wealth with the poorest. To this end, Cyprian referred to good works as an interest-bearing loan offered by man to God, for which he could expect repayment with interest, the accumulated interest constituting a treasure in heaven which the individual, as the creditor, could claim in the hereafter.[26]

Although the image of a debtor God was widely accepted by the Church Fathers, they did not all draw the same conclusions. Whereas for Cyprian the concept of a debtor God seemed far from being a mere metaphor, a good century and a half later, for Augustine, it appeared more and more like an analogy without absolute value. Although Augustine acknowledged that God had made himself a debtor, he did not conclude that this meant that man became his creditor. We should recall the historical context of this assertion, profoundly marked by Augustine's opposition to the contrary opinions of Pelagius, who extolled the merits of good works at the risk of erasing the role of divine grace in obtaining salvation.[27] Mindful of respecting God's superiority and emphasising the indispensable role of his grace, Augustine could not push the concept of a debtor God to its limit. This gave rise to the paradox of a debtor without a creditor, of a "God who pays debts without being indebted to anyone and who cancels the debts of others to himself without losing them."[28] This paradox was reprised by various theologians, including Thomas Aquinas. They underlined the fact that God had become man's debtor not on account of the latter's merits, but primarily by a voluntary decision to follow his plan for the world. God was subject to his own law, bound by the constitution (*ordinatio*) that he himself had promulgated.[29] The source of the divine obligation to pay debts would therefore be God's fidelity to himself, his willingness to keep his promise, without man's being able to claim any debt due for legal reasons.

Divine Promises

Francisco Suárez's remarkable analysis focused on precisely this point. Not satisfied with the paradoxical notion of a God who is a debtor without a creditor, he sought to demonstrate that a bond of justice, marked by the existence of a true debt claim on the part of a deserving individual, can actually exist between God and man. For this, he built on the notion of contract as promise, very much part of tradition, while radicalizing it. In his opinion, God, by his goodness, did not just promise salvation to men because they are bound to honour their promises to him. Motivated by his grace, God promised to reward man on the spiritual level as long as he did good works, so that the divine promise became conditional and reciprocal. This is a contract or covenant that binds God as well as man.[30] If man does good works, God is bound to keep his promise. He then proceeds to a remuneration which takes the form of a payment in the legal sense of the term, namely the settling of the debt. The recompense attributed is not simply a free gift.[31] Originally, however, the constitution of this contract was decided by a free act of the divine will. For Suárez, the order of grace continues to precede the order of justice.[32] It is God alone who, by his goodness, decided to create a covenant which he is obliged to respect by the virtue of justice. To the extent that God has made a promise to pay the price for good works done in his glory—in other words, to pay a genuine salary (*merces*) or premium (*praemium*)—man, his creation, receives a debt claim against him.[33]

Suárez rejected the opinion of Guillaume Durand de Saint-Pourçain, a scholastic theologian of the thirteenth century, which consisted in asserting that everything was grace, so that man could not claim any obligation from God as being due to him by justice. In Suárez's view, Durand de Saint Pourçain's view was the fruit of scrupulosity. He opposed it, saying that "even though meritorious works are principally gifts from God (they are so entirely as to their beginning, and rather essentially as to their consummation), still meritorious works belong to us and we are masters of them when it comes to cooperating and making free use of them; which is sufficient for us to acquire a right of justice (*ius iustitiae*) through them."[34] There is therefore no reason to doubt that man becomes a genuine creditor with a right to enforce the promise made by God. This promise is governed not only by the virtue of fidelity, obliging God to keep his word to himself, but also by the rules of justice, which ensure the balance between the rights and obligations of the debtor and the creditor. To quote Suárez again, "if the promise is made on condition that a proportionate good work is accomplished, by the only work of worthy value the man acquires a personal right; a right to obtain the promised thing that is so intimately linked to the good work that it would be true to say that such a promise is properly due on account of such a good work."[35]

In considering the debt incurred by God's conditional promise as a consequence not only of his fidelity to himself, but also of the rules of justice, Suárez went much further than Augustine and Thomas Aquinas. As God's fidelity is without parallel, and his justice perpetual, man can be certain that his good works will be rewarded. At a time of great political and religious upheaval, when the faithful were afflicted with a spiritual unease, Suárez brought to Catholics a certain confidence in their ability to take their spiritual destiny into their own hands and to work for their own salvation. In order to oppose the doctrine of salvation by faith alone, propagated by the Lutherans and Calvinists, Suárez strengthened the legal foundations of the traditional economy of salvation. In his view, "legal security" and "spiritual security" go hand in hand. It is here that the full theological implications of the doctrine of contracts developed by scholastics of the modern age can be seen. While it originally permitted a better understanding of the market, Suárez's reasoning illustrates how this contractual approach to human affairs subsequently helped articulate a very subtle theological mystery more effectively. In fact, at the core of Suárez's fourth opuscule on the justice of God is a concise treatise on the nature of contracts, which summarizes the discussions on the binding force of promises supported by the scholastics in their treatises *De iustitia et iure*, while applying it to the problem of the nature of divine promises.

Remuneration of Merit

"Through merit, it is as if man buys his recompense,"[36] explained Suárez. Merit is the price that individuals pay to obtain eternal life. Aware of the radical nature of his viewpoint, which he pushed to the extreme in order to better counteract the opposing claims of the Protestants, he attempted to be faithful to tradition by basing his assertions on patristic and biblical texts. He fully drew on the juridical imagination of the Church Fathers in their efforts to describe the principles of the economy of salvation. Cyprian, Basil the Great, Paulinus of Nola, and Bernard of Clairvaux were among his favourite authors. There are ubiquitous references to the image of God as a "righteous judge" who will bestow "the crown of justice" on those who have earned it. For Suárez, the image of the crown of justice, evoked in Paul's second epistle to Timothy, referred directly to the eternal life.[37] He supplemented the reference to this biblical passage with the interpretation given by the bishop Paulinus of Nola in the fifth century, for whom "the righteous judge will recognize that he owes you rewards for your virtues." He added a quotation from the Cistercian monk Bernard of Clairvaux (eleventh century), who attested that God is bound to fulfil his promise since it is just that he should pay back what he owes. Suárez's analysis is dotted with texts from the New Testament certifying that a just reward is due, on legal grounds, to those who work hard to obtain salvation. We need only think of the letters of St. Paul to the Romans and the Corinthians: "Now to him who works, the wages are not counted as grace but as debt" (Romans 4:4); "Every man shall receive his own reward according to his own labour" (1 Corinthians 3:8); "Be steadfast, immovable, always abounding in the work of the Lord, knowing that in the Lord your labour is not in vain" (1 Corinthians 15:58).

In order not to run the risk of accusations of Pelagianism, Suárez repeated several times that divine grace nevertheless precedes any form of legal logic. Many of his quotations from Augustine pose the rhetorical question of to whom the righteous judge would hand over his crown, if not to the one whom the merciful Father has previously endowed with grace. A special place is then given to the famous guarantee made by Paul to the Hebrews, according to which God is not unjust and therefore will not forget the works of the righteous (Hebrews 6:10). In his fifth opuscule, which takes the form of a long commentary on the letter to the Hebrews, Suárez interpreted this passage as meaning that salvation is a question of good works done in a state of grace.[38] For his analysis of all the subtleties involved in this complex interaction between divine assistance and human work, we need only refer to his treatise on grace, *De gratia*, the study of which, even if only superficially, would go far beyond the scope of this book.

The Sacred Contract between God and Man

An even more dizzying expression of how the legal foundations of the economy of salvation were reinforced by Jesuits in the early modern period can be found in Pedro de Oñate's extensive treatise on contracts. As the voluntaristic tendencies are highly conspicuous in *De contractibus* (1646–1654), it is probably not surprising that this is the case. As we have already noted, it is in this exceptional work that the scholastic notion of freedom of contract reached its apogee. The individual, by his will, must be able to dispose of his goods as freely as possible, and he chooses just as freely with whom and to what extent he commits himself. Freedom of contract is the sine qua non for Oñate for man to be able to participate fully in the activity of his Creator. With this guiding principle in mind, Oñate proceeded to an in-depth analysis of what he called "sacred contracts." There are six of these sacred contracts: (1) the contract between God the Father and his Son for the redemption of mankind through the blood of Christ; (2) the covenant between God and man for the attainment of salvation in exchange for merit; (3) the agreement between God and Adam to remain in paradise if Adam refrains from touching the tree of good and evil; (4) the vow by which man makes a formal promise to God; (5) the religious profession which commits man to his vows to God and his order; (6) marriage. Oñate situated these six contracts within a group of "gratuitous" or "lucrative contracts," or contracts in which one of the parties receives a benefit without any obligation to provide a consideration worthy of the name, such as gifts, free loans, or free deposits.

Building on Suárez's conclusions, Oñate argued that the bond between mankind and God, created by God's promise to reward merit, is governed by justice. The purity and perfection achieved by this divine justice are beyond human reality. For God, contracting a debt in no way implies a reduction in his wealth or the risk that he will find himself in a situation of inferiority. As such, God cannot be punished if he does not keep his promises. He is not constrained by judges in human courts. Nevertheless, Oñate insisted that God cannot escape the eternal law, the rational plan that underlies his creation. This plan demands that contracts be adhered to and that deceiving one's neighbour is forbidden. The conclusion that Oñate drew from this is of major importance. While the conception of commutative justice is somewhat different in the case of God, "faith in contracts is nevertheless no less sure and certain."[39] Like Suárez, whom he readily referred to as his "master" on this subject, Oñate strengthened the legal foundations of the economy of salvation in order to promote spiritual security. He nevertheless did not exclude the importance of actions of grace that go beyond the strict legal framework. Eternal salvation cannot be achieved by the actions of man alone. Without the merits of Christ, without the assistance of divine grace, without the prospect of an additional reward exceeding the value of human efforts, the gates of heaven will remain forever closed to mankind. However, the divine promise to reward good works is subject to the dictates of commutative justice. In this way, it offers a sure path to eternal bliss for the individual who, by his will, efforts, and merits, is ready to take his destiny in his hands.

The contractual nature of the covenant of salvation is not just metaphorical language. Oñate clarified the specific contours of that particular agreement. The contractual relationship between God and man takes the specific form of a *locatio conductio*, that is, the contract for hire, the forerunner of the labour contract: "The contract, governed by commutative justice, which was concluded with God, is a contract for hire. God, the tenant, hires workers for his worship and to work in his vineyard, that is, the Church. Man, the lessor, makes his work available in exchange for a wage, that is, eternal life."[40] Like Suárez in his treatise on grace, Oñate cited the parable of the labourers sent to the vineyard to substantiate his point (Matthew 20:1–16). While today this parable is cited, by Protestants but also within the Catholic Church, to highlight the differences between divine and human justice (God paying workers equal wages, regardless of how many hours they have worked), Suárez and Oñate's interpretation focused on the idea that the relationship between God and man can be compared to that of a landowner with his workers. The fact that the workers only working the last hour are paid the same as those who started work in the early morning is not an element of the parable that struck them in the first instance. It is probably no coincidence that, today, the parable is primarily known as "the parable of the workers of the eleventh hour," while Suárez and Oñate referred to "the parable of the workers in the vineyard" or "the parable of the farmer." In the texts of the two Jesuits, the emphasis is on the word "wages," clearly used in the parable. Oñate asserted that this wording was appropriate, since it is an actual contract where the wage is given, as a price, in exchange for the work done. He concluded his concise exegesis with an explanation reminiscent of the passage of Basil the Great quoted at the very start of this chapter, namely that the work to be done by the individual in God's vineyard is the implementation of his commandments.

The Race to Salvation

The radical nature of Suárez's assertions, adhered to by Oñate, was met with surprise, even within his own order. Leonardus Lessius was no exception. His unfortunate involvement in the notorious controversy in Louvain regarding grace and free will in the 1580s and 1590s would have made him realize the potentially debilitating effect of overly clear-cut positions on this extremely sensitive subject.[41] Moreover, the publication of his treatise on divine assistance and free will (*De gratia efficaci, decretis divinis, libertate arbitrii et praescientia Dei conditionata*), already completed in 1602, had been delayed for eight years owing to the suspicions of semi-Pelagianism hanging over his head. As a well-informed man of a certain age, perhaps he did not want to take any risks anymore with his later work on God's perfection (*De perfectionibus moribusque divinis*). Published in 1620, three years before his death, *De perfectionibus moribusque divinis* sought to give an account of the mysteries of faith, including divine justice. Although often overlooked, this treatise remains of great interest to us. In *The Kingdom and the Glory*, Giorgio Agamben highlighted its lasting influence on questions of the glorification of God and the economy of salvation.[42] Here, it is his remarkable reflections on the domain of God and his justice, contained respectively in the tenth and thirteenth books of the treatise, that capture our attention. While emphasizing the need to impose limits on the contractualist vision of salvation, Lessius proposed a highly lucid description of the imbuing of theological thought by market logic.

In his work on divine perfection, Lessius demonstrated impressive knowledge of the opinion put forward by Suárez, nevertheless without endorsing it. Summarizing Suárez's opinion, he explained that it was based on the idea that a perfect bond of justice exists between God and mankind, a bond that allows the individual to strengthen, in a sure and certain way, his claim vis-à-vis his Creator, by accumulating merits. In such a viewpoint, the struggle to obtain eternal life is fundamentally characterized by a competition, Lessius affirmed. Life on earth becomes the scene of a frantic race towards heavenly bliss. In Lessius' own words, earthly life provides the "stadium" (*stadium*) that hosts the "race" (*cursus*) for eternal life—a race in which as many good works (*opera*, also referred to as the *cursus in stadio*) as possible must be performed to win the prize of eternal life, referred to as a "crown" (*corona*) handed to the winners.[43] But, according to Lessius, this competition is already lost beforehand. The relationship of justice between God and mankind is part of a broader framework of divine gratuity that is resistant to a purely economic approach. In contrast to Suárez, Lessius denied that man could claim a perfect right against God, defined as a right that is completely beyond the power and will of the debtor.[44] Of course, man is supposed to work for his salvation, but human work will never be adequate to the divine goodness. In the end, all the glory goes to God's benevolence towards his useless servants. It would be an illusion to believe that by our labour (Lessius explicitly used the word *industria* here) we could fulfil our duty of servitude until the end.[45]

Extending economic logic to the field of the divine mysteries sometimes risks becoming too excessive. Lessius refused to qualify the relationship between God and man as a contract of services in the strictly legal sense of the term. While he fully recognized that God has promised to open the doors of his kingdom to those who work to honour his commandments, he did not see this as the beginning of an actual contract. The eternal law, God's order for the world and his divine plan for obtaining salvation, have clearly been referred to in the Bible by words such as "covenant" or "treaty," but contracts can only be referred to figuratively, Lessius explained, since the implementation of the divine plan does not depend on its acceptance by mankind. And yet, any contract, in the strictly legal sense of the term, presupposes a combination of an offer and acceptance thereof, an element at the basis of the scholastic doctrine of contracts. At most, man responds to God's promise by making a promise in turn: to observe the commandments, to honour God, to work in his vineyard. But this promise remains an inadequate response to God's generous promise. "All of this indicates a certain similarity, a certain affinity with true covenants," Lessius argued, "but it is not enough to establish a bond of justice in the strict sense of the term."[46] In Lessius' eyes, then, the covenant between God and mankind must be understood in a metaphorical sense.

Security, Freedom, and Divine Grace

While Lessius argued for a metaphorical interpretation of the juridical concepts underlying the economy of salvation, he remained very much mindful of the question of the security of salvation (*securitas salutis*).[47] Faced with the danger of defeatism, deemed inherent in Protestantism and its doctrine of predestination, he continually reiterated the need to positively appreciate good works. The beauty of Catholicism, according to Lessius, is that it offers the faithful the prospect of being able to predict their chances of obtaining eternal life, on account of the link, however imperfect, between meritorious efforts and divine reward. The individual can contribute, through the collaboration between his free will and the divine assistance, towards the direction that his supernatural destiny will take. The acceptance, of varying degrees among Catholic theologians, of a certain market logic in understanding the salvation of the soul, is likely to ease minds. This spiritual security was a major concern for Lessius. It is a common thread running through his various works of dogmatic and spiritual theology, starting with his treatise on grace and free will (*De gratia efficaci, decretis divinis, libertate arbitrii et praescientia Dei conditionata disputatio apologetica*, 1610). It is beyond the scope of this book to attempt an exhaustive examination of Lessius' ideas, or those of his colleagues, on this sensitive subject. This treatise interests us here only insofar as it constitutes the point where Lessius allows us to see the deep links between human freedom, meritorious work, and heavenly salvation—and the importance of legal language to articulate the interaction between them.

It should be emphasized that at no time did Lessius claim to eliminate grace as a necessary element for obtaining salvation. What he attempted to demonstrate is that the process of justification depends on both divine assistance and free will. In the same vein as his colleague Luis de Molina, Lessius was convinced that grace can act differently depending on whether or not it is accepted by the will of the individual.[48] The following is an example given by Lessius. Let us suppose that two individuals, Paul and Peter, have received the same divine grace. In Lessius' view, this does not mean that they will both be saved. For after receiving this grace, Paul can refuse it, while Peter accepts it. Grace is not effective by itself. It only becomes efficacious through the cooperation of the individual. To achieve its final objective, grace depends on consent, even though it is entirely at the root of the salvation initiative. In effect, Lessius explained that the so-called preventing divine assistance intervenes at three moments.[49] First, this divine assistance draws man to God, for example by offering him sudden intellectual enlightenment, whereby he can realize his sins. Second, divine assistance ensures that the human will has the strength to respond to this divine call if it so wishes. Insofar as the will effectively decides to consent to divine grace, the "preventing" grace brings its support one last time by accompanying the consent of the individual. Divine assistance is therefore necessary on three occasions, but, in the last instance, its effectiveness remains in the hands of free will. As Lessius affirmed, it is by mobilizing man's freedom that God has given him the gift of the security of his salvation: "You commanded that we be sure of your part [in the collaboration], since you have given us your assistance. Thanks to this assistance, we are sure and certain that justice will be done and that we will obtain salvation, unless we decide otherwise, neglecting the assistance offered and withdrawing from your grace. You have placed everything in our hands, as if the kingdom could be acquired by the forces of nature alone."[50]

Besides the fact that his discourse is full of references to the notions of freedom and security, Lessius drew on a contractualist logic to explain his ideas concerning the cooperation between divine grace and human will. He compared the need for consent to the free consent of a girl who is offered an engagement contract.[51] The man who proposes does not desire anything except that the girl becomes his fiancée, of course, but his desire is not unconditional. He wants the conclusion of the contract to depend on the voluntary consent of the girl. Similarly, God does not want to present man with a fait accompli. He expects the latter's free consent instead of imposing his will by force, because coercion and determinism are opposed to freedom. "God leaves everything to our freedom (*libertas*), so that we may consent," Lessius explained, "and so that we may resolve to work (*opus*) ourselves, by our freedom, which is substantiated by his grace."[52] Only under these conditions can a true relationship exist between God and man, especially since man, by his will, is the master of his acts.[53] Man must accept the grace, just as he must accept a promise in order for it to generate a binding force. The reference to an "accepted grace"[54] is not unlike the theory of the contract as an accepted promise. The interaction of the two contracting parties is essential to the conclusion of the contract. The intimate cooperation between man and his creator is similar to that between the promisor and the promisee in the field of contract law.

It was for insisting on the necessity of cooperation between divine grace and human will that, already in 1587, Lessius and his colleague Johannes Hamelius drew the wrath of Michel De Bay (Baius), a professor at Louvain's Faculty of Theology who had a more pessimistic view on human nature and the capacities of human beings to contribute to their salvation.[55] A few decades later, the criticism of Lessius was reaffirmed by other professors of the Theology Faculty of the University of Louvain such as Libertus Fromondus and Jacobus Janssonius.[56] Lessius' voluntaristic vision was radically opposed to the contrasting theory of "physical predetermination" to which some of the Thomists in Salamanca adhered and behind which the Jansenists subsequently hunkered down.[57] The most well-known and elaborate explanation of this adverse assertion was given by Domingo Báñez, an eminent Dominican theologian from Salamanca and confessor of Teresa of Avila. In his opinion, the divine assistance acts on the model of a physical predetermination or premotion, which means that once the preventive divine assistance is offered to the free will, the latter cannot oppose it. In the example given above, Peter could not have gone against divine grace. The diametrically opposed opinions of the Jesuits and the Dominicans gave rise to an unprecedented controversy that required the intervention of the Spanish authorities and the Holy See.[58] The Dominican friars accused the Jesuits of crypto-Pelagianism, while the Jesuits accused the Dominicans of crypto-Calvinism. In spite of the establishment of a commission called "on assistance" (*Congregatio de auxiliis*) in 1597, presided over by Pope Clement VIII and subsequently by Pope Paul V, the outcome of this affair remains unresolved to this day.

The Protestant Threat and the Praise of Industry

The absolute necessity, in the face of the Protestant threat, of insisting on the meritorious character of good works appears not only in Lessius' treatise on grace, but also, in 1609, in his work on choosing good faith and good religion, *Quae fides et religio sit capessenda*, an apologetic treatise containing a celebration of the genius of Catholicism, published just one year before his famous treatise on grace. Although little studied, this book provides an exceptional perspective on the pragmatic foundations of the economy of salvation. The praise of the meritorious character of works goes straight to the heart of the Christian religion, according to Lessius. "If all these things are the occasion of our loss through sin," he fulminated against the Protestants, "if there is nothing meritorious and useful in the works that is worthy of reward, then why would I accomplish them?"[59] This is a practical approach to religion, foreign to most modern individuals, but dear to the Jesuits involved in the struggle against Protestantism. The Christian faith encourages an active, ambitious, and unlimited search for the perfection of morals. The industry, ambition, and religious zeal that mark this pursuit (*studium*) are in grave danger, in Lessius' view, on account of the determinism engendered by the notion of predestination in the Protestant tradition. This admonition was subsequently reiterated by the Jesuits in their struggle against the Jansenists. In the idea of predestination without prior consideration of merits, the economy of salvation collapses. In Lessius' view, the only possible practical corollary to this kind of theory is the neglect of good works.

Since the utility of good works to obtain salvation is fundamentally called into question by the Protestant sects, the major incentive to perform good works evaporates. The economy of salvation in its entirety, based on the punishment of sins and the reward of virtues, is turned on its head.[60] The links between heaven and earth are severed. This provoked Lessius' indignation: "If there is nothing meritorious (*meritum*) in good works, if they do not make us more precious in the eyes of God, if they do not bring us rewards in heaven, then why should we bother to do them? Why should we spend our fortunes on works of mercy and assistance to the poor? Why should we pray? Why should we fast? Why tax the body? It is pointless to make the effort and worry about it when it doesn't bring us any benefit. Who can't see that this doctrine [of Luther] negates all endeavours to accomplish good works?"[61] The fact that the doctrine of predestination deprives the economy of salvation of all its meaning has serious consequences on the human level. Not only does man lose a strong incentive to pray, fast, and practice charity, he also faces considerable uncertainty regarding his heavenly destiny. In his arguments on predestination, annexed to his treatise on grace and free will, Lessius described great confusion within the community of the faithful, engendered by this new doctrine, which he believed would hollow out all the zeal from souls: "The reason why I began to write this disputation was that, for a long time, my experience has taught me that the souls of many individuals have been profoundly shaken by considering predestination. I know that certain souls have been plunged into a heavy depression, others have given up the pursuit of piety and no longer seek the perfection of religion, and others still are plagued by deep anxiety throughout their lives as they are wary of the fate to which God has preordained for them."[62]

The tranquillity of the soul is destroyed by the doctrine of predestination, since it removes from the soul all possibility of foreseeing, anticipating, and influencing its fate by making an inventory of its merits and sins. The "accounting of the hereafter" (*la comptabilité de l'au-delà*, to use a term made famous by Jacques Chiffoleau) collapses under the weight of a mystery even more mysterious than ever, because it is supposed to be entirely foreign to the categories of human thought. It is nevertheless this accounting that Lessius, as a good Jesuit, attempted to defend against the attacks of the Protestants. As long as the necessity of grace and the divine superiority are acknowledged, subjecting spiritual life to a commercial logic does not appear to be an outrageous idea to Lessius. On the contrary, it provides clarity, transparency and predictability. Moreover, Lessius did not only wish to defend the foundations of the economy of salvation against the Protestants. In a treatise from 1613, *De providentia numinis et animi immortalitate* (*On Divine Providence and the Immortality of the Soul*), he also addressed Machiavelli and the atheists, for whom the very idea of a supernatural order had lost all relevance. Lessius stressed the fact that at the end of its life, the soul will be obliged to give an account to divine providence which, after having accompanied and watched over it throughout its existence, "will add up the totals."[63] It is probably no coincidence that a close link could be made between the Jesuits' adoption of a modern accounting model for the administrative management of their order, and the perfection of "the spiritual accounting of the self"[64] in the practice of the Jesuit confessors.

It can be seen from this brief study that not only is the economy the fruit of a secularized theological paradigm, but also, as Giorgio Agamben has already demonstrated, that the articulation of the mysteries of faith has been imbued from the outset by economic-legal logic.[65] This affinity is all the more marked in the philosophy of Suárez, Lessius, and Oñate because in acquiring eternal salvation as well as material profits, they attach major importance to industry, good works, and merit. Moreover, key concepts in their analysis of contract law, such as freedom of contract or legal security, resurface in debates on grace and free will to think about the nature of the link between heaven and earth. The aim of this chapter was not to analyse in detail all the complexity of the question of the economy of salvation, and even less that of the relationship between grace and free will—such an undertaking would have been a disservice to the considerable efforts that scholars have devoted to analysing these delicate subjects.

In keeping with the narrower focus of this book, this chapter has limited itself to demonstrating that not only does there remain a theological logic at the heart of economic reason, but that, conversely, there remains an economic logic at the heart of theological reason. The link between these two rationalities is provided by legal thought. Contract law, in particular, played a key role in articulating the importance of will, freedom, and security, both in economics and in theology. In Suárez's view, the security of contracts provided individuals with the certainty of their right to a just reward for good works. In proportion to the merits accumulated through spiritual work,

God would pay the just wages of the workers in his vineyard. The bond of justice that binds man to his Creator was interpreted by Lessius in a more metaphorical sense than his younger colleague Pedro de Oñate. Nevertheless, Lessius, too, saw in the application of the logic of the market to the mystery of salvation an indispensable means of enhancing the individual's confidence in their ability to take their destiny in hand. Against the Protestants and proto-Jansenists, he affirmed that man should be able to influence his fate in the hereafter through his works. By accepting divine grace, man can ensure his salvation by his own will.

10
Business and Asceticism

Wealth, prestige, sensual delight, in large quantities, that is what the world promises.

—Leonardus Lessius

Following Weber's instinct that to understand Western economies, it is necessary to grasp their psychological dimension, historically linked to Christian spirituality, this book has highlighted key elements of Lessius' economic thought against the background of his role as a theologian and spiritual advisor. It may seem paradoxical that one of the main lessons to be drawn from this encounter is opposed to a widespread, yet flawed interpretation of *The Protestant Ethic and the Spirit of Capitalism*. It turns out, in effect, that Lessius, a Jesuit, made a significant contribution to the moral justification of the market and of the legal framework behind a capitalistic economy. Driven by a "spirit of meritocracy," he wished to reward economic prudence and industry. The merchant who knows how to play the market game must be able to profit from it without worrying about the salvation of his soul. Lessius was therefore the faithful heir of a scholastic tradition inclined to stimulate what Sylvain Piron has referred to as "the occupation of the world," this preoccupation with business that essentially comes down to being "occupied" or bus*y*, coupled with an accumulation or "occupation" of the goods of this world.

"The Lord wants man to apply himself to work and to demonstrate solicitude," Lessius explained, "so that, occupied in this exercise, he stays away from the pleasures and other sins that are the fruit of idleness" (see also chapter 5, p. 77). The ascetic spirit and the spirit of industry are therefore combined, a mixing of attitudes likely to promote the conduct of life necessary for the growth of the capitalist spirit, according to Weber. Had he known Lessius' writings, the jurist and pioneer of modern sociology would probably not have been surprised by the Jesuit's meritocratic attitude. Besides expressly rejecting "the absurd idea that the Reformation alone created the capitalist spirit," Weber acknowledged the favourable positions of

Money, Markets, and Merit. Wim Decock, Oxford University Press. © Oxford University Press (2025).
DOI: 10.1093/9780197827345.003.0011

the scholastics in promoting industrious behaviour and the accumulation of capital (see chapter 2, p. 29). Weber even went as far as to consider that rationalized asceticism had found its apogee among the Jesuits. The confrontation with Lessius' economic thought is therefore likely to call into question not so much Weber's assertions as the reductive interpretation circulating around it.

Furthermore, Lessius' "moral economy" contrasts with very common depictions, at least since the time of the Industrial Revolution, of the relationship between morality and economy. As Ute Frevert recalled, since the twentieth century, the notion of "moral economy" has served above all to convey ideologies critical of the capitalist spirit, denouncing its excesses, its aberrations, and even its opposition to the common good.[1] However, Lessius reveals another side of this "moral economy." Three centuries before the "social question" arose and crises broke out in the industrial areas of cities such as Liège or Manchester, it was obvious to Lessius that *industria* (in the original sense of "hard work") benefited the common good as much as the private interest. He adhered to the same notions of the virtuous circulation of money which Paolo Prodi and Giacomo Todeschini observed among medieval Franciscan theologians. Following the example of a Peter of John Olivi or a Fortunato Coppoli, Lessius developed a legal architecture and an economic morality, whose main objective was not to slow down economic activity. On the contrary, his ethics served above all to justify, legitimize, and liberate the market spirit. This final chapter seeks to better understand the reasons for this apparent paradox.

Nostalgia for Antwerp's Golden Age

Lessius' era was not characterized by the toxic smog hanging over the industrial areas of the late nineteenth century,[2] nor by the influence of computer algorithms orchestrating the financial markets at the start of the twenty-first century.[3] It is worth recalling how, at the turn of the seventeenth century, after the Netherlands was rent asunder following the revolts against Spanish domination, Lessius and his fellow citizens hoped to return to a period of calm and prosperity. Their primary concern was to stop the decline in commerce and the brain drain. Faced with the rise of Amsterdam, the new metropolis of world trade, which by 1610 had already managed to attract 450 grand mercantile families from the southern Netherlands,[4] the elites saw that the time had come to react. Many were convinced that trade and commerce had to be revived, to bring about a return to prosperity.

The sovereign princes, Archduke Albert of Austria and his wife Isabella, devised a plan to restore the political and economic order. The Perpetual Edict of 1611, intended to bolster legal security, is an example of that.[5] Benefiting from the climate of peace guaranteed by the Twelve Years' Truce (1609–1621), Albert and Isabella managed to assert themselves as the restorers of peace, at the cost of relative intolerance towards overt manifestations of Protestant beliefs, but nevertheless without pursuing a repressive religious policy.[6] By relying on their good relations with the ecclesiastical authorities, and in particular the Jesuit order, the Archdukes helped transform the Southern Netherlands into a bastion of the Counter-Reformation. The famous Jesuit church of Saint Ignatius in Antwerp (renamed "Carlo Borromeo Church" at the end of the eighteenth century), built between 1615 and 1621 with the support of the Archdukes and decorated by Peter Paul Rubens and Anthony Van Dyck, symbolizes the grandeur of the renewed alliance between the political, religious, and artistic elites.

In the first decades of the seventeenth century, the eyes of the rulers remained focused on the glorious past of the Southern Netherlands of the previous century. The nostalgia for Antwerp's golden age, the great metropolis of world trade under the reign of Charles V, can be felt even in the scholarly literature of the time. The work on Belgian commercial law by Franciscus Zypaeus, an ecclesiastical judge in the diocese of Antwerp, was the occasion for the author to look back with nostalgia on the historical contribution of commerce to the prosperity of the Low Countries.[7] The Jesuit theologian Carolus Scribani, a friend of the merchants of Antwerp, even went so far as to write two eulogies of the city of Antwerp and its illustrious origins, in which he mentioned the opulence brought to it thanks to its historical role as a metropolis of trade and finance.[8] From this reflection on the economic origins of the glorious past of cities such as Bruges, Ghent, and Antwerp, the conviction emerged that restoring prosperity required not only a renewed balance between political and religious forces, but also the revival of economic life, which in turn depended on a robust and accessible credit system.

It is in the context of this revival of the economic system that the establishment of the Mounts of Piety and the stimulation of commercial credit occupied a central place. To justify these financial innovations, the Archdukes received moral support from the Antwerp-native Leonardus Lessius, who, as we have shown, was fully aware of the benefits of commerce and money for the public good. Although the sources shed little light on any historical encounters between Lessius and the Archdukes, it has been claimed that Albert, a great defender of the Jesuits, sought his advice,[9] and we cannot entirely rule out that he would have chosen Lessius as his confessor if Madrid had not already imposed Iñigo de Brizuela, a Dominican friar of the School of Salamanca and a canonist by training, as his spiritual advisor. In any case, Lessius must have taken advantage of the occasional discord between Brizuela and Andrés de Soto, a Franciscan friar and the confessor of Isabel, within the court of the Archdukes in Brussels. An example of Lessius' attempts to recommend himself to the court is his *De iustitia et iure*, which is dedicated to Archduke Albert himself. Lessius presented his treatise as a "mirror for the prince," which should allow the Archduke to see in detail what justice and good government consist of from the perspective of "the first principles of nature," a nature which served sometimes to legitimize, sometimes to circumscribe the ambitions of the prince. Underlining the fact that Albert had all the qualities required to be a good prince, Lessius ended his dedication with a word of thanks for the support given by the sovereign and his wife to the educational projects of the Jesuits.

Asceticism and the Spirituality of Sobriety

Lessius has featured in this book as the herald of a current within the Catholic Church of the sixteenth and seventeenth centuries that was not afraid to highlight the positive sides of an economic order based on market logic. However, the doctrinal pluralism within the scholastic tradition as well as, more generally, the co-existence of divergent opinions within the Catholic Church at the dawn of the modern age, are worth being underlined—Italian-French historiography refers to "crossed heterodoxies" and "plural Catholicisms."[10] The bitter polemics between Jesuits and Jansenists during the seventeenth century can be cited as an example.[11] In *Les Provinciales* (1656–1657), the rigorous approach of Blaise Pascal clashes with the permissiveness of Lessius, regarded as a prince of "laxity". In his eighth letter, Pascal denounced the "subtle methods" used by Lessius and other Jesuits to justify certain commercial and banking practices. The French mathematical genius railed against the excessively legal turn taken by experts in economic ethics.

But rather than putting Lessius on trial through the caricatures put forward by Pascal, we should emphasize the limits that Lessius himself imposed on the logic of the market. While Lessius helped the Christian merchant extirpate himself of the moral blame associated with commerce, he did not push the latter into a blind race for money or submission to a materialistic God. In his view, the merchant's vocation was not to transform the world into commodities, nor to turn man into a slave of a hunger for gold, the *auri sacra fames* (see chapter 2, p. 30). Besides the obvious concern to protect the interests of the most vulnerable through his call to respect the virtue of charity, Lessius imposed a form of self-discipline on the merchant. Excess, in the economy as in life in general, is a vice contrary to the virtue of temperance (*temperantia*). While the concrete application of this virtue depends on the circumstances and the individual nature of each person, temperance advocates in a general way frugality, sobriety, and moderation. For Lessius, the analysis of temperance leads to praise of the ascetic life. We can therefore see the extent to which the economic thought of the scholastics remained inscribed in a moral universe which, regardless of the ambivalences therein, obliged individuals to seek a balance between business and contemplation.

Through many of his books, Lessius preached detachment from worldly affairs, highlighting the vanity of an unlimited pursuit of wealth, prestige, and carnal gratification. "The ineptitude of the human mind," he explained in his *Disputation on the Choice of a State of Life and Entry into Religion*, "consists in its unconcern for anything that touches eternal salvation, while its preoccupations and inventiveness in temporal and fleeting things are beyond the imagination" (see chapter 1, p. 20). Even in *On Justice and Law*, Lessius warned against the dangers of an excessive preoccupation (*nimia occupatio*) with worldly affairs. A person showing too much taste for temporal goods risks succumbing to the fear either of failing in the progressive accumulation of his fortune or of losing the goods already acquired.[12] Lessius stressed the dangers of excessive preoccupation (*nimia occupatio*) with the future, bearing witness to an overly secular mind, devoid of confidence in divine providence.[13] Being busy and occupied is necessary, but there are limits imposed by the virtue of temperance. It would seem that Lessius never forgot the sermon on death given in Louvain by Robert Bellarmine, in which he exhorted the busy Belgians to meditate on their divine fate as much as on their earthly prosperity (see chapter 1, p. 20).

For Lessius, neither market totalitarianism nor the unscrupulous exploitation of human and natural resources was an ideal. Indeed, the Jesuit himself was often the victim of excessive business and preoccupation. As such, his correspondence with Bellarmine reveals that the Jesuits were not immune to overexertion: they complained about the excessive workload and frequent and onerous external occupations (*occupationes externae*), and expressed their desire to devote more time to the contemplative life.[14] However, despite the difficulties, Lessius had an ideal of moderation in mind, looking after his health and that of others. With his friend Justus Lipsius, the great jurist and Stoic philosopher, he relaxed at the thermal springs at Spa, in the Principality of Liège. Moreover, a chronic illness contracted in his youth obliged him to be attentive to his body, and particularly to his diet.

This preoccupation with health and sobriety is reflected in Lessius' *Hygiasticon* of 1613, a remarkable book in which he urged individuals to practise frugality in order to best preserve their bodily and cognitive faculties until the twilight of life.[15] He took inspiration from the *Trattato de la vita sobria* (*Treatise on Sober Living*, 1558) by the Venetian Luigi Cornaro, a translation of which is given in the second part of his *Hygiasticon*. Whereas, in the dedication of his book, Lessius strove to be modest, warning the reader that he approached health from a spiritual and not medical perspective, the *Hygiasticon* nevertheless received the endorsement of Gerard de Vileers, professor at the Faculty of Medicine of Louvain. What is more, this book was a veritable success and was translated into several languages, including French (Pierre de Ram, rector of the University of Louvain between 1834 and 1865 and a great admirer of Lessius, had as many as five French versions at the time[16]). More recently, Cornaro's work and the *Hygiasticon* have been rediscovered by health historian Georges Vigarello.[17]

The sobriety preached in the manuals of food hygiene had become legendary at the time of Leonardus Lessius. The famous seventeenth-century scientist Francis Bacon was quick to criticize Cornaro for advising excessive sobriety, especially since he subscribed to the ancient theory of humours propagated by Galen.[18] At the start of his book, Lessius admitted to being aware of the fact that, for many people, living according to medical formulas meant living miserably (*qui medice vivit, misere vivit*). He explained that he aimed to propose a less radical alternative, while trying to convince his reader of the utility of frugality owing to its benefits: it offers a better guarantee of ageing without the loss of physical and mental capacities, not to mention its beneficial effect on the moral and spiritual life—without Ceres and Bacchus, Venus is less easily aroused.

Among the benefits of a strict diet, Lessius highlighted the neutralization of the body's acidification, strengthening of the immune system, mitigation of the negative effects of chronic diseases, a longer life, general improvement of physical condition, preservation of the senses, better control of emotions, passions and impulses, improvement of cognitive abilities, intellectual lucidity, and more openness to the spiritual dimension of life.[19]

While he admitted that the same recipes do not serve everyone, each temperament, each profession, each age requiring its own diet, Lessius advised his fellow individuals to limit their daily consumption of food to 330–380 grams, and that of drinks to the same amount, or a little more. His recommended dish is *panatella*, which would have been familiar to Italians as *pulticula*, a mixture of bread, water, and gravy, cooked together, combined if necessary with an egg or two. Lessius' general rule is that fatigue and feelings of heaviness in the stomach after eating are signs of a poor diet which require a change in eating habits, although not too sudden. Habits are like second nature, he warned, and nature should not be treated too violently. While he advocated avoiding fats, he played down the importance of the quality of different foods, considering that any beneficial food is potentially harmful if consumed in excess, while "heavy" foods (e.g., cheese, onions, beans, and peas) are likely to have beneficial effects if consumed in moderation. In the same way, he did not want to avoid the pleasures of an occasional festive banquet, provided that one imposed discipline on oneself for a few days before and after. Drawing on the authority of Plutarch and citing the example of Chinese, Japanese, and Turkish civilizations, he minimized the importance of consuming meat to have enough energy, even for those involved in physical labour (*occupatio corporis*). To those who exercise an intellectual profession (*occupatio mentis*), such as lawyers, professors, students, monks, and priests, he advised a purge twice a year.

The Spirit of Merit

While the recipes of frugality recommended by Lessius did not please everyone, they represented numerous opportunities to "accumulate merit" and gain salvation, in the spiritual as well as medical sense of the term. The one who submits to an austere diet not only guarantees improved health, but also the accumulation of credit with God. He therefore wins twice, according to Lessius, temporally and spiritually. The effort required for a sober life is a work rewarded by the Creator, as Lessius readily affirmed in order to encourage his reader to stay strong in moments of great temptation: "Practising temperance is not difficult in the absence of temptations. Nevertheless, being hungry in the middle of a banquet and controlling the voracity of the belly in front of all these stimulants demands work (*opus*) and effort (*labor*), especially on the part of the youngest and those who have not yet managed to tame their appetites. Consequently, this temperance is worth much merit (*meritum*) in the eyes of God."[20]

The valourization of merit is like a common thread through Lessius' various works. This is the initial principle binding his theological, legal, and economic ideas together. It is therefore not surprising that he wrote at the end of his *Hygiasticon* that the main purpose of his exhortation to sobriety was to enable people "to collect as many treasures of goods as possible," namely to increase their credit in the eyes of God.[21] Moreover, Lessius saw no contradiction between the pursuit of virtue and worldly success: he who first submits to God and to discipline reaps the fruits both in this world and in the hereafter. Sober people live their lives healthily on earth while guaranteeing a "superabundance of fruit" and the accumulation of their treasure of merits in their eternal life. On the other hand, the fate of the "lawless," of those who indulge in an "unordained life," of those who make themselves "slaves of their own sensual delights," is the opposite: while they submit to the temptations of this world and indulge in the vices of avarice, ambition, and lust, they harm their health and their eternal salvation.[22] Lessius would have been clearly opposed to Bernard Mandeville's famous assertion, published in 1714 in his *Fable of the Bees*, according to which human vices bring about material prosperity.

The centrality of a spirituality of merit in Lessius' work shows that it is difficult to grasp the particularity of his thought through the prism of modern ideological struggles. It was not Lessius' intention to answer the question of how the market economy can be combined with a welfare state. Nor did he seek to develop models for increasing national economic output. Of course, the Jesuit would have agreed with Antoine de Montchrestien, author of the first treatise on political economy worthy of the name in 1615, that it was in the interest of the authorities to stimulate business to combat idleness. But he would not have made it an absolute imperative, subjecting all human activity to growing the state's economic resources. Whereas modern political economy postulates that "man is born to live in continual exercise and occupation,"[23] to quote Montchrestien, a scholastic theologian like Lessius could not conceive of human life without taking into account its spiritual dimension. The Christian citizen is born into the world without being totally part of it, according to the famous adage from the Gospel of John 15:19. In the scholastic conception of the economy, there remains an ambiguity, a reserve, which is difficult to reconcile with the absolute, or even absolutist nature of the modern economic imperative. In this sense, the model of contemporary political economy goes beyond the scholastic paradigm.[24]

Fundamentally, the question Lessius answered was a spiritual one. It related to the need to comfort souls at one of the most dramatic periods in Western history, characterized by tremendous upheaval. The Jesuits, in particular, embarked on a frenetic pastoral mission intended to console souls shaken by the schisms of Christianity and the confrontation with a globalized world. As John O'Malley has noted, the founding documents of the Jesuit order abound in references to the term "consolation," going so far as to consider their pastoral mission to be essentially a "mission of consolation."[25] In the face of the disarray sown by the Protestant sects, Jesuits like Lessius proposed a return to the psychological security provided by Catholic theology, to the extent that it allowed the individual to augment his capacity to act on his destiny. The contractualist conception of the process of justification allows man to participate fully in the attainment of eternal life, even though he remains fundamentally dependent on the gracious offer of God. It allows him to regain a certain autonomy which is opposed to any defeatism. It allows him to accumulate merit.

As highlighted in the previous chapter, this mission to console reached its apogee in Lessius, who, in both his advisory and teaching activities, sought at all costs to empower the individual—let us recall that, in his role as administrator in the Society of Jesus, he fought to strengthen the school network of the Jesuits, a network reputed to have made a significant contribution to a merit-based scientific culture of excellence.[26] Bellarmine, who did not always agree with his colleague's radical defence of the meritocratic spirit, understood exactly what Lessius was driving at: "He tries in all his work to console people by teaching that salvation is in their hands."[27] Eleonora Rai, a historian, has observed the extent to which this optimistic attitude was appreciated by other Jesuits from the Low Countries who were contemporaries of Lessius, such as Cornelius a Lapide, a famous exegete, or Martin Becanus, confessor of Emperor Ferdinand II and a great adept of the law of contracts as developed by Lessius. According to Becanus, Lessius' doctrine "contributed greatly to the tranquillity of consciences," and Lapide affirmed that "the doctrine of Lessius is more benign, more likely to console, and more capable of inciting men to pursue a good and virtuous life, since it makes salvation depend entirely on the willingness of the individual and his free will, without taking anything away from divine grace. On the other hand, the opposing doctrine makes many people anxious, perplexed, negligent, not to mention those who fall into profound despair."[28]

To use a rather anachronistic term, we could assert that his concern for comforting troubled souls led Lessius to become the harbinger of a kind of "empowerment ethic" avant la lettre, activating the individual's strengths. This is an analysis that applies as much to his teachings on dogmatic theology as to his economic thought. On the economic level, the growing complexity of commercial life caused uncertainties and scruples that called for lenient treatment of penitents. Rather than automatically denouncing commercial and financial innovations, Lessius attempted to accompany the ordinary Christian and to heal him of his scruples. Everyone would be required to give up their business dealings, Lessius explained, if they were expected to follow the evangelical exhortations as closely as possible.[29] This would be absurd, because only non-Christians, or Christians of doubtful reputation, would then occupy the market. Instead of condemning mercantile activity, Lessius and other Jesuits sought to understand its dynamics, in order to give sound advice. At the same time, they developed a meritocratic criterion to distinguish between legitimate and illegitimate profits.

In Lessius' day, scrupulousness (*scrupulositas*) was regarded as a plague that struck the consciences of Christians as a spiritual illness.[30] This situation was not entirely new. At the start of the fifteenth century, the great Parisian theologian Jean Gerson launched an appeal against consciences that were too stringent and scrupulous. At the same time, Johannes Nider, a Dominican friar and author of a treatise on contracts, published a *Consolatorium timoratae conscientiae* (*Consolation of the Timid Conscience*).[31] Nider and Gerson had a considerable impact on modern scholasticism, in particular through the reading of their work by Konrad Summenhart at the turn of the sixteenth century. In overly perfectionist consciences, they perceived a danger that was serious and real: scrupulousness led to despair, paralysis, and sometimes suicide. The Jesuit pastoral ministry aimed to strengthen consolation strategies to remedy this spiritual affliction. Probabilism, a moral doctrine that allows individuals to take decisions in the face of uncertainty, played a prominent role in this therapeutic project.[32] Although denounced by his enemies as a cornerstone of laxity, Max Weber would later see it as the vehicle through which the Jesuits achieved "the indulgent and utilitarian adaptation to the world" (see also chapter 2, p. 29). In any case, probabilism is based on the sanctity of individual freedom.[33] The engraving on the title page of the *Treatise on Laws* (1611) by the Jesuit Juan de Salas, one of the advocates of moral probabilism, depicts a stocky man at a town gate, presumably Samson, carrying a doorpost on his left shoulder and another one under his right arm as he is fleeing a palace, probably the palace of Gaza.[34] The gate doors are accompanied by the text "I take my freedom with me" (Fig. 10.1, below).

Fig. 10.1 Juan de Salas, *Treatise on Laws*, 1611, engraving on the title page, "I take my freedom with me."

Leonardus Lessius reveals a hidden face of the "spirit of occupation" that has inspired Western legal and economic culture. This spirit praises the merits of the market in order to promote "the salvation of the economy" while articulating the "economy of salvation" according to the logic of the market. In both cases, the technique of the contract serves to consecrate the power of the will. In the eyes of Lessius, the tranquillity of the soul as well as the prosperity of the republic are not earned only thanks to good fortune. Man is not predestined for either wealth or divine glory. He can only be worthy by his active commitment and the accumulation of a treasure of merits. Thanks to the security of the promise made, the point of origin of an almost universalized contract law, expectations are stabilized: the one who works hard is sure to be rewarded. Using his industry, the merchant knows he can merit his wealth legitimately. By working together with God, man knows that he is capable of meriting eternal life, his reward for applying the rules of the ascetic life. Through a close reading of long-forgotten texts, it seems that Catholic ethics did not necessarily impede the progress of what Max Weber called the "spirit of capitalism." The good conscience of merchants is at least partly the fruit of the Jesuits' mission of consolation in the seventeenth century. Without ignoring its limitations, the Oracle of the Low Countries made a significant contribution to the legitimization of the market and the merits of industrious businessmen.

Notes

Prelims

1. The opening citation is from Max Weber, *The Protestant Ethic and the Spirit of Capitalism*, part 2, ch. 5 (transl. T. Parsons, p. 176).

Introduction

1. J.A. Schumpeter, *History of Economic Analysis*, edited from manuscript by Elizabeth Boody Schumpeter, with an introduction by Mark Perlman, London, Routledge, 1954, p. 93.
2. H.D. Kurz, "German and Austrian Schools," in G. Faccarello and H.D. Kurz (eds.), *Handbook of the History of Economic Analysis*, vol. 2 (Schools of Thought in Economics), Cheltenham, E. Elgar, 2016, p. 252–273.
3. Schumpeter, *History of Economic Analysis*, p. 94.
4. Schumpeter, *History of Economic Analysis*, p. 95.
5. Schumpeter, *History of Economic Analysis*, p. 101.
6. P.J. Roets, *The Economic Ideas of Bernard W. Dempsey, S.J.*, Milwaukee, Marquette University Press, 1991, 8–9.
7. J. Kirshner, "Raymond de Roover on Scholastic Economic Thought," in J. Kirshner (ed.), *Business, Banking and Economic Thought in Late Medieval and Early Modern Europe: Selected Studies of Raymond de Roover*, Chicago, Chicago University Press, 1974, p. 19.
8. J.A. Schumpeter, "Introduction," in B.W. Dempsey, *Interest and Usury*, London, 1948 [= Washington, DC, 1943], p. xviii.
9. Schumpeter, "Introduction," p. xviii.
10. Schumpeter, "Introduction," pp. ix–x.
11. M. Grice-Hutchinson, *The School of Salamanca: Readings in Spanish Monetary Theory, 1544–1605*, Oxford, Clarendon, 1952, pp. 89–96. See also S.J. Grabill (ed.), *Sourcebook in Late-Scholastic Monetary Theory: The Contributions of Martin de Azpilcueta, Luis de Molina SJ and Juan de Mariana SJ*, Lanham, Lexington, 2007, and the chapter "Martin de Azpilcueta: On Exchange (1556)" in E.W. Fuller (ed.), *A Source Book on Early Monetary Thought*, Cheltenham, E. Elgar, 2020, pp. 105–112.
12. F. Hayek, "The Pretence of Knowledge," Lecture to the Memory of Alfred Nobel, 11 December 1974, available at https://www.nobelprize.org/prizes/economic-sciences/1974/hayek/lecture/.
13. A.A. Chafuen, *Christians for Freedom: Late Scholastic Economics*, San Francisco, Ignatius Press, 1986, republished as *Faith and Liberty: The Economic Thought of the Late Scholastics*, Lanham, Lexington, 2003; see also B. Moreton, "Our Lady of Mont Pelerin: The 'Navarra School' of Catholic Neoliberalism," *Capitalism: A Journal of History and Economics*, 2 (2021), 88–153 (122, n. 125).
14. M.A. Rothbard, *An Austrian Perspective on the History of Economic Thought*, vol. 1: *Economic Thought before Adam Smith*, Cheltenham, E. Elgar, 1995, pp. 97–135.
15. Rothbard, *An Austrian Perspective on the History of Economic Thought*, vol. 1, p. 123.
16. Rothbard, *An Austrian Perspective on the History of Economic Thought*, vol. 1, p. 124.
17. R. De Roover, "Monopoly Theory Prior to Adam Smith: A Revision," *Quarterly Journal of Economics*, 65 (1951), 492–524.
18. R. De Roover, "The Concept of the Just Price: Theory and Economic Policy," *Journal of Economic History*, 18 (1958), 418–434. These statements should be nuanced considering the diversity of opinions among scholastics in the sixteenth century and the ideological context of De Roover's statements, which should be read against the background of the Cold War; see also M.Th. D'Emic, *Justice in the Marketplace in Early Modern Spain: Saravia, Villalón and the Religious Origins of Economic Analysis*, Lanham, Lexington, 2014.

19. Kirshner, "Raymond de Roover on Scholastic Economic Thought," pp. 20–21.
20. R. De Roover, "Scholastic Economics: Survival and Lasting Influence from the Sixteenth Century to Adam Smith," *Quarterly Journal of Economics*, 69 (1955), 161–190 (173).
21. J.T. Noonan Jr., *The Scholastic Analysis of Usury*, Cambridge, MA, Harvard University Press, 1957.
22. Noonan, *The Scholastic Analysis of Usury*, p. 222.
23. B. Gordon, *Economic Analysis before Adam Smith: Hesiod to Lessius*, London/Basingstoke, Macmillan, 1975, p. 248.
24. Gordon, *Economic Analysis before Adam Smith*, p. 258.
25. Gordon, *Economic Analysis before Adam Smith*, p. 251.
26. Gordon, *Economic Analysis before Adam Smith*, p. 253.
27. O.I. Langholm, *The Legacy of Scholasticism in Economic Thought: Antecedents of Choice and Power*, Cambridge, Cambridge University Press, 1998, p. 162.
28. Langholm, *The Legacy of Scholasticism in Economic Thought*, p. 164.
29. W. Decock, "Lessius and the Breakdown of the Scholastic Paradigm," *Journal of the History of Economic Thought*, 31 (2009), 57–78.
30. P. Evangelisti, *La pensée économique au Moyen Âge: Richesse, pauvreté, marchés et monnaie*, Paris, Garnier, 2021.
31. O. De-Juan and F. Monsalve, "Morally Ruled Behaviour: The Neglected Contribution of Scholasticism," *The European Journal of the History of Economic Thought*, 13 (2006), pp. 99–112. See also Decock, "Lessius and the Breakdown of the Scholastic Paradigm," 57–58.
32. E.g., G. Todeschini, *Richesse franciscaine: De la pauvreté volontaire à la société de marché*, Paris, Verdier, 2008; G. Todeschini, *Les marchands et le temple: La société chrétienne et le cercle vertueux de la richesse du Moyen Âge à l'époque moderne* (préface de Thomas Piketty), Paris, Albin Michel, 2017; S. Piron, introduction to S. Piron (ed.), R. Thornton (transl.), M. Cusato (transl.), *Peter of John Olivi, A Treatise on Contracts*, Bonaventure, NY, Franciscan Institute, 2016.
33. R. Sturn, "Agency, Exchange, and Power in Scholastic Thought," *The European Journal of the History of Economic Thought*, 24 (2017), 640–669 (649).
34. R.B. Ekelund and R.F. Hébert, *History of Economic Theory and Method*, Sixth ed., Chicago, Waveland Press, 2013; S. Medema, *The Economics Book. From Xenophon to Cryptocurrency*, 250 Milestones in the History of Economics, New York, Sterling, 2019.
35. M. Blaug, *Economic Theory in Retrospect*, Fifth ed., Cambridge, Cambridge University Press, 1997, pp. 29–31.
36. I. Chaplygina and A. Lapidus, "Economic Thought in Scholasticism," in *Handbook of the History of Economic Analysis*, vol. 2, pp. 20–42.
37. F. Monsalve, "Economics and Ethics: Juan de Lugo's Theory of the Just Price, or the Responsibility of Living in Society," *History of Political Economy*, 42 (2010), 495–519; F. Monsalve, "Scholastic Just Price vs. Current Market Price: Is It Merely a Matter of Labeling?," *The European Journal of the History of Economic Thought*, 21 (2014), 4–20; F. Monsalve, "Late Spanish Doctors on Usury, and the Evolving Scholastic Tradition," *Journal of the History of Economic Thought*, 36 (2014), 215–235.
38. A. Lapidus, "Hugo Grotius on Usury: Acknowledging the End of the Scholastic Argument," *The European Journal of the History of Economic Thought*, 30 (2023), 1031–1049; A. Lapidus, "Hugo Grotius on Exchange and Price," *The European Journal of the History of Economic Thought*, 31 (2024), 633–649.
39. E.S. Noell, "Smith and a Living Wage: Competition, Economic Compulsion, and the Scholastic Legacy," *History of Political Economy*, 38 (2006), 151–174. See also E.S. Noell, "In Pursuit of the Just Wage: A Comparison of Reformation and Counter-Reformation Economic Thought," *Journal of the History of Economic Thought*, 23 (2001), 467–489.
40. E.g., F. Gómez Camacho, "Later Scholastics: Spanish Economic Thought in the XVIth and XVIIth Centuries," in T. Lowry and B. Gordon (eds.), *Ancient and Medieval Economic Ideas and Concepts of Social Justice*, Leiden, Brill, 1998, pp. 503–560; D. Alonso Lasheras, *Luis de Molina's* De iustitia et iure: *Justice as Virtue in an Economic Context*, Leiden, Brill, 2011; R. Schüßler, "The Economic Thought of Luis de Molina," in A. Aichele and M. Kaufmann (eds.), *A Companion to Luis de Molina*, Leiden, Brill, 2014, pp. 257–288.
41. B. Schefold, *Great Economic Thinkers from Antiquity to the Historical School: Translations from the Series Klassiker der Nationalökonomie*, London/New York, Routledge, 2016.

42. B. Schefold (ed.), *Leonardus Lessius'* De iustitia et iure: *Vademecum zu einem Klassike de spätscholastischen Wirtschaftsanalyse*, Düsseldorf, Verlag Wirtschaft und Finanzen, 1999.
43. T. Van Houdt, "Lack of Money: A Reappraisal of Lessius' Contribution to the Scholastic Analysis of Money-Lending and Interest-Taking," *The European Journal of the History of Economic Thought*, 5 (1998), 1–35.
44. L. Baeck, *The Mediterranean Tradition in Economic Thought*, London, Routledge, 1994.
45. W. Decock, *Theologians and Contract Law: The Moral Transformation of the Ius Commune (c. 1500–1650)*, Leiden, Brill, 2013.
46. E.g., W. Decock and C. Birr, *Recht und Moral in der Scholastik der Frühen Neuzeit*, Berlin, de Gruyter, 2016.
47. G. Haberler, "Joseph Alois Schumpeter 1883–1950," *Quarterly Journal of Economics*, 64 (1950), 333–372 (335).
48. Schumpeter, *History of Economic Analysis*, p. 98.
49. T. Velardo, "From the Primitive Mentality to the Civilization of Capitalism: Joseph Schumpeter, Reader of Lucien Lévy-Bruhl," *The European Journal of the History of Economic Thought*, published online 19 November 2024.
50. S.O. Becker, J. Rubin, and L. Woessmann, "Religion and Growth," *Journal of Economic Literature*, 62 (2024), 1094–1142 (1100).
51. F. Trivellato, "The Ghosts of Max Weber in the Economic History of Preindustrial Europe," *Capitalism: A Journal of History and Economics*, 4 (2023), 332–376.
52. W. Decock, "From Law to Paradise: Confessional Catholicism and Legal Scholarship," *Rechtsgeschichte/Legal History*, 18 (2011), 12–34. For an updated version, see "Jesuits and Jurisprudence," in R.A. Maryks (ed.), *Jesuit Historiography Online* (2019), https://doi.org/10.1163/2468-7723_jho_COM_209877.
53. Sturn, "Agency, Exchange, and Power in Scholastic Thought," 643; B.J. Friedman, "The Influence of Religious Thinking on Economic Thinking: America's Social Gospel, with Thoughts on Rerum Novarum," *The European Journal of the History of Economic Thought*, 9 December 2024, https://doi.org/10.1080/09672567.2024.2433960.
54. E. Nelson, *The Theology of Liberalism. Political Philosophy and the Justice of God*, Cambridge, MA, Harvard University Press, 2019; D. Markovits, *The Meritocracy Trap: How America's Foundational Myth Feeds Inequality, Dismantles the Middle Class, and Devours the Elite*, New York, Penguin, 2019; M. Sandel, *The Tyranny of Merit: What's Become of the Common Good?*, New York, Farrar, Straus & Giroux, 2020.
55. G. Campagnolo and Ch. Vivel, "Before Schumpeter: Forerunners of the Theory of the Entrepreneur in 1900s German Political Economy—Werner Sombart, Friedrich von Wieser," *The European Journal of the History of Economic Thought*, 19 (2012), 908–943 (924).

Chapter 1

1. J. Barrientos García, *Repertorio de moral económica (1536-1670): La Escuela de Salamanca y su proyección*, Pamplona, eunsa, 2011.
2. Schumpeter, *History of Economic Analysis*, p. 144.
3. Schumpeter, "Introduction," in Dempsey, *Interest and Usury*, pp. viii and x.
4. Gordon, *Economic Analysis before Adam Smith: Hesiod to Lessius*, p. 244.
5. Rothbard, *An Austrian Perspective on the History of Economic Thought*, vol. 1, p. 124.
6. R. De Roover, *Leonardus Lessius als economist: De economische leerstellingen van de latere scholastiek in de Zuidelijke Nederlanden*, Brussels, Paleis der Academiën, 1969. On De Roover's English articles from the 1950s, see the Introduction.
7. T. Van Houdt, *Leonardus Lessius over lening, interest en woeker: De iustitia et iure, lib. 2, cap. 20: editie, vertaling en commentaar*, Brussels, Paleis der Academiën, 1998.
8. B. Schefold (ed.), *Leonardus Lessius'* De iustitia et iure: *Vademecum zu einem Klassiker der spätscholastischen Wirtschaftsanalyse*, Düsseldorf, Verlag Wirtschaft und Finanzen, 1999.
9. V. Brants, *La faculté de droit de l'Université de Louvain à travers cinq siècles*, Paris/Brussels, new edition (undated [1917]), p. 351, n. 1.
10. E. Rai, "The 'Odor of Sanctity': Veneration and Politics in Leonardus Lessius's Cause for Beatification," *Journal of Jesuit Studies*, 3, 2016, 238–258.
11. K. Van Sull, *Leonardus Lessius (1554–1623)*, Wetteren, 1923; French version: *Léonard Lessius, de la Compagnie de Jésus (1554–1623)*, Louvain-Paris-Brussels, 1930.

12. These factual elements are taken from T. Van Houdt and W. Decock, *Leonardus Lessius: Traditie en vernieuwing*, Antwerp, Lessius Hogeschool, 2005, pp. 11–54.
13. R. Bellarmine, *Conciones habitae Lovanii*, Cologne, 1615, *De quattuor novissimis*, concio 1, p. 424.
14. L. Lessius, *Disputatio de statu vitae deligendo et religionis ingressu*, Antwerp, 1613 [dedication].
15. L. Lessius, *Quae fides et religio sit capessenda consultatio*, Antwerp, 1609 [dedication], p. 4.
16. Lessius, *Quae fides et religio sit capessenda consultatio*, p. 131.
17. P. Brown, *The Ransom of the Soul: Afterlife and Wealth in Early Western Christianity*, Cambridge, MA, Harvard University Press, 2015.
18. W. Decock & C. Birr, *Recht und Moral in der Scholastik der Frühen Neuzeit (c. 1500–1650)*, Berlin, De Gruyter/Oldenbourg, 2016.
19. S. Piron, *L'Occupation du monde*, Brussels, Zones sensibles, 2018, pp. 162–164.
20. J. P. Coujou (ed.), *Francisco de Vitoria, La Justice*, Paris, Dalloz, 2014.
21. E. J. Van Eijl, "La controverse louvaniste autour de la grâce et du libre arbitre à la fin du xvie siècle," in M. Lamberigts (ed.), *L'augustinisme à l'ancienne faculté de théologie de Louvain*, Louvain, Peeters, 1994, pp. 207–282.
22. Ignatius of Loyola, *Spiritual Exercises*, § 367.
23. E. Rai, "*Ex meritis praevisis*. Predestination, Grace and Free Will in intra-Jesuit Controversies (1587–1613)," *Journal of Early Modern Christianity*, 7 (2020), 111–150.
24. In a rather rudimentary way, I have attempted to demonstrate the connections between views about grace and free will, on the one hand, and views about market ethics, on the other, in W. Decock, "Grazia divina e giustizia commutativa: un confronto tra Bañez e Lessius," in K. Härter & C. Nubola (ed.), *Grazia e giustizia: Figure della clemenza fra tardo medioevo ed età contemporanea*, Bologna, Il Mulino, 2011, pp. 361–388.
25. A. M. Artola, "El sistema inspiracionista de Leonardo Lessio S.I.," *Archivo Teológico Granadino*, 37, 1974, 5–44.
26. Like in the *Journal of Interior Motions* of Ignatius of Loyola, for which P.-A. Fabre provided the critical edition and a new translation (Brussels/Namur, Lessius, 2007).

Chapter 2

1. His doctoral thesis in 1889 was devoted to the medieval history of commercial companies. In 1891, he pursued a habilitation in Roman law with a second thesis on Roman agricultural policy. See the introduction in G. Dilcher and S. Lepsius (ed.), *Zur Geschichte der Handelsgesellschaften im Mittelalter* (Max Weber Gesamtausgabe, i/1), Tübingen, Mohr Siebeck, 2008, pp. 8–29 and pp. 57–89.
2. Th. C. Ertman (ed.), *Max Weber's Economic Ethic of the World Religions: An Analysis*, Cambridge, Cambridge University Press, 2017.
3. For an overview, see W. Schluchter and U. Bube (eds.), *Die protestantische Ethik und der Geist des Kapitalismus; Die protestantischen Sekten und der Geist des Kapitalismus, Schriften 1904-1920*, Max Weber–Gesamtausgabe, i/18, Tübingen, Mohr Siebeck, 2016.
4. Response to the first reply of Karl Fischer, in M. Weber, *L'Éthique protestante et l'esprit du capitalisme*, translated and edited by Jean-Pierre Grossein, Paris, Gallimard, 2004, p. 323.
5. Scholastics on whom texts by Franz Keller and Werner Sombart must have drawn his attention; see Piron, *L'Occupation du monde*, p. 133.
6. M. Weber, *The Protestant Ethic and the Spirit of Capitalism, translated by Talcott Parsons, with a Foreword by Richard Tawney*, London/New York, Allen & Unwin/Scribner, 1930, pp. 197 and 202.
7. Weber, *The Protestant Ethic* (transl. Parsons), pp. 82–83.
8. Weber, *The Protestant Ethic* (transl. Parsons), p. 81.
9. Response to the first reply of Felix Rachfahl, in Weber, *L'Éthique protestante et l'esprit du capitalisme* (transl. Grossein), p. 352.
10. M. Weber, *Zur Psychophysik der industriellen Arbeit, Schriften und Reden 1908-1912*, W. Schluchter and S. Frommer (eds.), Max Weber Gesamtausgabe i/11, Tübingen, Mohr Siebeck, 1995, p. 362, n. 95.
11. P. Ghosh, *Max Weber and The Protestant Ethic: Twin Histories*, Oxford, Oxford UP, 2014, p. 135.
12. Response to the first reply of Rachfahl, in M. Weber, *L'Éthique protestante et l'esprit du capitalisme* (transl. Grossein), p. 350.

13. Weber, *The Protestant Ethic* (transl. Parsons), pp. 153–154.
14. Weber, *The Protestant Ethic* (transl. Parsons), p. 49.
15. Weber, *The Protestant Ethic* (transl. Parsons), pp. 56–57.
16. Weber, *The Protestant Ethic* (transl. Parsons), p. 170.
17. Weber, *The Protestant Ethic* (transl. Parsons), pp. 161–162.
18. Weber, *The Protestant Ethic* (transl. Parsons), p. 163.
19. Weber, *The Protestant Ethic* (transl. Parsons), p. 170.
20. Weber, *The Protestant Ethic* (transl. Parsons), p. 172.
21. Weber, *The Protestant Ethic* (transl. Parsons), p. 174.
22. Weber, *The Protestant Ethic* (transl. Parsons), p. 181.
23. Response to the second reply of Karl Fischer, in Weber, *L'Éthique protestante et l'esprit du capitalisme* (transl. Grossein), p. 343.
24. Ghosh, *Max Weber and the Protestant Ethic*, p. 78, who does not agree with these efforts, which are illustrated by K. Jaspers, *Max Weber: Deutsches Wesen im politischen Denken, im Forschen und Philosophieren*, Oldenburg, Stalling, 1932.
25. Weber, *The Protestant Ethic* (transl. Parsons), p. 191.
26. M. Dumoulin, "Émile de Laveleye, un professeur renommé puis oublié," in V. Genin (ed.), *Une Fabrique des Sciences humaines: L'université de Liège dans la mêlée (1817–2017)*, Brussels, General State Archives, 2018, pp. 109–122.
27. https://orbi.uliege.be/handle/2268/209200.
28. "Émile de Laveleye et la théorie de la supériorité protestante (1875)," lecture given by Vincent Genin at the Belgian-Dutch Colloquium on the History of Law at the University of Liege, 14 June 2019.
29. E. de Laveleye, "Le protestantisme et le catholicisme dans leurs rapports avec la liberté et la prospérité des peoples," *Revue de Belgique*, 15 January 1875, pp. 5–41. An English translation was published in 1876 (https://archive.org/stream/cihm_04559#page/n3/mode/2up). The reference to the category of "Latin communities" to explain economic developments remains popular; see B. Colmant, *Économie européenne: L'influence des religions*, Louvain-la-Neuve, Anthemis, 2008, and *Capitalisme européen: l'ombre de Jean Calvin*, Brussels, Académie royale de Belgique, 2013.
30. E. de Laveleye, "Le protestantisme et le catholicisme," pp. 9–10.
31. Weber, *The Protestant Ethic* (transl. Parsons), p. 35.
32. Piron, *L'Occupation du monde*, p. 129.
33. H.M. Robertson, *Aspects of the Rise of Economic Individualism: A Criticism of Max Weber and His School*, Cambridge/New York, Cambridge UP/Macmillan, 1973.
34. J. Brodrick, *The Economic Morals of the Jesuits: An Answer to Dr H.M. Robertson*, Oxford, Oxford UP, 1934.
35. M. Novak, *The Catholic Ethic and the Spirit of Capitalism*, New York, Macmillan/The Free Press, 1993, p. 18.
36. See the brief conceptual history in J. Kocka and M. van der Linden (eds.), *Capitalism: The Reemergence of an Historical Concept*, London, Bloomsbury, 2016, pp. 1–10.
37. Weber, *The Protestant Ethic* (transl. Parsons), p. 155.
38. Weber, *The Protestant Ethic* (transl. Parsons), p. 183.
39. Weber, *The Protestant Ethic* (transl. Parsons), p. 97.
40. Response to the second reply of Karl Fischer, in Weber, *L'Éthique protestante et l'esprit du capitalisme* (transl. Grossein), p. 332.
41. G. Agamben, *Le règne et la gloire (Homo sacer, 2.2)*, Paris, Éditions du Seuil, 2008, p. 177.
42. E. Leites (ed.), *Conscience and Casuistry in Early Modern Europe*, Cambridge, Cambridge University Press, 1988; H. E. Braun and E. Vallance (eds.), *Contexts of Conscience in Early Modern Europe, 1500–1700*, Basingstoke, Palgrave, 2004.
43. Weber, *The Protestant Ethic* (transl. Parsons), p. 156.
44. Another telling example is the *Resolutions and Decisions of Divers Practical Cases of Conscience* by the Anglican bishop Joseph Hall (1574–1656), which drew more and less openly on Lessius and other Catholic theologians. See D. McGinnis, "Charity and Commerce: Joseph Hall's Reception of Catholic Casuistry and Economic Thought," *Renaissance and Reformation Review*, 21 (2019), 203–217.

45. R. Baxter, *A Christian Directory or a Body of Practical Divinity*, London, 1846, 1, 4, 1, pp. 310–312 (https://www.gutenberg.org/files/41633/ 41633-h/41633-h.htm). As for the recipes proposed by Lessius, see here chapter 10, p. 166.
46. Weber, *The Protestant Ethic* (transl. Parsons), p. 201.
47. W. Decock, *Theologians and Contract Law: The Moral Transformation of the* Ius Commune *(ca. 1500-1650)*, Leiden/Boston, Brill/Nijhoff, 2013, p. 16.

Chapter 3

1. Weber, *The Protestant Ethic* (transl. Parsons), pp. 48–49.
2. A. Supiot, *Homo juridicus: Essai sur la fonction anthropologique du Droit*, Paris, Éditions du Seuil, 2005, pp. 135–175; see also, by the same author, "The Dogmatic Foundations of the Market," *Industrial Law Journal*, 29, 2000, 321–345.
3. *Liber Extra* 1,35,1. See also F. Spies, *De l'observation des simples conventions en droit canonique*, Paris, Sirey, 1928, p. 24.
4. Dig. 2,14,7,4: "*nuda pactio obligationem non parit, sed parit exceptionem.*"
5. *Decretum Gratiani* C.22 q.5 c.12—the biblical phrases come from the Book of Wisdom (Wisdom 1, 11).
6. Cicero, *De officiis*, 1,23.
7. Supiot, *Homo juridicus*, pp. 154, 155, and 157.
8. A. Loysel, *Institutes coustumieres ou manuel de plusieurs et diverses reigles, sentences, et proverbes tant anciens que modernes du droict coustumier et plus ordinaire de la France*, Paris, 1607, l. 3, tit. 1, line 2, p. 30.
9. Decock, *Theologians and Contract Law*, p. 154, n. 547.
10. Loysel, *Institutes coustumieres*, Paris, 1637, p. 64.
11. P. Legendre, "L'inscription du droit canon dans la théologie: Remarques sur la seconde scolastique," in S. Kuttner et K. Pennington (eds.), *Proceedings of the Fifth International Congress of Medieval Canon Law*, Vatican City, Vatican Press, 1980, p. 449.
12. Decock, *Theologians and Contract Law*, pp. 142–143.
13. L. Lessius, *De iustitia et iure*, Antwerp, 1621, 2,17,4,19,197.
14. L. de Molina, *De iustitia et iure*, Mainz, 1602, 2,2,257,18.
15. Decock, *Theologians and Contract Law*, pp. 163–164.
16. Here, as afterwards, the text draws on passages in Decock, *Theologians and Contract Law.*
17. Supiot, *Homo juridicus*, p. 138.
18. As highlighted by P. Grossi in "La proprietà nel sistema privatistico della Seconda Scolastica" (in P. Grossi [ed.], *La Seconda Scolastica nella formazione del diritto privato moderno*, Milan, Giuffrè, 1973) and by M.-F. Renoux-Zagamé in *Origines théologiques du concept moderne de propriété*, Geneva, Droz, 1987.
19. Quoted in Decock, *Theologians and Contract Law*, p. 170.
20. Decock, *Theologians and Contract Law*, p. 168.
21. Article 1134 of the Code civil (original version from 1804): https://gallica.bnf.fr/ark:/12148/bpt6k1061517/f278.image. See also the current article 1103 of the French Civil Code.
22. For a critical reading of the "voluntarist" interpretations given to articles 1134–1135 since the very end of the nineteenth century, see J. Gordley, "Myths of the French Civil Code," *American Journal of Comparative Law*, 42, 1994, 459–505.
23. Decock, *Theologians and Contract Law*, p. 512.
24. Decock, *Theologians and Contract Law*, p. 291. For the first quotation, cf. R.J. Pothier, *Traité des obligations*, Paris/Orleans, Masson, 1761, vol. 1, p. 414.
25. J. Krynen, *Le théâtre juridique: Une histoire de la construction du droit*, Paris, Gallimard, 2018, p. 271.
26. Lessius, *De iustitia et iure*, 2,18,8,51,223–224.
27. A. Boureau, *Le désir dicté: Histoire du vœu religieux dans l'Occident médiéval*, Paris, Les Belles Lettres, 2014.
28. Decock, *Theologians and Contract Law*, pp. 178–179.
29. Pothier, *Traité des obligations*, vol. 1, pp. 7–8.
30. Lessius, *De iustitia et iure*, 2,18,5,30, quoted in Decock, *Theologians and Contract Law*, p. 186.

31. L. Lessius, *De iustitia et iure*, 2,18,6,40, quoted in W. Decock, *Theologians and Contract Law*, p. 191.
32. Decock, *Theologians and Contract Law*, p. 178.
33. Pothier, *Traité des obligations*, vol. 1, p. 9.
34. Supiot, *Homo juridicus*, p. 16.
35. Lessius, *De iustitia et iure*, 2,16,9, quoted in W. Decock, "Trust beyond Faith: Re-Thinking Contracts with Heretics and Excommunicates in Times of Religious War," *Rivista internazionale di diritto comune*, 27, 2016, pp. 301–328.

Chapter 4

1. This chapter offers an expanded version of W. Decock, "L'usure face au marché: Lessius (1554–1623) et l'escompte des lettre obligataires," in A. Girollet (ed.), *Le droit, les affaires et l'argent: Célébration du bicentenaire du Code de commerce*, Dijon, Université de Bourgogne, 2008, pp. 221–238.
2. F. Zypaeus, *Notitia iuris belgici*, Antwerp, 1675, lib. 4, p. 61.
3. V. Andreas, *Bibliotheca belgica*, Louvain, 1623, p. 575.
4. Molina, *De iustitia et iure*, 2,2,361.
5. Lessius, *De iustitia et iure*, 2,21,8*pr* and 9*pr*.
6. L. Fontaine, *L'économie morale: Pauvreté, crédit et confiance dans l'Europe préindustrielle*, Paris, Gallimard, 2008, pp. 190–222. See also P. Vismara, *Oltre l'usura: La Chiesa moderna e il prestito a interesse*, Soveria Mannelli, Rubbettino, 2004.
7. These alternatives have been described in detail by J.T. Noonan in *The Scholastic Analysis of Usury*, Cambridge, MA, Harvard University Press, 1957, the benchmark book for understanding the scholastic doctrine of usury; to be complemented, for modern scholasticism, with in particular O.I. Langholm, *The Legacy of Scholasticism in Economic Thought: Antecedents of Choice and Power*, Cambridge, Cambridge University Press, 1998, pp. 59–76, and F. Gómez Camacho, *Economía y filosofía moral*, Madrid, Síntesis, 1998, pp. 213–291.
8. Noonan, *The Scholastic Analysis of Usury*, pp. 340–342.
9. Dempsey, *Interest and Usury*, p. 112.
10. J.M. Keynes, *The General Theory of Employment, Interest, and Money*, New York, Harcourt, Brace, 1936, p. 351.
11. Piron, *L'Occupation du monde*, pp. 170–176.
12. L. Armstrong, *The Idea of a Moral Economy: Gerard of Siena on Usury, Restitution and Prescription*, Toronto, University of Toronto Press, 2016.
13. J. Davis, *Medieval Market Morality: Life, Law and Ethics in the English Marketplace, 1200–1500*, Cambridge, Cambridge University Press, 2012, pp. 411–413.
14. B. Frydman, *Le sens des lois: Histoire de l'interprétation et de la raison juridique*, Brussels, Bruylant, 2005, pp. 216–221.
15. S. Goltzberg, "Le contournement de la loi est-il hypocrite? Statut de la ruse dans la loi juive," *Cahiers philosophiques*, 145, 2016, 97–110.
16. T. Bauer, *A Culture of Ambiguity. An Alternative History of Islam*, New York, Columbia University Press, 2021.
17. For example, J. Lejeune, "Religion, morale et capitalisme dans la société liégeoise du XVIIe siècle," *Revue belge de philologie et d'histoire*, 22, 1943, pp. 109–154, demonstrating that the Principality of Liège was prosperous and favourable to the spirit of capitalism while the souls of its citizens were firmly in the hands of religious orders, especially the Jesuits.
18. J. Kaye, *A History of Balance, 1250-1375. The Emergence of a New Model of Equilibrium and its Impact on Thought*, Cambridge, Cambridge University Press, 2014, p. 22; see also Ian P. Wei, *Intellectual Culture in Medieval Paris: Theologians and the University, c. 1100–1330*, Cambridge, Cambridge University Press, 2012, p. 321.
19. Schumpeter, *History of Economic Analysis*, p. 95.
20. R. De Roover, *L'Évolution de la lettre de change, XIVe–XVIIIe siècles*, Paris, Éditions de l'Ehess, 1953, pp. 83–142; Herman Van der Wee, "Anvers et les innovations de la technique financière aux XVIe–XVIIe siècles," *Annales: Économies, Sociétés, Civilisations*, 5, 1967, 1067–1089.
21. H. Van der Wee, "Antwerpens bijdrage tot de ontwikkeling van de moderne geld- en banktechniek," *Tijdschrift voor Economie*, 4, 1965, pp. 496–497.

22. E. Aerts, "The Absence of Public Exchange Banks in Medieval and Early Modern Flanders and Brabant (1400–1800): A Historical Anomaly to Be Explained," *Financial History Review*, 18, 2011, p. 91.
23. Lessius, *De iustitia et iure*, 2,21,8,71–72.
24. Lessius, *De iustitia et iure*, 2,20,3,18, and 20.
25. Lessius, *De iustitia et iure*, 2,21,8,71.
26. Aristotle, *Pol.* 1,10,5 (1258b).
27. Rolandinus de Passageriis, *Collectio contractuum*, part 1, cap. 3 (*de debitis et creditis*), in *Summa totius artis notariae*, Venice, 1546, pp. 83–84. The argument of usury as a sale of time was overturned a few decades later by Peter of John Olivi, as noted by Piron in *L'Occupation du monde*, p. 172.
28. E. Marmursztejn, *L'autorité des maîtres: Scolastique, normes et société au XIIIe siècle*, Paris, Les Belles Lettres, 2007, p. 194.
29. Thomas Aquinas, *Summa Theologiae*, 2,2,78,1, responsio, also quoted in J. Kaye, *Economy and Nature in the Fourteenth Century: Money, Market Exchange and the Emergence of Scientific Thought*, Cambridge, Cambridge University Press, 1998, p. 86.
30. Thomas Aquinas, *Summa Theologiae*, 2,2,78,2,2.
31. Lessius, *De iustitia et iure*, 2,21,8,66.
32. M. de Azpilcueta (Dr Navarrus), *Enchiridion sive Manuale confessariorum et poenitentium*, Antwerp, 1575, ch. 17, nr. 231, p. 375.
33. J. Wamesius, *Responsa sive consilia de iure pontificio*, Louvain, 1618, vol. 2, consil. 594, nr. 2, p. 605. See also W. Druwé, "Loans and Credit in the Canon Law Consilia of Wamesius (1524–1590)," *Tijdschrift voor Rechtsgeschiedenis*, 85, 2017, 230–271.
34. Lessius, *De iustitia et iure*, 2,22,3,14.
35. Lessius, *De iustitia et iure*, 2,22,3,14; 2,22,4,26 and 2,22,4,27b.
36. Lessius, *De iustitia et iure*, 2,23,1,4 and 2,23,4,37.
37. Gordon, *Economic Analysis before Adam Smith*, pp. 250–252; R. Beutels, *Leonardus Lessius (1554–1623): Portret van een Zuidnederlandse laat-scholastieke econoom*, Wommelgem, Den Gulden Engel, 1987, pp. 42–45; B. Schefold, "Von der praktischen Tugend der Gerechtigkeit zur Wirtschaftstheorie," in *Leonardus Lessius'* De iustitia et iure, p. 29.
38. Peter of John Olivi, *Traité des contrats*, translated and presented by S. Piron, Paris, Les Belles Lettres, 2012, p. 224.
39. Lessius, *De iustitia et iure*, 2,23,4,30.
40. Lessius, *De iustitia et iure*, 2,20,14,123.
41. In particular, T. Van Houdt, B. Gordon, M. Rothbard, B. Schefold, and P. Vismara. See T. Van Houdt, "'Lack of Money': A Reappraisal of Lessius' Contribution to the Scholastic Analysis of Money-Lending and Interest-Taking," *The European Journal of the History of Economic Thought*, 5, 1998, 1–35.
42. Lessius, *De iustitia et iure*, 2,20,14,124.
43. Dig. 50, 17, 204, quoted in Lessius, *De iustitia et iure*, 2,21,8,69, and in Azpilcueta, *Enchiridion*, 17,231.
44. Lessius, *De iustitia et iure*, 2,21,8,72.
45. Wamesius, *Responsa*, 2,594,9–10, p. 606.
46. Lessius, *De iustitia et iure*, 2, 21, 8, 73.
47. Chafuen, *Faith and Liberty: The Economic Thought of the Late Scholastics*, pp. 123–124.
48. A more thorough introduction to probabilism can be found in S. Tutino, *Uncertainty in Post-Reformation Catholicism: A History of Probabilism*, Oxford, Oxford University Press, 2018.
49. L. Lessius, *De beatitudine, de actibus humanis, de incarnatione Verbi, de sacramentis et censuris praelectiones theologicae posthumae. Accesserunt eiusdem variorum casuum conscientiae resolutiones* [= *Auctarium*] (ed. J. Wijns), Louvain, 1645, quaest. 19, art. 6, num. 45. For a more in-depth analysis on the distinction between probable and certain opinions, see R. Schüßler, *The Debate on Probable Opinions in the Scholastic Tradition*, Leiden/Boston, Brill, 2019, pp. 46–55 and pp. 145–147.
50. Van Houdt, *Leonardus Lessius over lening, intrest en woeker*, p. 250.
51. For a very enlightening introduction to the subject of extrinsic titles and their development in Lessius, see T. Van Houdt, "Money, Time, and Labour: Leonardus Lessius and the Ethics of Money-Lending and Interest-Taking," *Ethical Perspectives*, 2.1, 1995, 11–27.

52. Lessius, *De iustitia et iure*, 2,20,11,80.
53. Noonan, *The Scholastic Analysis of Usury*, p. 264. The finer points of the argument leading to this general application are described in Lessius, *De iustitia et iure*, 2,20,14, and were analyzed by Toon Van Houdt in "Implicit Intention and the Conceptual Shift from *interesse* to Interest: An Underestimated Chapter from the History of Scholastic Economic Thought," *Lias*, 33, 2006, 37–58.
54. Noonan, *The Scholastic Analysis of Usury*, pp. 286–289.
55. Cf. Lessius, *De iustitia et iure*, 2,20,14,123–125.
56. L. Fontaine, *Le marché. Histoire et usages d'une conquête sociale*, Paris, Gallimard, 2014, pp. 39 and 259.
57. Lessius, *Auctarium*, s.v. *restitutio*, case 5, nr. 11, p. 262.

Chapter 5

1. Ambrose, *De officiis*, 3, 6, 39. In reality, with these words, Ambrose of Milan condemns the speculative thirst of the merchants. On Ambrose, see now P. Boucheron, *La trace et l'aura: Vies posthumes d'Ambroise de Milan (IVe–XVIe siècles)*, Paris, Seuil, 2019.
2. For references, see W. Decock and J. Hallebeek, "Pre-Contractual Duties to Inform in Early Modern Scholasticism," *Tijdschrift voor Rechtsgeschiedenis*, 78, 2010, 89–133.
3. Lessius, *De iustitia et iure*, 2,21,5.
4. A. der Weduwen, *Dutch and Flemish Newspapers of the Seventeenth Century, 1618–1700*, Leiden/Boston, Brill, 2017, vol. 1, pp. 7–8.
5. G. A. Bredero, *De Spaanschen Brabander*, v. 1095–1097: "Ghy bent een man die all dingh eerst pleech te weten, ghy bent des morgens vroech voor dach al op de brugh, daar neem jy de tijngjes uyt de nest eer sy zijn vlugh," https://www.dbnl.org/arch/bred001spaa08_01/pag/bred001spaa08_01.pdf.
6. N. Schobesberger et al., "European Postal Networks," in J. Raymond and N. Moxham (ed.), *News Networks in Early Modern Europe*, Leiden, Brill, 2016, pp. 19–63.
7. J.A. Van Houtte, "Les postes dans les Pays-Bas méridionaux sous la maîtrise des Tour et Taxis," in L. Janssens and M. Meurrens (eds.), *La poste des Tour et Taxis, 1489–1794*, Brussels, General State Archives, 1992.
8. J. de la Vega, *Confusión de confusiones: Dialogos curiosos entre un philosopho agudo, un mercader discreto, y un accionista erudito descriviendo el negocio de la acciones, su origen, su ethimologia, su realidad, su juego, y su enredo*, Amsterdam, 1688 (see the bilingual Spanish-Dutch edition published by M. F. J. Smith and G. J. Geers at Nijhoff in 1939: https://www.dbnl.org/tekst/vega002conf01_01/vega002conf01_01_0009.php).
9. De la Vega, *Confusión de confusiones*, Dialogo segundo, pp. 27–28.
10. Der Weduwen, *Dutch and Flemish Newspapers of the Seventeenth Century, 1618–1700*, p. 5.
11. Decock and Hallebeek, "Pre-Contractual Duties to Inform in Early Modern Scholasticism," p. 116.
12. Decock and Hallebeek, "Pre-Contractual Duties to Inform in Early Modern Scholasticism," p. 126.
13. Decock and Hallebeek, "Pre-Contractual Duties to Inform in Early Modern Scholasticism," pp. 103 and 117.
14. Lessius, *De iustitia et iure*, 2,21,3,10.
15. R. Bellarmine, *Tractatus de iustitia*, notes of lectures given at the Jesuit College, preserved in the Royal Library of Belgium (ms. 1734,1); Molina, *De iustitia et iure*, 2,347,3. On Bellarmine's lecture notes, see S. Roelofs, "Robert Bellarmine (1542–1621) and the Law and Morality of the Market: A Brief Introduction," *Rivista Internazionale di diritto comune*, 33 (2022), 269–279.
16. Lessius, *De iustitia et iure*, 2,21,3,8.
17. Lessius, *De iustitia et iure*, 2,21,4,33.
18. M. Martinat, *Le juste marché: Le système annonaire romain aux XVIe et XVIIe siècles*, Rome, École française de Rome, 2004, pp. 60–67.
19. Lessius, *De iustitia et iure*, 2,21,4,35.

20. See also T. Van Houdt, "Spelen om geld: Gokken, wedden en loten in het moraaltheologische discours in de Zuidelijke Nederlanden," *De zeventiende eeuw*, 15, 1999, 61–73.
21. Lessius, *De iustitia et iure*, 2,21,4,29.
22. Lessius, *De iustitia et iure*, 2,21,4,29.
23. J.T. Noonan, *The Scholastic Analysis of Usury*, pp. 86–87; J. Kirshner (ed.), *Business, Banking and Economic Thought in Late Medieval and Early Modern Europe: Selected Studies*, Chicago, University of Chicago Press, 1974, pp. 15–16; O.I. Langholm, *Price and Value in the Aristotelian Tradition: A Study in Scholastic Economic Sources*, Oxford, Oxford University Press, 1979, pp. 75–79.
24. Lessius, *De iustitia et iure*, 1,1,1.
25. Lessius, *De iustitia et iure*, 1,2,4,23, and 28.
26. Piron, *L'Occupation du monde* and S. Piron, *Généalogie de la morale économique (L'occupation du monde, 2)*, Brussels, Zones sensibles, 2020.
27. Lessius, *De iustitia et iure*, 1,2,4,31.
28. Lessius, *De iustitia et iure*, 1,2,1.
29. Lessius, *De iustitia et iure*, 2,21,5,40.
30. Lessius, *De iustitia et iure*, 2,21,10,80.
31. M. Schmoeckel, "Nescience and the Conscience of Judges: An Example of Religion's Influence on Legal Procedure," in C. Zwierlein (ed.), *The Dark Side of Knowledge: Histories of Ignorance, 1400 to 1800*, Leiden/Boston, Brill, 2016, pp. 70–87.
32. W. Decock, "The Judge's Conscience and the Protection of the Criminal Defendant: Moral Safeguards against Judicial Arbitrariness," in G. Martyn et al. (eds.), *From the Judge's Arbitrium to the Legality Principle*, Berlin, Duncker & Humblot, 2013, pp. 69–94.
33. J. de Lugo, *De iustitia et iure*, Lyon, 1642, 2,26,4,40,312.
34. F. Hayek, "The Pretence of Knowledge," Lecture to the Memory of Alfred Nobel, 11 December 1974.
35. Decock and Hallebeek, "Pre-Contractual Duties to Inform in Early Modern Scholasticism" 122.
36. Lessius, *Auctarium*, s.v. *contractus*, case 7, nr. 13, p. 182.
37. A. Bondolfi, "'Tu ne témoigneras pas faussement contre ton prochain' (Exode, 20, 16): Quelques considérations historiques sur le prétendu caractère absolu du huitième (neuvième) commandement," *Revue d'éthique et de théologie morale*, 37, 2005, 29–77.
38. Lessius, *De iustitia et iure*, 2,21,5,43.
39. Lessius, *Auctarium*, s.v. *contractus*, case 9, nr. 16, p. 182, quoted in W. Decock, "Lessius and the Breakdown of the Scholastic Paradigm," *Journal of the History of Economic Thought*, 31, 2009, 57–78.
40. Decock, "Lessius and the Breakdown of the Scholastic Paradigm," p. 63.
41. "*Charitas bene ordinata incipit a se ipso*"; see, e.g., Summenhart and Aragón, quoted in Decock and Hallebeek, "Pre-Contractual Duties to Inform in Early Modern Scholasticism," 103 and 122. On the Augustinian origins of this theme and its interpretation, controversial in modern times, see A. Frigo, "Charité bien ordonnée commence par soi-même. Notes sur la genèse d'un adage," *Freiburger Zeitschrift für Philosophie und Theologie*, 59, 2012, 234–248.
42. See, in this respect, the discussions in Summenhart and Mair, analyzed in Decock and Hallebeek, "Pre-Contractual Duties to Inform in Early Modern Scholasticism," pp. 102–103 and pp. 117–118.
43. Lessius, *De iustitia et iure*, 2,21,5,43.
44. Decock and JHallebeek, "Pre-Contractual Duties to Inform in Early Modern Scholasticism," 103 and 117–118.
45. Molina, *De iustitia et iure*, 2,354,4, quoted in Decock, "Lessius and the Breakdown of the Scholastic Paradigm," 66.
46. Lessius, *De iustitia et iure*, 2,21,5,46 and 48.
47. Quoted in Decock and Hallebeek, "Pre-Contractual Duties to Inform in Early Modern Scholasticism," 120.
48. A. Supiot, "Face à l'insoutenable. Les ressources du droit de la responsabilité," in A. Supiot and M. Delmas-Marty (eds.), *Prendre la responsabilité au sérieux*, Paris, Presses universitaires de France, 2015, pp. 9–35.

Chapter 6

1. L. Fontaine, *Le marché. Histoire et usages d'une conquête sociale*, Paris, Gallimard, 2014, pp. 130–133.
2. Ch. Bergfeld, "Die Stellungnahme der Spanischen Spätscholastiker zum Versicherungsvertrag," in P. Grossi (ed.), *La seconda scolastica nella formazione del diritto privato moderno*, Florence, Giuffrè, 1973, pp. 457–471.
3. However, we should not overlook Summenhart's surprisingly hostile attitude towards insurance; cf. G. Ceccarelli, "Risky Business: Theological and Canon Thought on Insurance from the Thirteenth to the Seventeenth Century," *Journal of Medieval and Early Modern Studies*, 31, 2001, 607–658.
4. Ceccarelli, "Risky Business," p. 611.
5. Molina, *De iustitia et iure*, Mainz, 1602, 2,507,1145.
6. Author of the first autonomous treatise on insurance law, first published in 1552 but preserved in a manuscript dating from 1488. Cf. T. Van Houdt, "Petrus Santerna: Pionnier de l'assurance," *Bulletin du crédit communal*, 180, 1992, 15–26.
7. Molina, *De iustitia et iure*, 2,507,1145.
8. Molina, *De iustitia et iure*, 2,507,1147.
9. Lessius, *De iustitia et iure*, 2,28,4,26.
10. G. Cabral, *Os decisionistas portugueses entre o direito comume o direito pátrio*, São Paulo, Faculdade de Direito, Universidade de São Paulo, 2013, PhD thesis, pp. 117–195.
11. *Consuetudines compilatae*, part iv, tit. 11, sect. 3, art. 91 and 93, obliging, respectively, insurers to take an oath to attest their good faith in the event of insurance taken after the arrival of the ship, and policyholders in the case of a claim that has occurred.
12. G. Rossi, *Insurance in Elizabethan England: The London Code*, Cambridge, Cambridge University Press, 2016, pp. 219–221.
13. E. Leoninus, *Centuria consiliorum*, Antwerp, 1584, Cons. 22, nr. 5, p. 132; see also A. Wijffels, "Business Relations between Merchants in Sixteenth-Century Belgian Practise-Orientated Civil Law Literature," in V. Piergiovanni (ed.), *From Lex Mercatoria to Commercial Law*, Berlin, Duncker & Humblot, 2004, pp. 256–259.
14. Leoninus, *Centuria consiliorum*, Cons. 22, nr. 8, p. 135.
15. The parasang is a Persian unit of distance corresponding to a distance between 5 and 6 km. In the dictionaries of the day, a *parasanga* corresponds to thirty stadia, which amounts to 3,750 steps; cf. F. Pomey, *Indiculus universalis latino-gallicus*, Nürnberg, 1671, p. 628. However, in Spain, the *leuca* would have corresponded to 4,000 steps; cf. H. Spelmann, *Glossarium archaiologicum*, London, 1687, p. 356. Molina seems to use *leuca* and *parasanga* interchangeably.
16. Molina, *De iustitia et iure*, 2,507,1147.
17. Lessius, *De iustitia et iure*, 2,28,4,24.
18. Lessius, *De iustitia et iure*, 2,28,4,27.
19. P. Quattrone, "Governing Social Orders, Unfolding Rationality, and Jesuit Accounting Practices: A Procedural Approach to Institutional Logics," *Administrative Science Quarterly*, 20, 2015, pp. 1–35. A similar approach can be witnessed in the debates on the accumulation of merit in the spiritual domain; see here chapter 9.
20. Lessius, *De iustitia et iure*, 2,28,4,30.
21. Wamesius, *Responsa-*, vol. 2, consil. 594, nr. 5, p. 605.
22. Lessius, *De iustitia et iure*, 2,21,10,79.
23. Noonan, *The Scholastic Analysis of Usury*, pp. 286–289.
24. Molina, *De iustitia et iure*, 2,304,8,234.
25. Lessius, *Auctarium*, s.v. *mutuum*, case3, nr. 8, p. 224.
26. Lessius, *De iustitia et iure*, 2,20,13,111.
27. Lugo, *De iustitia et iure*, 2,26,7,1,96, p. 324: "Ubi enim reperitur hodie debitum ita in tuto positum, ut in securitate aequivaleat pecuniae praesenti?" See also Noonan, *The Scholastic Analysis of Usury*, p. 288.
28. Lessius, *De iustitia et iure*, 2,21,9,74.
29. Lessius, *Auctarium*, s.v. *mutuum*, case 3, nr. 8, p. 224.
30. Lessius, *Auctarium*, case 3, nr. 8, p. 224.
31. Lessius, *Auctarium*, cas 3, nr. 9, p. 224.
32. Molina, *De iustitia et iure*, 2,361,460.

33. Langholm, *Economics in the Medieval Schools*, pp. 232–234.
34. Lessius, *De iustitia et iure*, 2,21,9,76.
35. J. Malderus, *De virtutibus theologicis et iustitia et religione commentaria ad Secundam Secundae D. Thomae*, Antwerp, 1616, tract. 5, cap. 2, dub. 5, p. 422.
36. Decock and Hallebeek, "Pre-Contractual Duties to Inform in Early Modern Scholasticism," p. 121.
37. Lessius, *De iustitia et iure*, 2,21,9,81,284.

Chapter 7

1. It is beyond the scope of this book to address the complex question of the relationship between the creation of cartels among German companies and the rise of Hitler. See Werner Plumpe, "Les entreprises sous le nazisme: Bilan intermédiaire," *Histoire, économie et société*, 24, 2005, pp. 453–472.
2. M. Hermanns, "Joseph Höffner—Lebensstationen eines Sozialethikers," in K. Gabriel and H.-J. Grosse Kracht (eds.), *Joseph Höffner (1906–1987): Soziallehre und Sozialpolitik*, Paderborn, Schöningh, 2005, pp. 13–36.
3. J. Höffner, *Christentum und Menschenwürde: Das Anliegen der spanischen Kolonialethik im Goldenen Zeitalter*, Trier, Paulinus, 1947.
4. J. Chappel, "Catholicism and the Economy of Miracles in West Germany, 1920–1960," *New German Critique*, 42, 2015, pp. 9–40.
5. J. Höffner, "Der Wettbewerb in der Scholastik," *OrDO: Jahrbuch für die Ordnung von Wirtschaft und Gesellschaft*, 5, 1953, pp. 181–202.
6. S. Gregg, "The Forgotten Story of the German Economic Miracle," https://acton.org/pub/commentary/2016/07/06/forgotten-story-german- economic-miracle.
7. Chappel, "Catholicism and the Economy of Miracles," p. 36. Nevertheless, this history continues to irk many Catholic theologians, who seem not to have any interest in highlighting these historical links between Catholicism and economic liberalism. For example, Höffner and the scholastics are ignored in M.A. Saddle's work, *Interrupting Capitalism: Catholic Social Thought and the Economy*, Oxford, Oxford UP, 2018.
8. A. Müller-Armack, *Religion und Wirtschaft: Geistesgeschichtliche Hintergründe unserer europäischen Lebensform*, Stuttgart, Kohlhammer, 1959.
9. S. Gregg, *Wilhelm Röpke's Political Economy*, Cheltenham, Elgar, 2010, p. 93. On Röpke's conservative liberalism, see also R. Fèvre, "Retour sur le libéralisme conservateur de Wilhelm Röpke," *Revue européenne des sciences sociales*, 53, 2015, 147–190.
10. T. Petersen, "Theologische Einflüsse auf die deutsche Nationalökonomie im 19. und 20. Jahrhundert: Drei Fallbeispiele," *Zeitschrift für Wirtschafts- und Unternehmensethik*, 12, 2011, pp. 318–330.
11. This article is available online: https://www.institutcoppet.org/leconomie-politique-daniel-villey.
12. D. Villey, "Die Marktwirtschaft im katholischen Denken," *OrDO: Jahrbuch für die Ordnung von Wirtschaft und Gesellschaft*, 7, 1955, 23–69.
13. P. Commun, *Les ordolibéraux: Histoire d'un libéralisme à l'allemande*, Paris, Les Belles Lettres, 2016, pp. 227–228. For an in-depth analysis of ordoliberalism in the English language, see also R. Fèvre, *A Political Economy of Power: Ordoliberalism in Context, 1932–1950*, Oxford Studies in the History of Economics, Oxford, Oxford University Press, 2022.
14. N. Goldschmidt, "Walter Eucken's Place in the History of Ideas," *Review of Austrian Economics*, 26, 2013, 127–147; G. Franco, "Glaube und Wirtschaft: Zur normativen Bedeutung des Ordo-Begriffes bei Walter Eucken," *Journal for Markets and Ethics*, 5, 2018, 23–38.
15. J. Drexl, "La constitution économique européenne: L'actualité du modèle ordolibéral," *Revue internationale de droit économique*, 25, 2011, 419–454.
16. F. Böhm, "Freiheit und Ordnung in der Marktwirtschaft," *OrDO: Jahrbuch für die Ordnung von Wirtschaft und Gesellschaft*, 22, 1971, 20.
17. N. Thirion, "Des rapports entre le marché et la puissance publique. De l'état-providence à l'état régulateur," in N. Thirion (ed.), *Crise et droit économique*, Brussels, Larcier, 2014, pp. 237–257.
18. F. Böhm, "Privatrechtsgesellschaft und Marktwirtschaft," *OrDO: Jahrbuch für die Ordnung von Wirtschaft und Gesellschaft*, 17, 1966, 75, also quoted in Drexl, "La constitution économique européenne," p. 436.

19. H. Thieme, "Natürliches Privatrecht und Spätscholastik," *Zeitschrift der Savigny—Stiftung für Rechtsgeschichte, Germanistische Abteilung*, 70, 1953, 230–266.
20. For example, Burckhardt Löber studied the contribution of the scholastics to the development of corporate law, and Günther Nufer explored the scholastic doctrine of unjust enrichment and the duty of restitution. See Decock and Birr, *Recht und Moral*, pp. 80–81.
21. Lessius, *De iustitia et iure*, 2,21,21,144, p. 295.
22. J. Höffner, *Wirtschaftsethik und Monopole im fünfzehnten und sechzehnten Jahrhundert*, Freiburger Staatswissenschaftliche Schriften, 2, Jena, G. Fischer, 1941, pp. 137–139. R. De Roover, "Monopoly Theory prior to Adam Smith: A Revision," *Quarterly Journal of Economics*, 65.4, 1951, 492–524. B. Gordon, *Economic Analysis before Adam Smith*, p. 266–270. See now also W. Vandermeulen, "Modest Building Blocks. The State of the Art of Monopoly Thinking at the Turn of the Middle Ages and the Early Modern Period in the Works of Lawyers and Theologians", *Tijdschrift voor Rechtsgeschiedenis*, 91 (2023), 427-470.
23. Cod. 4,59,2.
24. D.V. Cowen, "Survey of the Law Relating to the Control of Monopoly in South Africa," *South African Journal of Economics*, 18, 1950, 124–147, half of which is devoted to the criminalization of monopolies in Roman and Roman-Dutch law.
25. Cod. 4,59 (Denis Godefroy edition), https://iiif.lib.harvard.edu/manifests/view/drs:427005513$533i: "De monopoliis et conventu negotiatorum illicito vel artificio ergolaborum nec-non balneatorum prohibitis et pactionibus illicitis." Modern editions write: "De monopoliis et de conventu negotiatorum illicito vel artificum ergolaborumque nec non balneatorum prohibitis illicitisque pactionibus." Moreover, whereas a constitution of the emperor Zeno of 473 precedes that of 483 in the modern editions, the edition of Godefroy contains only that of 483. See also B. W. Frier (ed.), *The Codex of Justinian: A New Annotated Translation*, Cambridge, Cambridge University Press, 2016, vol. 2, pp. 1045–1046, which provides a translation of two constitutions.
26. B. Mertens, *Im Kampf gegen die Monopole: Reichtagsverhandlungen und Monopolprozesse im frühen 16. Jahrhundert*, Tübingen, Mohr, 1996, pp. 29–36 and pp. 73–80.
27. Mertens, *Im Kampf gegen die Monopole*, pp. 61–63.
28. Silvester, *Summa*, s.v. *monopolium*.
29. Molina, *De iustitia et iure*, 2,345,385.
30. In the Latin text and its translation (B. W. Frier [ed.], *The Codex of Justinian*, vol. 2, p. 1045) the fine of 50 gold pounds is reserved for the participants in the agreement, while the administrators are fined 40 gold pounds. Molina's interpretation corresponds more closely to the Latin text in Godefroy's edition.
31. The *Lex Julia de annona* is included in Dig. 48,12,2.
32. Dig. 47,11,6, following the translation by S.P. Scott, available online at https://droitromain.univ-grenoble-alpes.fr/Anglica/D47_Scott.htm.
33. C. Prieto and D. Bosco, *Droit européen de la concurrence: Ententes et abus de position dominante*, Brussels, Bruylant, 2013, p. 42, n. 37.
34. *Placaat ende Euwig Edict van Keyser Karel de V. van den 4. October 1540 tegens banquerouten, monopolien, woekeren, etc.*, art. 7.
35. J. De Damhouder, *Praxis rerum criminalium*, Antwerp, 1562, ch. 132.
36. Both examples are from J. Puttevils, *Merchants and Trading in the Sixteenth Century: The Golden Age of Antwerp*, London, Routledge, 2015, p. 68.
37. *Decretum Gratiani*, C. 14, q. 4, c. 11.
38. O.I. Langholm, "Monopoly and Market Irregularities in Medieval Economic Thought: Traditions and Texts to AD 1500." *Journal of the History of Economic Thought*, 28, 2006, 395–411. The references to medieval canonists in the remainder of this paragraph are also taken from this article, pp. 401–403.
39. Azpilcueta, *Enchiridion*, 23,91.
40. Lessius, *De iustitia et iure*, 2,21,21,151,296.
41. J. de Medina, *De restitutione et contractibus*, Salamanca 1550, f. 106v, par. *Sed obijciet.*
42. Molina, *De iustitia et iure*, 345,388,c.
43. T. De Vio Cajetanus, *Summula peccatorum*, Antwerp, 1575, s.v. *venditio*, p. 544.
44. Molina, *De iustitia et iure*, 345,385,e.
45. J.C. Boyajian, *Portuguese Trade in Asia under the Habsburgs, 1580–1640*, London/Baltimore, Johns Hopkins University Press, 1993, pp. 90–95.

46. Lessius, *De iustitia et iure*, 2,21,21,149,295.
47. Lessius, *De iustitia et iure*, 2,21,21,148,295.
48. L. Pfister, "Les conditions d'octroi des privilèges d'imprimerie en France (1500–1630)," in E. Keller-Rahbé, H. Pommier, and D. Régnier- Roux (eds.), *Privilèges de librairie en France et en Europe: XVIe–XVIIe siècles*, Paris, Classiques Garnier, 2017, pp. 49–92.
49. P. Durand and T. Habrand, *Histoire de l'édition en Belgique, XVe–XXIe siècle*, Paris/Brussels, Les Impressions Nouvelles, 2018, pp. 50–61.
50. Molina, *De iustitia et iure*, 345, 385,d–e.
51. "Ut melius atque ornatius excudat." Letter from Lessius to John Moretus I dated 16 January 1609, quoted in I. Maclean, *Scholarship, Commerce and Religion: The Learned Book in the Age of Confessions, 1560–1630*, Cambridge, MA, Harvard University Press, 2012, p. 307.
52. D. Imhof, *Jan Moretus and the Continuation of the Plantin Press: A Bibliography of the Works Published and Printed by Jan Moretus I in Antwerp (1589–1610)*, Leiden/Boston, Brill, 2014, vol. 1, p. 310.
53. Lugo, *De iustitia et iure*, 2,26,12,171, p. 342.
54. Even though he recognizes the importance of monopolistic privileges in scholastic thought; see Höffner, *Wirtschaftsethik und Monopole*, pp. 143–145.
55. P. de Oñate, *De contractibus*, Rome, 1646, vol. 3, tract. 21, disp. 67, sect. 1, p. 141.

Chapter 8

1. There is extensive literature on this topic; see N. L. Barile, "Renaissance Monti di Pietà in Modern Scholarship: Themes, Studies, and Historiographic Trends," *Renaissance and Reformation/Renaissance et Réforme*, 35, 2012, 85–114.
2. M. G. Muzzarelli, *Il denaro e la salvezza: L'invenzione del Monte di Pietà*, Bologna, Il Mulino, 2001, p. 90.
3. H. Holzapfel, *Die Anfänge der Montes Pietatis (1462–1515)*, Munich, Lentner, 1903.
4. G. Todeschini, *Richesse franciscaine: De la pauvreté volontaire à la société de marché*, Lagrasse, Verdier, 2008 [2004].
5. M. Greilsammer, *L'usurier chrétien, un Juif métaphorique? Histoire de l'exclusion des prêteurs lombards (XIIIe–XVIIe siècle)*, Rennes, Presses universitaires de Rennes, 2012, pp. 258–259. See also G. Todeschini, "Christian Perceptions of Jewish Economic Activity in the Middle Ages," in Michael Toch (ed.), *Wirtschaftsgeschichte der mittelalterlichen Juden: Fragen und Einschätzungen*, Munich, De Gruyter, 2008, pp. 1–16; F. Trivellato, *The Promise and Peril of Credit*, Princeton, Princeton University Press, 2019; and R. Dorin, *No Return: Jews, Christian Usurers, and the Spread of Mass Expulsion in Medieval Europe*, Princeton, Princeton University Press, 2023.
6. P. Soetaert, *De Bergen van Barmhartigheid in de Spaanse, de Oostenrijkse en de Franse Nederlanden (1618–1795)*, Brussels, Gemeentekrediet, 1986, p. 95 and 102.
7. J. Lejeune, "Religion, morale et capitalisme dans la société liégeoise du XVIIe siècle," *Revue belge de philologie et d'histoire*, 22, 1943, 109 154.
8. C. Zwierlein, *The Political Thought of the French League and Rome (1585–1589): "De justa populi gallici ab Henrico tertio defectione" and "De justa Henrici tertii abdicatione" (Jean Boucher, 1589)*, Geneva, Droz, 2016.
9. Lessius, *De iustitia et iure*, Appendix ad 2,20,23 De monte pietatis, p. 809.
10. Lessius, *De iustitia et iure*, Appendix ad 2,20,23 De monte pietatis, p. 809.
11. Lessius, *De iustitia et iure*, Louvain, 1605, 2,20,23,194.
12. Lessius, *De iustitia et iure*, Louvain, 1605, 2,20,23,189.
13. Greilsammer, *L'usurier chrétien, un Juif métaphorique?*, pp. 233, 246, and 266.
14. Quoted in T. Van Houdt, N. Golvers, and P. Soetaert, *Tussen woeker en weldadigheid. Leonardus Lessius over de Bergen van Barmhartigheid* (1621), Leuven, Acco, 1992, p. 121.
15. Soetaert, *De Bergen van Barmhartigheid*, p. 331.
16. S. Amadori, *Nelle bisacce di Bernardino da Feltre: Gli scritti giuridici in difesa dei monti di pietà*, Bologna, Compositori, 2007, p. 140.
17. Lessius, *De iustitia et iure*, Appendix ad 2,20,23 De monte pietatis, 1,5,813.
18. Lessius, *De iustitia et iure*, 1621, 2,20,23,193,271.
19. "Qui sentit onus, sentire debet commodum, et e contra" in *Liber Sextus* 5,12, line 55; Lessius, *Notae in Manuale Navarri anno 1596 praelectae in Collegio Societatis Jesu*, Royal Library of Belgium, ms. 4518, f. 1v.

20. One only needs to think of successions, where the heir is in principle supposed to bear the debts of the deceased to the extent that he accepts the assets. J.-B. Dantoine, *Les règles du droit canon*, Liège, 1772, pp. 49–54.
21. Lessius, *De iustitia et iure*, 2,20,23,193,271. See also Lessius, *De iustitia et iure*, Appendix ad 2,20,23 De monte pietatis, 1,6,813.
22. The exposition of the triple contract on the following pages is based on W. Decock, "In Defense of Commercial Capitalism: Lessius, Partnerships and the Contractus Trinus," in B. Van Hofstraeten and W. Decock (eds.), *Companies and Company Law in Late Medieval and Early Modern Europe*, Iuris scripta historica, 29, Leuven, Peeters, 2016, pp. 55–90.
23. I. Birocchi, "Tra elaborazioni nuove e dottrine tradizionali: Il contratto trino e la natura contractus," *Quaderni fiorentini per la storia del pensiero giuridico moderno*, 19, 1990, 243–322.
24. Lessius, *De iustitia et iure*, 2,25,3,33.
25. Lessius, *De iustitia et iure*, 2,25,3,30.
26. B. de Siena, *Quadragesimale de evangelio aeterno*, sermo 39, art. 1, cap. 4, quoted in F. Boldrini, "Sacri Montes e fraudolenta cambia: Credito e usura nell'opera di frate Orfeo Cancellieri, predicatore francescano e giurista nell'Italia del XVI secolo," *Rivista internazionale di diritto comune*, 24, 2013, 279–326.
27. Lessius, *De iustitia et iure*, 2,25,3,26.
28. See here chapter 4.
29. Lessius, *De iustitia et iure*, 2,20,11,80; see also Decock, "L'usure face au marché," p. 235.
30. Lessius, *De iustitia et iure*, 2,25,3,32,341.
31. A. Wijffels, "*Policy considerations*, en amont de l'argument conséquentialiste," conference held on 8 June 2017 at the Collège de France: https://www.college-de-france.fr/site/alain-wijffels/course-2017-06-08-17h00.htm.
32. T. Simon, "Gemeinwohltopik in der mittelalterlichen und frühneuzeitlichen Politiktheorie," in H. Münkler and H. Bluhm (eds.), *Gemeinwohl und Gemeinsinn: Historische Semantiken politischer Leitbegriffe*, Berlin, Akademie Verlag, 2001, pp. 129–146.

Chapter 9

1. H. J. Berman, *Law and Revolution, II: The Impact of the Protestant Reformations on the Western Legal Tradition*, Cambridge, MA, Harvard University Press, 2003.
2. G. Todeschini, *Il prezzo della salvezza: Lessici medievali del pensiero economico*, Rome, La Nuova Italia Scientifica, 1994, and *Les marchands et le temple: La société chrétienne et le cercle vertueux de la richesse du Moyen Âge à l'Époque moderne*, Paris, Albin Michel, 2017 [2002]; O.I. Langholm, *The Merchant in the Confessional: Trade and Price in the Pre-Reformation Penitential Handbooks*, Leiden/Boston, Brill, 2003.
3. Basilius, Homilia 12, *In principium Proverbiorum*, no. 16: "omnes qui vitam evangelicam incedimus, mercatores sumus, per opera mandatorum nobis possessionem coelestem comparantes." The Latin text quoted by Suárez is slightly different from that published in the modern edition by Migne (PG 31, 112, p. 419), without the meaning being different.
4. G. Génelle, *La vie économique et sociale dans l'Afrique romaine tardive d'après les sermons de saint Augustin*, Lille, Atelier national de reproduction des thèses, 2005.
5. E. Chevreau, "La *traiecticia pecunia*: Un mode de financement du commerce international," *Mémoires de la Société pour l'histoire du droit*, 65, 2008, 37–47.
6. J. Gaudemet, *Le droit romain dans la littérature chrétienne occidentale du IIIe au Ve siècle*, Milan, Giuffrè, 1978. See also L. Waelkens, *Amne adverso: Roman Legal Heritage in European Culture*, Louvain, Leuven University Press, 2015, pp. 69–72.
7. T. Faitini, "Redemption between Law and Theology: The Theological Translation of the Roman *redemptio* in the Patristics," in W. Druwé et al. (eds.), *Ius commune graeco-romanum: Essays in Honor of Prof. Dr. Laurent Waelkens*, Louvain, Peeters, 2018, pp. 24–36.
8. B. Hamm, "Den Himmel kaufen: Heilskommerzielle Perspektiven des 14. bis 16. Jahrhunderts," in B. Hamm, *Religiosität im späten Mittelalter*, Tübingen, Mohr Siebeck, 2011, pp. 301–334.
9. C. Colombus, "Lettre sur le quatrième et dernier voyage" (7 July 1503), in Christopher Colombus, *La découverte de l'Amérique. Vol. 2. Relations de voyages (1493–1504)*, Paris, La Découverte, 1984, p. 208.
10. P. Brown, *The Ransom of the Soul: Afterlife and Wealth in Early Western Christianity*, Cambridge, MA, Harvard University Press, 2015.

11. P.-A. Fabre and C. Maire (eds.), *Les antijésuites: Discours, figures et lieux de l'antijésuitisme à l'époque moderne*, Rennes, Presses Universitaires de Rennes, 2010; P.-A. Fabre and J.E. Franco, "The Dynamics of Anti-Jesuitism in the History of the Society of Jesus," in R. Maryks (ed.), *Jesuit Historiography Online*, 2018, http://dx.doi. org/10.1163/2468-7723_jho_COM_192530.
12. D.R. Kelley, "Fides historiae: Charles Dumoulin and the Gallican View of History," *Traditio*, 22, 1966, 347–402.
13. Brown, *The Ransom of the Soul*, p. 28.
14. S. Piron, "La dette de Panurge," *L'Homme*, 162, 2002, 262.
15. V. Goossaert, "Bureaucratie, taxation et justice: Taoïsme et construction de l'État au Jiangnan (Chine), XVIIe–XIXe siècles," *Annales: Histoire, Sciences Sociales*, 65, 2010, 999–1027.
16. Brown, *The Ransom of the Soul*, p. 27.
17. G. Anderson, *Sin: A History*, New Haven, Yale University Press, 2009, pp. 144–147.
18. Anderson, *Sin: A History*, pp. 160–163.
19. Brown, *The Ransom of the Soul*, p. 93.
20. J. Rivière, "Mérite," *Dictionnaire de théologie catholique*, Paris, 1928, vol. 10, part 1, col. 574–785.
21. Ignatius of Loyola, *Spiritual Exercises*, § 367.
22. Rivière, "Mérite," col. 576.
23. Decock, "Trust beyond Faith," p. 310.
24. F. Suarez, *Conselhos e pareceres*, Coimbra, Universidade de Coimbra, 1948; see also L. Brunori and W. Decock, "The Pragmatic Suárez. Private Law in the Work of the Doctor Eximius," in D. Bauer and R. Lesaffer (eds.), *History, Casuistry and Custom in the Legal Thought of Francisco Suárez (1548–1617)*, Leiden/Boston, Brill, 2021, pp. 54–75.
25. F. Suárez, *Opuscula theologica*, Opusc. 4, disp. 2, sect. 2, in *Opera omnia* (ed. C. Berton), Paris, Vivès, 1858, vol. xi, pp. 425–426.
26. E. V. Rebenack, *Thasci Caecili Cypriani de opere et eleemosynis, A Translation with an Introduction and a Commentary*, PhD thesis, Washington, DC, Catholic University of America Press, 1962, p. 128.
27. A. Dupont, *Gratia in Augustine's Sermones ad Populum during the Pelagian Controversy: Do Different Contexts Furnish Different Insights?*, Leiden/Boston, Brill, 2012, p. 141.
28. Augustine, Confessiones, 1, 4 (PL 32, p. 663): "Reddis debita, nulli debens; donas debita, nihil perdens."
29. One might see here an application of the adage that one must suffer the law one has made (*patere legem quam ipse fecisti*), which was supposed to apply to God as well as to ecclesiastical authorities long before it became a basic principle of administrative law; Supiot, *Homo juridicus*, p. 99, n. 4. It is probably no accident that the adage was first formulated as such by medieval canonists (*Liber Extra*, 1,2,6).
30. Suárez, Opusc. 6, sect. 2, no. 18, p. 534.
31. Suárez, Opusc. 6, sect. 2, no. 36, p. 541.
32. Suárez, Opusc. 4, disp. 2, sect. 2, no. 55, p. 432.
33. Suárez, Opusc. 6, sect. 1, no. 16, pp. 519–520.
34. Suárez, Opusc. 4, disp. 2, sect. 2, no. 56, p. 432. See also Suárez, Opusc. 4, disp. 2, sect. 2, no. 43, p. 429.
35. Suárez, Opusc. 4, disp. 2, sect. 2, no. 53, p. 431.
36. F. Suárez, *De gratia*, lib. 12, cap. 28, no. 1, in *Opera omnia*, vol. x, p. 174.
37. Suárez, *De gratia*, in *Opera omnia*, vol. x, lib. 12, cap. 28, no. 1, p. 174.
38. Suárez, Opusc. 5, disput. 1, no. 12, p. 440.
39. P. de Oñate, *De contractibus lucrativis*, Rome, 1646, vol. 2, tract. 8, disp. 25, sect. 1, no. 18, p. 31: "Nec ideo minus certa et secura est fides contractus."
40. Oñate, *De contractibus lucrativis*, vol. 2, tract. 8, disp. 25, sect. 13 no. 79, p. 42.
41. Van Eijl, "La controverse louvaniste autour de la grâce et du libre arbitre", pp. 207–282.
42. Agamben, *Le règne et la gloire*, pp. 326–328.
43. L. Lessius, *De perfectionibus moribusque divinis*, Antwerp, 1620, lib. 13, cap. 2, no. 7, p. 357.
44. Lessius, *De perfectionibus*, 13,1,6, p. 356.
45. Lessius, *De perfectionibus*, 10,6,59, p. 158.
46. Lessius, *De perfectionibus*, 13,2,11, p. 360.
47. E.g., Lessius, *Quae fides et religio sit capessenda*, pp. 129 and 134.
48. Molina, *Des secours de la grâce*, edition, translation and notes by P. Nicolas, preface by J. Schmutz, Paris, Les Belles Lettres, 2016, p. xlix.

49. L. Lessius, *De gratia efficaci, decretis divinis, libertate arbitrii et praescientia Dei conditionata disputatio apologetica*, Antwerp, 1610, cap. 2, num. 10, p. 6; cap. 10, num. 13.
50. Lessius, *De praedestinatione et reprobatione angelorum et hominum disputatio*, Antwerp 1610, sect. 7, p. 376.
51. Lessius, *De praedestinatione*, sect. 5, p. 338.
52. Lessius, *De gratia efficaci*, cap. 12, p. 140.
53. Lessius, *De gratia efficaci*, cap. 5, p. 53, "voluntas domina suorum actorum."
54. Lessius, *De gratia efficaci*, cap. 6, p. 63, "gratia accepta."
55. Baius' lectures on grace and free are examined in J. Van Der Biest, *An Augustinian Revolution in the Lecture Hall? Michael Baius (1513–1589) as Regius Professor of Theology in Leuven*, doct. diss., Leuven, 2024.
56. On the engagement of Lessius' enemies in Louvain with his doctrines on grace and free will, see L. Van den Eede, "Controversy in the Classroom: Jacobus Janssonius (1547–1625) versus Leonardus Lessius on Grace, Free Will and Predestination," *Journal of Early Modern Christianity*, 11, 2024, 413–443; L.A. De Preter and W. François, "'Capite nobis vulpes' (Song 2:15): The Struggle of Libertus Fromondus (1587–1653) with Leonardus Lessius' Theological Legacy," *Journal of Early Modern Christianity*, 11, 2024, 445–466.
57. S. Hermann De Franceschi, *Entre saint Augustin et saint Thomas: Les jansénistes et le refuge thomiste (1653–1663): à propos des 1ère, 2e et 18e Provinciales*, Paris, Classiques Garnier, 2017, p. 18.
58. P. Broggio, *La teologia e la politica: Controversie dottrinali, Curia romana e monarchia spagnola tra Cinque e Seicento*, Florence, Olschki, 2009.
59. Lessius, *Quae fides et religio sit capessenda*, consideration 1, p. 11.
60. Lessius, *Quae fides et religio sit capessenda*, consideration 2, pp. 18–19.
61. Lessius, *Quae fides et religio sit capessenda*, consideration 9, reason 8, pp. 106–107.
62. Lessius, *De praedestinatione*, notice to the reader, p. 239.
63. L. Lessius, *De providentia Numinis et animi immortalitate*, Antwerp, 1613, preface.
64. Quattrone, "Governing Social Orders, Unfolding Rationality, and Jesuit Accounting Practices," pp. 1–35. See also here chapter 5, "Information and Speculation."
65. Agamben, *Le règne et la gloire*, p. 19.

Chapter 10

1. U. Frevert, "Moral Economies, Present and Past: Social Practices and Intellectual Controversies," in U. Frevert (ed.), *Moral Economies*, Göttingen, Vandenhoeck & Ruprecht, 2019, pp. 13–44.
2. A. Zimmer, *Brouillards toxiques: Vallée de la Meuse—1930—contre-enquête*, Brussels, Zones sensibles, 2016.
3. A. Laumonier, *6/5*, Brussels, Zones sensibles, 2013-2014.
4. O. Gelderblom, *Zuid-Nederlandse kooplieden en de opkomst van de Amsterdamse stapelmarkt (1578–1630)*, Hilversum, Verloren, p. 242.
5. D. Leider and G. Martyn, "Édit perpétuel: Vers plus de sécurité juridique, 1611–2011," Brussels, General State Archives, 2011, http://arch.arch.be/docs/catalogues/catalogue_edit_perpetuel.pdf.
6. W. Thomas, "The Treaty of London, The Twelve Years Truce and Religious Toleration in Spain and the Netherlands (1598–1621)," in Randall Lesaffer (ed.), *The Twelve Years Truce (1609): Peace, Truce, War and Law in the Low Countries at the Turn of the 17th Century*, Leiden/Boston, Brill, 2014, pp. 277–297.
7. Zypaeus, *Notitia iuris belgici*, lib. 4, p. 61.
8. C. Scribani, *Antverpia*, Antwerp, 1610, pp. 22–28, and C. Scribani, *Origines Antverpiensium*, Antwerp, 1610, p. 122.
9. Van Houdt, Golvers, and Soetaert, *Tussen woeker en weldadigheid. Leonardus Lessius over de Bergen van Barmhartigheid*, p. 19.
10. G. Fragnito and A. Tallon (eds.), *Hétérodoxies croisées: Catholicismes pluriels entre France et Italie, XVIe–XVIIe siècles*, Rome, École française de Rome, 2015.
11. P.-A. Fabre and C. Maire (eds.), *Les antijésuites: Discours, figures et lieux de l'antijésuitisme à l'époque moderne*, Rennes, Presses Universitaires de Rennes, 2010; P.-A. Fabre and J.E. Franco, "The Dynamics of Anti-Jesuitism in the History of the Society of Jesus," in R. Maryks (ed.), *Jesuit Historiography Online*, 2018, http://dx.doi. org/10.1163/2468-7723_jho_COM_192530.

12. Lessius, *De iustitia et iure*, 1,2,4,28,11.
13. Lessius, *De iustitia et iure*, 1,2,4,30.
14. P.F.X. De Ram, "La vie et les écrits de Léonard Lessius de la Compagnie de Jésus," *Revue catholique de Louvain*, 4, April 1861, 189–206.
15. L. Lessius, *Hygiasticon seu vera ratio valetudinis bonae una cum sensuum, iudicii et memoriae integritate ad extremam senectutem conservandae*, Antwerp, 1613.
16. De Ram, "La vie et les écrits de Léonard Lessius de la Compagnie de Jésus," p. 204.
17. *Luigi Cornaro-Léonard Lessius: La sobriété ou conseils pour vivre longtemps*, text presented by G. Vigarello, Grenoble, Éditions Jérôme Millon, 2014 [1991].
18. T. Van Houdt, "Over boeken en gezondheid: Enkele gezondheidsboekjes uit de Nederlanden," *Geschiedenis der Geneeskunde*, 2.3, 1995, 163–168.
19. Lessius, *Hygiasticon*, pp. 32–49, for the benefits of frugality, and pp. 49–68, for a detailed explanation of its advantages for the soul.
20. Lessius, *Hygiasticon*, no. 8, p. 9.
21. Lessius, *Hygiasticon*, no. 56, p. 64: "ut . . . maximos bonorum thesauros sibi congregare possint." The ambiguity of the term *bonorum*, which can mean both "goods" and "good things/practices," should be borne in mind.
22. For the use of these terms, see Lessius, *Hygiasticon*, pp. 44, 64, 70, and 71.
23. A. de Montchrestien, *Traicté de l'oeconomie politique*, Paris, 1615, book 1, p. 21, https://gallica.bnf.fr/ark:/12148/bpt6k106383n/f143.image.
24. J.-C. Perrot, *Une histoire intellectuelle de l'économie politique, XVIIe–XVIIIe siècles*, Paris, Éditions de l'Ehess, 1992, pp. 64–65
25. J.W. O'Malley, *The First Jesuits*, Cambridge, MA, Harvard University Press, 1993, p. 82.
26. W. Clark, "The Pursuit of the Prosopography of Science," in R. Porter (ed.), *The Cambridge History of Science*, Cambridge, Cambridge University Press, 2003, vol. 4, p. 218.
27. The Latin text is quoted in Rai, "*Ex meritis praevisis*," p. 142.
28. Rai, "*Ex meritis praevisis*," p. 142.
29. Lessius, *De beatitudine . . . praelectiones theologicae posthumae*, 19, 6, 7, 44, cited in Decock, *Theologians and Contract Law*, p. 82.
30. Tutino, *Uncertainty in Post-Reformation Catholicism*, p. 21.
31. T. Brogl, "'Yeglichs nāch sín vermugen': Johannes Nider's Idea of Conscience," in S. Müller and C. Schweiger (eds.), *Between Creativity and Norm-Making: Tensions in the Early Modern Era*, Leiden/Boston, Brill, 2013, pp. 61–76.
32. Probabilism makes it possible to pursue an action with a clear conscience when there is a strong enough reason or authority to support the legitimacy of that action, regardless of whether another view is more likely or "probable". See Decock, *Theologians and Contract Law*, pp. 73–82.
33. Schüßler, *The Debate on Probable Opinions in the Scholastic Tradition*, p. 415.
34. The story is related in Judges 16:3. Image also used for the cover of Decock and Birr, *Recht und Moral in der Scholastik der Frühen Neuzeit*.

Bibliography

Pre-modern Sources

Ambrose, *De officiis* (ed. M. Testard), Paris, 1984–1992

Andreas, V., *Bibliotheca belgica*, Louvain, 1623

Aragón, P. de, *In secundam secundae commentaria de iustitia et iure*, Salamanca, 1590

Aristotle, *Ethica Nicomachea* (ed. I. Bywater), Oxford, 1970 [= 1894]

Aristotle, *Politica* (ed. W.D. Ross), Oxford, 1973 [= 1957]

Augustine, *Confessions* (ed. C.J.-B. Hammond), Cambridge, MA, 2014, vol. 1

Azpilcueta, M. de (Dr Navarrus), *Enchiridion sive Manuale confessariorum et poenitentium*, Antwerp, 1575

Baxter, R., *A Christian Directory or a Body of Practical Divinity*, London, 1673

Bellarmine, R., *Conciones habitae Lovanii*, Cologne, 1615

Bellarmine, R., *Tractatus de iustitia*, notes of lectures given at the Jesuit College, preserved at the Royal Library of Belgium (ms. 1734, 1)

Cajetan, Th. de Vio, *Summula peccatorum*, Antwerp, 1575

Cicero, *De officiis* (ed. M. Testard), Paris, 1965–1970

Corpus Iustinianaeum cum commentariis Accursii, scholiis Contii, paratitlis Cujacii, et quorundam aliorum doctorum virorum observationibus, Novae accesserunt ad ipsum Accursium Dionysii Gothofredi notae, Lyons 1604 [= 1588] (= ed. Gothofredi)

Corpus iuris civilis, ed. P. Krüger- Th. Mommsen, Dublin-Zürich 1968[16]

Corpus iuris canonici emendatum et notis illustratum, Gregorii XIII iussu editum, Rome 1582 (= ed. Gregoriana)

Corpus iuris canonici, ed. E. Friedberg, Leipzig 1879-1881

Damhouder, J. de, *Praxis rerum criminalium*, Antwerp, 1562

Dantoine, J.-B., *Les règles du droit canon*, Liège, 1772

Gratian, *Decretum*, see *Corpus iuris canonci*

Hall, J., *The Resolutions and Decisions of Divers Practical Cases of Conscience*, London, 1649

Justinian, see *Corpus Iustinianaeum*

Leoninus, E., *Centuria consiliorum*, Antwerp, 1584

Lessius, L., *Notae in Manuale Navarri anno 1596 praelectae in Collegio Societatis Jesu*, preserved at the Royal Library of Belgium (ms. 4518)

Lessius, L., *Quae fides et religio sit capessenda consultatio*, Antwerp, 1609

Lessius, L., *De gratia efficaci, decretis divinis, libertate arbitrii et praescientia Dei conditionata disputatio apologetica*, Antwerp, 1610

Lessius, L., *De praedestinatione et reprobatione angelorum et hominum disputatio*, Antwerp, 1610

Lessius, L., *Defensio potestatis Summi Pontificis*, Antwerp, 1611
Lessius, L., *De Antichristo et eius praecursoribus, cum appendice De Calvino*, Antwerp, 1611
Lessius, L., *Disputatio de statu vitae deligendo et religionis ingressu*, Antwerp, 1613
Lessius, L., *Discussio decreti Magni Concilii Lateranensis*, Antwerp, 1613
Lessius, L., *De providentia numinis et animi immortalitate*, Antwerp, 1613
Lessius, L., *Hygiasticon*, Antwerp, 1613
Lessius, L., *De summo bono et aeterna beatitudine hominis*, Antwerp, 1616
Lessius, L., *De perfectionibus moribusque divinis*, Antwerp, 1620
Lessius, L., *De iustitia et iure ceterisque virtutibus cardinalibus*, Antwerp 1621
Lessius, L., *Quinquaginta nomina Dei seu divinarum perfectionum compendiaria expositio*, Antwerp, 1640
Lessius, L., *De beatitudine, de actibus humanis, de incarnatione Verbi, de sacramentis et censuris praelectiones theologicae posthumae. Accesserunt variorum casuum conscientiae resolutiones*, ed. I. Wijns, Louvain 1645
Loysel, A., *Institutes coustumieres*, Paris, 1607 (also: *Institutes coustumieres*, Paris, 1637)
Lugo, J. de, *De iustitia et iure*, Lyon, 1642
Malderus, J., *De virtutibus theologicis et iustitia et religione*, Antwerp, 1616
Medina, J. de, *De poenitentia, restitutione et contractibus*, Salamanca 1550
Mercado, T., *Suma de tratos y contratos*, Seville, 1587
Molina, L. de, *De iustitia et iure*, Mainz, 1602
Montchrestien, A. de, *Traicté de l'oeconomie politique*, Paris, 1615
Oñate, P. de, *De contractibus*, Rome, 1646
Olivi, Peter of John, *Traité des contrats* (ed. S. Piron), Paris, 2012
Pomey, F., *Indiculus universalis latino-gallicus*, Nürnberg, 1671
Pothier, Robert-Joseph, *Traité des obligations, selon les règles tant du for de la conscience que du for extérieur*, Paris/Orléans, 1761
Rolandinus de Passageriis, *Collectio contractuum*, Venice, 1546
Sánchez, T., *Disputationes de sancto matrimonii sacramento*, Antwerp, 1620
Scribani, C., *Antverpia*, Antwerp, 1610
Scribani, C., *Origines Antverpiensium*, Antwerp, 1610
Soto, D. de, *De iustitia et iure*, Salamanca, 1556
Spelmann, H., *Glossarium archaiologicum*, London, 1687
Suárez, F., *De legibus et Deo legislatore*, Coimbra, 1612
Suárez, F., *De divina gratia*, Lyon, 1628
Suárez, F., *Opuscula theologica*, in: *Opera omnia* (ed. C. Berton), Paris, Vivès, 1858
Suárez, F., *Conselhos e pareceres*, Coimbra, Universidade de Coimbra, 1948
Summenhart, K., *Opus septipertitum de contractibus*, Augsburg, 1515
Thomas Aquinas, *Summa theologiae* (ed. Leonina), Rome, 1888–1906
Vega, J. de la, *Confusión de confusiones*, Amsterdam, 1688
Wamesius, J., *Responsa sive consilia de iure pontificio*, Louvain, 1618
Wiggers, J., *De iure et iustitia*, Louvain, 1661
Zypaeus, F., *Notitia iuris belgici*, Antwerp, 1635

Modern Literature

Aerts E., "The Absence of Public Exchange Banks in Medieval and Early Modern Flanders and Brabant (1400–1800): A Historical Anomaly to be Explained," *Financial History Review*, 18 (2011), 91–117

Agamben G., *Le règne et la gloire* (Homo sacer, 2.2), Paris, Éditions du Seuil, 2008

Alonso Lasheras D., *Luis de Molina's* De iustitia et iure: *Justice as Virtue in an Economic Context*, Leiden, Brill, 2011

Amadori S., *Nelle bisacce di Bernardino da Feltre: Gli scritti giuridici in difesa dei monti di pietà*, Bologna, Compositori, 2007

Anderson G., *Sin: A History*, New Haven, Yale University Press, 2009

Anderson G., *Charity: The Place of the Poor in the Biblical Tradition*, New Haven, Yale University Press, 2013

Armstrong L., *The Idea of a Moral Economy: Gerard of Siena on Usury, Restitution and Prescription*, Toronto, University of Toronto Press, 2016

Artola A.M., "El sistema inspiracionista de Leonardo Lessio S.I.," *Archivo teológico granadino*, 37 (1974), 5–44

Baeck L., *The Mediterranean Tradition in Economic Thought*, London, Routledge, 1994

Barile N.L., "Renaissance Monti di Pietà in Modern Scholarship: Themes, Studies, and Historiographic Trends," *Renaissance and Reformation/Renaissance et Réforme*, 35 (2012), 85–114

Barrientos García J., *Repertorio de moral económica (1536–1670): La Escuela de Salamanca y su proyección*, Pamplona, eunsa, 2011

Bauer T., *A Culture of Ambiguity. An Alternative History of Islam*, New York, Columbia University Press, 2021 (= *Die Kultur der Ambiguität: Eine andere Geschichte des Islams*, Berlin, Verlag der Weltreligionen im Insel Verlag, 2011)

Becker S.O., J. Rubin, and Woessmann L., "Religion and Growth," *Journal of Economic Literature*, 62 (2024), 1094–1142

Bergfeld, Ch., "Die Stellungnahme der Spanischen Spätscholastiker zum Versicherungsvertrag," in P. Grossi (ed.), *La seconda scolastica nella formazione del diritto privato moderno*, Florence, Giuffrè, 1973, pp. 457–471

Berman H., *Law and Revolution, I: The Formation of the Western Legal Tradition*, Cambridge, MA, Harvard University Press, 1983

Berman H., *Law and Revolution II: The Impact of the Protestant Reformations on the Western Legal Tradition*, Cambridge, MA, Harvard University Press, 2003

Beutels, R., *Leonardus Lessius (1554–1623): Portret van een Zuidnederlandse laatscholastieke econoom: Een bio-bibliografisch essay*, Wommelgem, Den Gulden Engel, 1987

Birocchi I., "Tra elaborazioni nuove e dottrine tradizionali: Il contratto trino e la natura contractus," *Quaderni fiorentini per la storia del pensiero giuridico moderno*, 19 (1990), 243–322

Blaug M., *Economic Theory in Retrospect*. Fifth ed., Cambridge, Cambridge University Press, 1997

Böhm F., "Freiheit und Ordnung in der Marktwirtschaft," *OrDO: Jahrbuch für die Ordnung von Wirtschaft und Gesellschaft*, 22 (1971), 11–27

Böhm F., "Privatrechtsgesellschaft und Marktwirtschaft," *OrDO: Jahrbuch für die Ordnung von Wirtschaft und Gesellschaft*, 17 (1966), 75–151

Boldrini, F., "Sacri Montes e fraudolenta cambia: Credito e usura nell'opera di frate Orfeo Cancellieri, predicatore francescano e giurista nell'Italia del XVI secolo," *Rivista internazionale di diritto comune*, 24 (2013), 279–326

Bondolfi, A., "'Tu ne témoigneras pas faussement contre ton prochain' (Exode, 20, 16): Quelques considérations historiques sur le prétendu caractère absolu du huitième (neuvième) commandement," *Revue d'éthique et de théologie morale*, 37 (2005), 29–77

Boucheron, P., *La trace et l'aura: Vies posthumes d'Ambroise de Milan (IVe–XVIe siècles)*, Paris, Seuil, 2019

Boureau A., *Le désir dicté: Histoire du vœu religieux dans l'Occident médiéval*, Paris, Les Belles Lettres, 2014

Boyajian C.J., *Portuguese Trade in Asia under the Habsburgs, 1580–1640*, London/Baltimore, Johns Hopkins UP, 1993

Brants V., *La faculté de droit de l'Université de Louvain à travers cinq siècles*, Paris/Brussels, new edition (undated [1917]), p. 351, n. 1

Brodrick J., *The Economic Morals of the Jesuits. An Answer to Dr H.M. Robertson*, Oxford, Oxford UP, 1934

Broggio P., *La teologia e la politica: Controversie dottrinali, Curia romana e monarchia spagnola tra Cinque e Seicento*, Florence, Olschki, 2009

Brogl T., "'Yeglichs nāch sín vermugen': Johannes Nider's Idea of Conscience," in S. Müller and C. Schweiger (eds.), *Between Creativity and Norm-Making: Tensions in the Early Modern Era*, Leiden/Boston, Brill, 2013, pp. 61–76

Brown P., *The Ransom of the Soul: Afterlife and Wealth in Early Western Christianity*, Cambridge, MA, Harvard University Press, 2015

Brunori L., *Societas quid sit: La société commerciale dans l'élaboration de la Seconde Scolastique*, Paris, Mare & Martin, 2015

Brunori L. and W. Decock, "The Pragmatic Suárez. Private Law in the Work of the Doctor Eximius," in D. Bauer and R. Lesaffer (eds.), *History, Casuistry and Custom in the Legal Thought of Francisco Suárez (1548-1617)*, Leiden/Boston, Brill, 2021, pp. 54-75

Cabral G., "Os decisionistas portugueses entre o direito comum e o direito pátrio," PhD thesis, São Paulo, Faculdade de Direito, Universidade de São Paulo, 2013

Campagnolo G. and Ch. Vivel, "Before Schumpeter: Forerunners of the Theory of the Entrepreneur in 1900s German Political Economy—Werner Sombart, Friedrich von Wieser," *The European Journal of the History of Economic Thought*, 19 (2012), 908–943

Ceccarelli G., "Risky Business: Theological and Canon Thought on Insurance from the Thirteenth to the Seventeenth Century," *Journal of Medieval and Early Modern Studies*, 31 (2001), 607–658

Ceccarelli G., *Il gioco e il peccato: Economia e rischio nel tardo medioevo*, Bologna, Il Mulino, 2003

Ceccarelli G., *Risky Markets: Marine Insurance in Renaissance Florence*, Leiden/Boston, Brill, 2021

Chafuen A.A., *Christians for Freedom: Late Scholastic Economics*, San Francisco, Ignatius Press, 1986

Chafuen A.A., *Faith and Liberty: The Economic Thought of the Late Scholastics*, Lanham, Lexington Books, 2003

Chaplygina I. and Lapidus A., "Economic Thought in Scholasticism," in G. Faccarello and H.D. Kurz (eds.), *Handbook of the History of Economic Analysis*, vol. 2, Cheltenham, E. Elgar, 2016, pp. 20–42

Chappel J., "Catholicism and the Economy of Miracles in West Germany, 1920–1960," *New German Critique*, 42 (2015), 9–40

Chevreau E., "La traiecticia pecunia: Un mode de financement du commerce international," *Mémoires de la Société pour l'histoire du droit*, 65 (2008), 37–47

Clark W., "The Pursuit of the Prosopography of Science," in Porter R. (ed.), *The Cambridge History of Science*, Cambridge, Cambridge UP, 2003

Colmant B., *Économie européenne: L'influence des religions*, Louvain-la-Neuve, Anthemis, 2008

Colmant B., *Capitalisme européen: L'ombre de Jean Calvin*, Brussels, Académie royale de Belgique, 2013

Commun P., *Les ordolibéraux: Histoire d'un libéralisme à l'allemande*, Paris, Les Belles Lettres, 2016

Coujou J.-P. (ed.), *Francisco de Vitoria, La Justice*, Paris, Dalloz, 2014

Cowen, D.V., "Survey of the Law Relating to the Control of Monopoly in South Africa," *South African Journal of Economics*, 18 (1950), 124–147

Davis J., *Medieval Market Morality: Life, Law and Ethics in the English Marketplace, 1200–1500*, Cambridge, Cambridge University Press, 2012

Decock W., "Lessius and the Breakdown of the Scholastic Paradigm," *Journal of the History of Economic Thought*, 31 (2009), 57–78

Decock W., "From Law to Paradise: Confessional Catholicism and Legal Scholarship," *Rechtsgeschichte/Legal History*, 18 (2011), 12–34

Decock W., "The Judge's Conscience and the Protection of the Criminal Defendant: Moral Safeguards against Judicial Arbitrariness," in Martyn G. et al. (eds.), *From the Judge's Arbitrium to the Legality Principle*, Berlin, Duncker & Humblot, 2013, pp. 69–94

Decock W., *Theologians and Contract Law: The Moral Transformation of the Ius Commune (c. 1500–1650)*, Leiden/Boston, Brill/Nijhoff, 2013

Decock W., "The Catholic Spirit of Capitalism? Contrasting Views on Profit-Making through Capital Investment in the Age of Reformations," in W. Decock, J. Ballor, M. Germann, and L. Waelkens (eds.), *Law and Religion: The Legal Teachings of the Protestant and Catholic Reformations*, Göttingen, V&R, 2014, 22–44

Decock W., "Domingo de Soto: *De iustitia et iure* (1553–1554)," in S. Dauchy et al. (eds.), *The Formation and Transmission of Western Legal Culture: 150 Books That Made the Law in the Age of Printing*, Berlin, Springer, 2016, 84–86

Decock W. (ed.), N. De Sutter (transl.), *Leonardus Lessius on Sale, Securities and Insurance*, Grand Rapids, CLP Academic, 2016

Decock W., "Luis de Molina: *De iustitia et iure* (1593–1609)," in S. Dauchy et al. (eds.), *The Formation and Transmission of Western Legal Culture: 150 Books That Made the Law in the Age of Printing*, Berlin, Springer, 2016, 129–131

Decock W., "Spanish Scholastics on Money and Credit: Economic, Legal and Political Aspects," in W. Ernst and D. Fox (eds.), *Money in the Western Legal Tradition: Middle Ages to Bretton Woods*, Oxford, Oxford UP, 2016, 267–283

Decock W., "Trust beyond Faith. Re-Thinking Contracts with Heretics and Excommunicates in Times of Religious War," *Rivista internazionale di diritto comune*, 27 (2016), 301–328

Decock W., "Law, Religion and Debt Relief: Balancing above the 'Abyss of Despair' in Early Modern Canon Law and Theology," *American Journal of Legal History*, 57 (2017), 125–141

Decock W., "Knowing before Judging: Law and Economic Analysis in Early Modern Jesuit Ethics," *Journal of Markets and Morality*, 21 (2018), 309–330

Decock W., "Law of Property and Obligations: Neoscholastic Thinking and Beyond," in H. Pihlajamäki et al. (eds)., *The Oxford Handbook of European Legal History*, Oxford, Oxford UP, 2018, pp. 611–631

Decock W., "Martin de Azpilcueta (Dr Navarrus)," in R. Domingo and J. Martínez-Torrón (eds.), *Great Christian Jurists in Spanish History*, Cambridge, Cambridge UP, 2018, 115–132

Decock W., "L'esprit catholique du capitalisme: Éthique et investissement selon Musculus et Lessius," in L. Brunori (ed.), *Histoire de l'économie sans travail. Volume Sources I. intellectuelles, acteurs, résolution des conflits*, Paris, Garnier, 2019, pp. 57–85

Decock W., "Jesuits and Jurisprudence," in R.A. Maryks (ed.), *Jesuit Historiography Online* (2019), https://doi.org/10.1163/2468-7723_jho_COM_209877

Decock W., "Princes and Prices: Regulating the Grain Market in Scholastic Economic Thought," in J.A. Tellkamp (ed.), *A Companion to Early Modern Spanish Imperial Political and Social Thought*, Leiden/Boston, Brill, 2020, 172–196

Decock W., "Thomas Cajetan (1469–1536)," in O. Condorelli and R. Domingo (eds.), *Law and the Christian Tradition in Italy: The Legacy of the Great Jurists*, London, Routledge, 2021, 230–244

Decock W., "'Mercatores isti regulandi': Monopolies and Moral Regulation of the Market in Pedro de Oñate's *De contractibus*," *Tijdschrift voor Rechtsgeschiedenis*, 90 (2022), 462–488

Decock W., "Hugo Grotius, Monopolies and the Shift in Business Morality in the Early Modern Low Countries," *Yale Journal of Law and the Humanities*, 35 (2024), 450–464

Decock W. and C. Birr, *Recht und Moral in der Scholastik der Frühen Neuzeit*, Berlin, de Gruyter, 2016

Decock W. and J. Hallebeek, "Pre-Contractual Duties to Inform in Early Modern Scholasticism," *Tijdschrift voor Rechtsgeschiedenis*, 78 (2010), 89–133

De-Juan O. and F. Monsalve, "Morally Ruled Behaviour: The Neglected Contribution of Scholasticism," *The European Journal of the History of Economic Thought*, 13 (2006), 99–112

de Laveleye E., "Le protestantisme et le catholicisme dans leurs rapports avec la liberté et la prospérité des peuples," *Revue de Belgique*, 15 January 1875, pp. 5–41

D'Emic M.Th., *Justice in the Marketplace in Early Modern Spain: Saravia, Villalón and the Religious Origins of Economic Analysis*, Lanham, Lexington, 2014

Dempsey B.W., *Interest and Usury*, London, 1948 (= Washington, DC, 1943)

De Preter, A. and W. François, "'Capite nobis vulpes' (Song 2:15): The Struggle of Libertus Fromondus (1587–1653) with Leonardus Lessius' Theological Legacy," *Journal of Early Modern Christianity*, 11 (2024), 445–466

De Ram, P.F.X., "La vie et les écrits de Léonard Lessius de la Compagnie de Jésus," *Revue catholique de Louvain*, 4 (1861), 189–206

De Roover R., "Monopoly Theory prior to Adam Smith: A Revision," *Quarterly Journal of Economics*, 65 (1951), 492–524

De Roover R., *L'Évolution de la lettre de change, XIVe–XVIIIe siècles*, Paris, Éditions de l'EHESS, 1953

De Roover R., "Scholastic Economics: Survival and Lasting Influence from the Sixteenth Century to Adam Smith," *Quarterly Journal of Economics*, 69 (1955), 161–190

De Roover R., "The Concept of the Just Price: Theory and Economic Policy," *Journal of Economic History*, 18 (1958), 418–434

De Roover R., *Leonardus Lessius als economist: De economische leerstellingen van de latere scholastiek in de Zuidelijke Nederlanden*, Brussels, Paleis der Academiën, 1969

De ruysscher D., "From Usages of Merchants to Default Rules: Practices of Trade, Ius Commune and Urban Law in Early Modern Antwerp," *Journal of Legal History*, 33 (2012), 3–29

De ruysscher D., "Antwerp 1490–1590: Insurance and Speculation," in A.B. Leonard (ed.), *Marine Insurance: Origins and Institutions, 1300–1850*, London, Palgrave Macmillan, 2015, 78–105

De ruysscher D. and J. Puttevils, "The Art of Compromise: Legislative Deliberations on Marine Insurance Institutions in Antwerp (c. 1550–c. 1570)," *BMGN—Low Countries Historical Review*, 130 (2015), 25–49

der Weduwen, A., *Dutch and Flemish Newspapers of the Seventeenth Century, 1618–1700*, Leiden/Boston, Brill, 2017

Dilcher G. and Lepsius S. (eds.), *Zur Geschichte der Handelsgesellschaften im Mittelalter* (Max Weber Gesamtausgabe, i/1), Tübingen, Mohr Siebeck, 2008

Dorin R., *No Return: Jews, Christian Usurers, and the Spread of Mass Expulsion in Medieval Europe*, Princeton, Princeton University Press, 2023

Drexl J., "La constitution économique européenne: L'actualité du modèle ordoliberal," *Revue internationale de droit économique*, 25 (2011), 419–454

Druwé W., "Loans and Credit in the Canon Law Consilia of Wamesius (1524–1590)," Tijdschrift voor Rechtsgeschiedenis, 85 (2017), 230–271

Dumoulin M., "Émile de Laveleye, un professeur renommé puis oublié," in V. Genin (ed.), *Une Fabrique des Sciences humaines: L'université de Liège dans la mêlée (1817–2017)*, Brussels, General State Archives, 2018, pp. 109–122

Dupont A., *Gratia in Augustine's Sermones ad Populum during the Pelagian Controversy: Do Different Contexts Furnish Different Insights?*, Leiden/Boston, Brill, 2012

Durand P. and T. Habrand, *Histoire de l'édition en Belgique, XVe–XXIe siècle*, Paris/Brussels, Les Impressions Nouvelles, 2018

Duve Th., "The School of Salamanca. A Case of Global Knowledge Production," in Th. Duve, J.L. Egío, and C. Birr (eds.), *The School of Salamanca: A Case of Global Knowledge Production*, Leiden/Boston, Brill, 2021, pp. 1–42

Ekelund R.B. and R.F. Hébert, *History of Economic Theory and Method.* Sixth ed., Chicago, Waveland Press, 2013

Ertman T.C. (ed.), *Max Weber's Economic Ethic of the World Religions: An Analysis*, Cambridge, Cambridge UP, 2017

Evangelisti P., *La pensée économique au Moyen Âge: Richesse, pauvreté, marchés et monnaie*, Paris, Garnier, 2021

Fabre P.-A. and J.E. Franco, "The Dynamics of Anti-Jesuitism in the History of the Society of Jesus," in R. Maryks (ed.), *Jesuit Historiography Online*, 2018, org/10.1163/2468-7723_jho_COM_192530

Fabre P.-A. and C. Maire (eds.), *Les antijésuites: Discours, figures et lieux de l'antijésuitisme à l'époque moderne*, Rennes, Presses Universitaires de Rennes, 2010

Faitini T., "Redemption between Law and Theology: The Theological Translation of the Roman redemptio in the Patristics," in W. Druwé et al. (eds.), *Ius commune graeco-romanum: Essays in Honor of Prof. Dr. Laurent Waelkens*, Leuven, Peeters, 2018, pp. 24–36

Fèvre R., "Retour sur le libéralisme conservateur de Wilhelm Röpke," *Revue européenne des sciences sociales*, 53 (2015), 147–190

Fèvre R., *A Political Economy of Power: Ordoliberalism in Context, 1932–1950* (Oxford Studies in the History of Economics), Oxford, Oxford University Press, 2022

Fontaine L., *L'économie morale: Pauvreté, crédit et confiance dans l'Europe préindustrielle*, Paris, Gallimard, 2008

Fragnito G. and A. Tallon (eds.), *Hétérodoxies croisées: Catholicismes pluriels entre France et Italie, XVIe–XVIIe siècles*, Rome, École française de Rome, 2015

Franco G., "Glaube und Wirtschaft: Zur normativen Bedeutung des Ordo-Begriffes bei Walter Eucken," *Journal for Markets and Ethics*, 5 (2018), 23–38

Frevert U., "Moral Economies, Present and Past: Social Practices and Intellectual Controversies," in U. Frevert (ed.), *Moral Economies*, Göttingen, Vandenhoeck & Ruprecht, 2019, pp. 13–44

Friedman B.J., "The Influence of Religious Thinking on Economic Thinking: America's Social Gospel, with Thoughts on Rerum Novarum," *The European Journal of the History of Economic Thought*, 9 December 2024, https://doi.org/10.1080/09672567.2024.2433960

Frier, B.W. (ed.), *The Codex of Justinian: A New Annotated Translation*, Cambridge, Cambridge UP, 2016

Frigo, A., "Charité bien ordonnée commence par soi-même: Notes sur la genèse d'un adage," *Freiburger Zeitschrift für Philosophie und Theologie*, 59 (2012), 234–248

Frydman B., *Le sens des lois: Histoire de l'interprétation et de la raison juridique*, Brussels, Bruylant, 2005

Fuller E.W. (ed.), *A Source Book on Early Monetary Thought*, Cheltenham, E. Elgar, 2020, pp. 105–112

Fusaro M., "The Burden of Risk: Early Modern Maritime Enterprise and Varieties of Capitalism," *Business History Review*, 94 (2020), 179–200

Gaudemet J., *Le droit romain dans la littérature chrétienne occidentale du IIIe au Ve siècle*, Milan, Giuffrè, 1978

Gelderblom O., *Zuid-Nederlandse kooplieden en de opkomst van de Amsterdamse stapelmarkt (1578–1630)*, Hilversum, Verloren, 2000

Gelderblom O., *Cities of Commerce: The Institutional Foundations of International Trade in the Low Countres, 1250–1650*, Princeton, Princeton UP, 2013

Génelle G., "La vie économique et sociale dans l'Afrique romaine tardive d'après les sermons de saint Augustin," Lille, Atelier national de reproduction des thèses, 2005

Ghosh P., *Max Weber and The Protestant Ethic: Twin Histories*, Oxford, Oxford UP, 2014

Goldschmidt N., "Walter Eucken's Place in the History of Ideas," *Review of Austrian Economics*, 26 (2013), 127–147

Goltzberg S., "Le contournement de la loi est-il hypocrite? Statut de la ruse dans la loi juive," *Cahiers philosophiques*, 145 (2016), 97–110

Gómez Camacho F., *Economía y filosofía moral*, Madrid, Síntesis, 1998

Gómez Camacho F., "Later Scholastics: Spanish Economic Thought in the XVIth and XVIIth Centuries," in Lowry T. and Gordon B. (eds.), *Ancient and Medieval Economic Ideas and Concepts of Social Justice*, Leiden, Brill, 1998, pp. 503–560

Goossaert V., "Bureaucratie, taxation et justice: Taoïsme et construction de l'État au Jiangnan (Chine), XVIIe–XIXe siècles," *Annales: Histoire, Sciences Sociales*, 65 (2010), 999–1027

Gordon, B., *Economic Analysis before Adam Smith: Hesiod to Lessius*, London/Basingstoke, Macmillan, 1975

Grabill S.J. (ed.), *Sourcebook in Late-Scholastic Monetary Theory: The Contributions of Martin de Azpilcueta, Luis de Molina SJ and Juan de Mariana SJ*, Lanham, Lexington, 2007

Gregg S., *Wilhelm Röpke's Political Economy*, Cheltenham, Elgar, 2010

Gregg S., "The Forgotten Story of the German Economic Miracle," https://acton.org/pub/commentary/2016/07/06/forgotten-story-german-economic-miracle

Greilsammer M., *L'usurier chrétien, un Juif métaphorique? Histoire de l'exclusion des prêteurs lombards (XIIIe–XVIIe siècle)*, Rennes, Presses universitaires de Rennes, 2012

Grice-Hutchison M., *The School of Salamanca: Readings in Spanish Monetary Theory, 1544–1605*, Oxford, Clarendon, 1952

Grossi, P., "La proprietà nel sistema privatistico della Seconda Scolastica," in P. Grossi (ed.), *La Seconda Scolastica nella formazione del diritto privato moderno*, Milan, Giuffrè, 1973, pp. 117–222

Haberler G., "Joseph Alois Schumpeter 1883–1950," *Quarterly Journal of Economics*, 64 (1950), 333–372

Hamm, B., "Den Himmel kaufen: Heilskommerzielle Perspektiven des 14. bis 16. Jahrhunderts," in B. Hamm, *Religiosität im späten Mittelalter*, Tübingen, Mohr Siebeck, 2011, pp. 301–334

Hayek F., "The Pretence of Knowledge," Lecture to the Memory of Alfred Nobel, 11 December 1974, available at https://www.nobelprize.org/prizes/economic-sciences/1974/hayek/lecture/.

Hermann De Franceschi S., *Entre saint Augustin et saint Thomas: Les jansénistes et le refuge thomiste (1653–1663): à propos des 1ère, 2e et 18e Provinciales*, Paris, Classiques Garnier, 2017

Hermanns M., "Joseph Höffner—Lebensstationen eines Sozialethikers," in Gabriel, K. and H.J. Grosse Kracht (eds.), *Joseph Höffner (1906–1987): Soziallehre und Sozialpolitik*, Paderborn, Schöningh, 2005, pp. 13–36

Höffner J., *Wirtschaftsethik und Monopole im fünfzehnten und sechzehnten Jahrhundert* (Freiburger Staatswissenschaftliche Schriften, 2), Jena, Fischer G., 1941

Höffner J., *Christentum und Menschenwürde: Das Anliegen der spanischen Kolonialethik im Goldenen Zeitalter*, Trier, Paulinus, 1947

Höffner J., "Der Wettbewerb in der Scholastik," *OrDO: Jahrbuch für die Ordnung von Wirtschaft und Gesellschaft*, 5 (1953), 181–202

Holzapfel H., *Die Anfänge der Montes Pietatis (1462–1515)*, Munich, Lentner, 1903

Imhof, D., *Jan Moretus and the Continuation of the Plantin Press: A Bibliography of the Works Published and Printed by Jan Moretus I in Antwerp (1589–1610)*, Leiden/Boston, Brill, 2014

Jaspers K., *Max Weber: Deutsches Wesen im politischen Denken, im Forschen und Philosophieren*, Oldenburg, Stalling, 1932

Kaye J., *Economy and Nature in the Fourteenth Century: Money, Market Exchange and the Emergence of Scientific Thought*, Cambridge, Cambridge UP, 1998

Kaye J., *A History of Balance, 1250–1375. The Emergence of a New Model of Equilibrium and Its Impact on Thought*, Cambridge, Cambridge University Press, 2014

Kelley, D.R. "Fides historiae: Charles Dumoulin and the Gallican View of History," *Traditio* 22 (1966), 347–402

Keynes J.M., *The General Theory of Employment, Interest and Money*, New York, Harcourt, Brace, 1936

Kirshner J., "Raymond de Roover on Scholastic Economic Thought," in Kirshner J. (ed.), *Business, Banking and Economic Thought in Late Medieval and Early Modern Europe: Selected Studies of Raymond de Roover*, Chicago, Chicago University Press, 1974, pp. 15–36

Kocka J. and M. van der Linden (eds.), *Capitalism: The Reemergence of an Historical Concept*, London, Bloomsbury, 2016

Krynen J., *Le théâtre juridique: Une histoire de la construction du droit*, Paris, Gallimard, 2018

Kurz H.D., "German and Austrian Schools," in G. Faccarello and H.D. Kurz (eds.), *Handbook of the History of Economic Analysis*, vol. 2 (Schools of Thought in Economics), Cheltenham, E. Elgar, 2016, pp. 252–273

Langholm O.I., *Price and Value in the Aristotelian Tradition: A Study in Scholastic Economic Sources*, Oxford, Oxford UP, 1979

Langholm O.I., *Economics in the Medieval Schools: Wealth, Exchange, Value, Money and Usury according to the Paris Theological Tradition, 1200–1350*, Leiden/Boston, Brill, 1992

Langholm O.I., *The Legacy of Scholasticism in Economic Thought: Antecedents of Choice and Power*, Cambridge, Cambridge UP, 1998

Langholm O.I., *The Merchant in the Confessional: Trade and Price in the Pre-Reformation Penitential Handbooks*, Leiden/Boston, Brill, 2003

Langholm O.I., "Monopoly and Market Irregularities in Medieval Economic Thought: Traditions and Texts to AD 1500," *Journal of the History of Economic Thought*, 28 (2006), 395–411

Lapidus, A., "Hugo Grotius on Usury: Acknowledging the End of the Scholastic Argument," *Th European Journal of the History of Economic Thought*, 30 (2023), 1031–1049

Lapidus, A., "Hugo Grotius on Exchange and Price," *The European Journal of the History of Economic Thought*, 31 (2024), 633–649

Legendre P., "L'inscription du droit canon dans la théologie: Remarques sur la seconde scolastique," in Kuttner S. and Pennington K. (eds.), *Proceedings of the Fifth International Congress of Medieval Canon Law*, Vatican City, Vatican Press, 1980, pp. 443–454

Leites E. (ed.), *Conscience and Casuistry in Early Modern Europe*, Cambridge, Cambridge University Press, 1988

Lejeune J., "Religion, morale et capitalisme dans la société liégeoise du XVIIe siècle," *Revue belge de philologie et d'histoire*, 22 (1943), 109–154

Lequenne, M. et al. (eds.), *Christoph Colomb, La découverte de l'Amérique. Vol. 2. Relations de voyages (1493–1504)*, Paris, La Découverte, 1984

Leyder, D. and G. Martyn, *Édit perpétuel: Vers plus de sécurité juridique, 1611–2011*, Brussels, General State Archives, 2011

Maclean, I., *Scholarship, Commerce and Religion: The Learned Book in the Age of Confessions, 1560–1630*, Cambridge, MA, Harvard UP, 2012

Markovits D., *The Meritocracy Trap: How America's Foundational Myth Feeds Inequality, Dismantles the Middle Class, and Devours the Elite*, New York, Penguin, 2019

Marmursztejn E., *L'autorité des maîtres: Scolastique, normes et société au XIIIe siècle*, Paris, Les Belles Lettres, 2007, p. 194

Martinat M., *Le juste marché: Le système annonaire romain aux XVIe et XVIIe siècles*, Rome, École française de Rome, 2004

McGinnis D., "Charity and Commerce: Joseph Hall's Reception of Catholic Casuistry and Economic Thought," *Renaissance and Reformation Review*, 21 (2019), 203–217

Medema S., *The Economics Book: From Xenophon to Cryptocurrency, 250 Milestones in the History of Economics*, New York, Sterling, 2019

Mertens B., *Im Kampf gegen die Monopole: Reichtagsverhandlungen und Monopolprozesse im frühen 16. Jahrhundert*, Tübingen, Mohr, 1996

Molina L., *Des secours de la grâce*, edition, translation and notes by Nicolas P., preface by Schmutz J., Paris, Les Belles Lettres, 2016

Monsalve F., "Economics and Ethics: Juan de Lugo's Theory of the Just Price, or the Responsibility of Living in Society," *History of Political Economy*, 42 (2010), 495–519

Monsalve F., "Late Spanish Doctors on Usury, and the Evolving Scholastic Tradition," *Journal of the History of Economic Thought*, 36 (2014), 215–235

Monsalve F., "Scholastic Just Price vs. Current Market Price: Is It Merely a Matter of Labeling?," *The European Journal of the History of Economic Thought*, 21 (2014), 4–20

Moreton, B., "Our Lady of Mont Pelerin: The 'Navarra School' of Catholic Neoliberalism," *Capitalism: A Journal of History and Economics*, 2 (2021), 88–153

Müller-Armack, A., *Religion und Wirtschaft: Geistesgeschichtliche Hintergründe unserer europäischen Lebensform*, Stuttgart, Kohlhammer, 1959

Muzzarelli M.G., *Il denaro e la salvezza: L'invenzione del Monte di Pietà*, Bologna, Il Mulino, 2001

Nelson E., *The Theology of Liberalism: Political Philosophy and the Justice of God*, Cambridge, MA, Harvard University Press, 2019

Noell E.S., "In Pursuit of the Just Wage: A Comparison of Reformation and Counter-Reformation Economic Thought," *Journal of the History of Economic Thought*, 23 (2001), 467–489

Noell E.S., "Smith and a Living Wage: Competition, Economic Compulsion, and the Scholastic Legacy," *History of Political Economy*, 38 (2006), 151–174

Noonan Jr J.T., *The Scholastic Analysis of Usury*, Cambridge, MA, Harvard University Press, 1957

Novak M., *The Catholic Ethic and the Spirit of Capitalism*, New York, Macmillan/The Free Press, 1993

O'Malley J.W., *The First Jesuits*, Cambridge, MA, Harvard University Press, 1993

Perrot J.-C., *Une histoire intellectuelle de l'économie politique, XVIIe–XVIIIe siècles*, Paris, Éditions de l'EHESS, 1992

Petersen T., "Theologische Einflüsse auf die deutsche Nationalökonomie im 19. und 20. Jahrhundert: Drei Fallbeispiele," *Zeitschrift für Wirtschafts- und Unternehmensethik*, 12 (2011), 318–330

Pfister L., "Les conditions d'octroi des privilèges d'imprimerie en France (1500–1630)," in E. Keller-Rahbé et al. (eds.), *Privilèges de librairie en France et en Europe: XVIe–XVIIe siècles*, Paris, Classiques Garnier, 2017, p. 49–92

Piron S., "La dette de Panurge," *L'Homme*, 162 (2002), 255–270

Piron S. (ed.), Thornton R. (transl.), Cusato M. (transl.), *Peter of John Olivi: A Treatise on Contracts*, Bonaventure, NY, Franciscan Institute, 2016

Piron S., *L'Occupation du monde*, Brussels, Zones sensibles, 2018

Piron S., *Généalogie de la morale économique* (L'occupation du monde, 2), Brussels, Zones sensibles, 2020

Plumpe W., "Les entreprises sous le nazisme: Bilan intermédiaire," *Histoire, économie et société*, 24 (2005), 453–472

Popescu O., *Studies in the History of Latin American Economic Thought*, London, Routledge, 1997

Prak M. and J. Luiten Zanden, *Pioneers of Capitalism: The Netherlands 1000–1800*, Princeton, Princeton University Press, 2022

Prieto, C. and D. Bosco, *Droit européen de la concurrence: Ententes et abus de position dominante*, Brussels, Bruylant, 2013

Prodi P., *Settimo non rubare: Furto e mercato nella storia dell'Occidente*, Bologna, Il Mulino, 2009

Puttevils J., *Merchants and Trading in the Sixteenth Century: The Golden Age of Antwerp* (Perspectives in Economic and Social History, 38), London, Pickering & Chatto, 2015

Puttevils J., "Invoking Fortuna and Speculating on the Future Lotteries in the 15th and 16th Century Low Countries," *Quaderni Storici*, 52 (2017), 699–725

Puttevils J., "Sixteenth-Century Antwerp, A Hyper-Market for All? The Case of Low Countries Merchants," in B. Blondé and J. Puttevils (eds.), *Antwerp in the Renaissance*, Turnhout, Brepols, 2020, pp. 29–54

Quattrone P., "Governing Social Orders, Unfolding Rationality, and Jesuit Accounting Practices: A Procedural Approach to Institutional Logics," *Administrative Science Quarterly*, 20 (2015), 1–35

Rai E., "The 'Odor of Sanctity': Veneration and Politics in Leonardus Lessius's Cause for Beatification," *Journal of Jesuit Studies*, 3 (2016), 238–258

Rai E., "Ex meritis praevisis: Predestination, Grace and Free Will in Intra-Jesuit Controversies (1587–1613)," *Journal of Early Modern Christianity*, 7 (2020), 111–150

Rebenack V.E., *Thasci Caecili Cypriani de opere et eleemosynis, A Translation with an Introduction and a Commentary*, PhD thesis, Washington, DC, Catholic University of America Press, 1962

Renoux-Zagamé, M.-F., *Les origines théologiques du concept moderne de propriété*, Geneva, Droz, 1987

Rivière J., "Mérite," *Dictionnaire de théologie catholique*, Paris, 1928, vol. 10, part 1, col. 574–785

Robertson H.M., *Aspects of the Rise of Economic Individualism: A Criticism of Max Weber and His School*, Cambridge/New York, Cambridge University Press/Macmillan, 1973

Roelofs S., "Robert Bellarmine (1542–1621) and the Law and Morality of the Market: A Brief Introduction," *Rivista internazionale di diritto comune*, 33 (2022), 269–279

Roets P.J., *The Economic Ideas of Bernard W. Dempsey, S.J.*, Milwaukee, Marquette University Press, 1991

Rossi G., *Insurance in Elizabethan England: The London Code*, Cambridge, Cambridge University Press, 2016

Rothbard M.N., *An Austrian Perspective on the History of Economic Thought*, vol. 1, *Economic Thought before Adam Smith*, Auburn, Ludwig von Mises Institute, 2006 [1995]

Saddle M.A., *Interrupting Capitalism: Catholic Social Thought and the Economy*, Oxford, Oxford University Press, 2018

Sandel M., *The Tyranny of Merit: What's Become of the Common Good?*, New York, Farrar, Straus & Giroux, 2020

Schefold B. (ed.), *Leonardus Lessius'* De iustitia et iure: *Vademecum zu einem Klassiker der spätscholastischen Wirtschaftsanalyse*, Düsseldorf, Verlag Wirtschaft und Finanzen, 1999

Schefold B., "Von der praktischen Tugend der Gerechtigkeit zur Wirtschaftstheorie," in B. Schefold (ed.), *Leonardus Lessius'* De iustitia et iure: *Vademecum zu einem Klassiker der spätscholastischen Wirtschaftsanalyse*, Düsseldorf, Verlag Wirtschaft und Finanzen, 1999, pp. 5–32

Schefold B., *Great Economic Thinkers from Antiquity to the Historical School: Translations from the Series Klassiker der Nationalökonomie*, London/New York, Routledge, 2016

Schlag M., "Moraltheologische Vor- und Rahmenbedingungen der spätscholastischen Wirtschaftsethik," *Zeitschrift der Savigny-Stiftung für Rechtsgeschichte, Germanistische Abteilung*, 132 (2015), 82–115

Schluchter W. and U. Bube (eds.), *Die protestantische Ethik und der Geist des Kapitalismus; Die protestantischen Sekten und der Geist des Kapitalismus, Schriften 1904–1920* (Max Weber-Gesamtausgabe, i/18), Tübingen, Mohr Siebeck, 2016

Schmoeckel M., "Nescience and the Conscience of Judges: An Example of Religion's Influence on Legal Procedure," in C. Zwierlein (ed.), *The Dark Side of Knowledge: Histories of Ignorance, 1400 to 1800*, Leiden/Boston, Brill, 2016, pp. 70–87

Schobesberger N. et al., "European Postal Networks," in J. Raymond and N. Moxham (eds.), *News Networks in Early Modern Europe*, Leiden, Brill, 2016, pp. 19–63

Schüßler R., "The Economic Thought of Luis de Molina," in A. Aichele and M. Kaufmann (eds.), *A Companion to Luis de Molina*, Leiden, Brill, 2014, pp. 257–288

Schüßler R., *The Debate on Probable Opinions in the Scholastic Tradition*, Leiden/Boston, Brill, 2019

Schumpeter J.A., "Introduction," in B.W. Dempsey, *Interest and Usury*, London, 1948 (= Washington, DC, 1943), pp. vii–x

Schumpeter J.A., *History of Economic Analysis*, edited from manuscript by Elizabeth Boody Schumpeter, with an introduction by Mark Perlman, London, Routledge, 1954

Simon T., "Gemeinwohltopik in der mittelalterlichen und frühneuzeitlichen Politiktheorie," in H. Münkler and H. Bluhm (eds.), *Gemeinwohl und Gemeinsinn: Historische Semantiken politischer Leitbegriffe*, Berlin, Akademie Verlag, 2001, pp. 129–146

Soetaert P., *De Bergen van Barmhartigheid in de Spaanse, de Oostenrijkse en de Franse Nederlanden (1618–1795)*, Brussels, Gemeentekrediet, 1986

Spies F., *De l'observation des simples conventions en droit canonique*, Paris, Sirey, 1928

Sturn R., "Agency, Exchange, and Power in Scholastic Thought," *The European Journal of the History of Economic Thought*, 24 (2017), 640–669

Supiot, A., "The Dogmatic Foundations of the Market," *Industrial Law Journal*, 29 (2000), 321–345

Supiot, A., *Homo juridicus: Essai sur la fonction anthropologique du Droit*, Paris, Éditions du Seuil, 2005

Supiot, A., "Face à l'insoutenable: Les ressources du droit de la responsabilité," in A. Supiot and M. Delmas-Marty (eds.), *Prendre la responsabilité au sérieux*, Paris, Presses universitaires de France, 2015, pp. 9–35

Thieme H., "Natürliches Privatrecht und Spätscholastik," *Zeitschrift der Savigny-Stiftung für Rechtsgeschichte, Germanistische Abteilung*, 70 (1953), 230–266

Thirion N., "Des rapports entre le marché et la puissance publique: De l'état-providence à l'état régulateur," in N. Thirion (ed.), *Crise et droit économique*, Brussels, Larcier, 2014, pp. 237–257

Thomas W., "The Treaty of London, The Twelve Years Truce and Religious Toleration in Spain and the Netherlands (1598–1621)," in R. Lesaffer (ed.), *The Twelve Years Truce (1609): Peace, Truce, War and Law in the Low Countries at the Turn of the 17th Century*, Leiden/Boston, Brill, 2014, pp. 277–297

Todeschini G., *Il prezzo della salvezza: Lessici medievali del pensiero economico*, Rome, La Nuova Italia Scientifica, 1994

Todeschini G., "Christian Perceptions of Jewish Economic Activity in the Middle Ages," in Michael Toch (ed.), *Wirtschaftsgeschichte der mittelalterlichen Juden: Fragen und Einschätzungen*, Munich, De Gruyter, 2008, pp. 1–16

Todeschini G., *Richesse Franciscaine: De la pauvreté volontaire à la société de marché*, Paris, Verdier, 2008

Todeschini G., *Les marchands et le temple: La société chrétienne et le cercle vertueux de la richesse du Moyen Âge à l'Époque moderne*, Paris, Albin Michel, 2017 [2002]

Trivellato F., *The Promise and Peril of Credit: What a Forgotten Legend about Jews and Finance Tells Us about the Making of European Commercial Society*, Princeton, Princeton University Press, 2019

Trivellato F., "The Ghosts of Max Weber in the Economic History of Preindustrial Europe," *Capitalism: A Journal of History and Economics*, 4 (2023), 332–376

Tutino, S., *Uncertainty in Post-Reformation Catholicism: A History of Probabilism*, Oxford, Oxford University Press, 2018

Van den Eede L., "Controversy in the Classroom: Jacobus Janssonius (1547–1625) versus Leonardus Lessius on Grace, Free Will and Predestination," *Journal of Early Modern Christianity*, 11 (2024), 413–443

Van Der Biest, J., "An Augustinian Revolution in the Lecture Hall? Michael Baius (1513–1589) as Regius Professor of Theology in Leuven," unpublished doct. diss., Leuven, 2024

Vandermeulen, W., "Modest Building Blocks. The State of the Art of Monopoly Thinking at the Turn of the Middle Ages and the Early Modern Period in the Works of Lawyers and Theologians," *Tijdschrift voor Rechtsgeschiedenis*, 91 (2023), 427-470

Van der Wee H., *The Growth of the Antwerp Market and the European Economy (Fourteenth-Sixteenth Centuries)*, The Hague, Nijhoff, 1963

Van der Wee H., "Antwerpens bijdrage tot de ontwikkeling van de moderne geld- en banktechniek," *Tijdschrift voor Economie*, 4 (1965), 488–500

Van der Wee H., "Anvers et les innovations de la technique financière aux XVIe–XVIIe siècles," *Annales: Économies, Sociétés, Civilisations*, 5 (1967), 1067–1089

Van Eijl J.E., "La controverse louvaniste autour de la grâce et du libre arbitre à la fin du XVIe siècle," in M. Lamberigts (ed.), *L'augustinisme à l'ancienne faculté de théologie de Louvain*, Leuven, Peeters, 1994, pp. 207–282

Van Hofstraeten B., "Het contractus trinus in vroegmodern Antwerpen," *Pro memorie*, 18 (2016), 131–152

Van Hofstraeten B., "The Organization of Mercantile Capitalism in the Low Countries: Private Partnerships in Early Modern Antwerp (1480–1620)," *Tijdschrift voor Sociale en Economische Geschiedenis*, 13 (2016), 1–24

Van Hofstraeten B., "Recording Customs in Early Modern Antwerp, a Commercial Metropolis," *Rechtsgeschichte/Legal History*, 24 (2016), 288–301

Van Houdt, T., "Petrus Santerna: Pionnier de l'assurance," *Bulletin du crédit communal*, 180 (1992), 15–26

Van Houdt, T., "Money, Time, and Labour: Leonardus Lessius and the Ethics of Money-Lending and Interest-Taking," *Ethical Perspectives*, 2 (1995), 11–27

Van Houdt, T., "Over boeken en gezondheid: Enkele gezondheidsboekjes uit de Nederlanden," *Geschiedenis der Geneeskunde*, 2 (1995), 163–168

Van Houdt, T., "'Lack of Money': A Reappraisal of Lessius' Contribution to the Scholastic Analysis of Money-Lending and Interest-Taking," *The European Journal of the History of Economic Thought*, 5 (1998), 1–35

Van Houdt, T., *Leonardus Lessius over lening, interest en woeker: De iustitia et iure, lib. 2, cap. 20: Editie, vertaling en commentaar*, Brussels, Paleis der Academiën, 1998

Van Houdt, T., "Spelen om geld: Gokken, wedden en loten in het moraaltheologische discours in de Zuidelijke Nederlanden," *De zeventiende eeuw*, 15 (1999), 61–73

Van Houdt, T., "Implicit Intention and the Conceptual Shift from Interesse to Interest: An Underestimated Chapter from the History of Scholastic Economic Thought," *Lias*, 33 (2006), 37–58

Van Houdt, T., "Leonardus Lessius," in W. Decock and J.W. Oosterhuis (eds.), *Great Christian Jurists in the Low Countries*, Cambridge, Cambridge UP, 2021, pp. 64–79

Van Houdt, T. and W. Decock, *Leonardus Lessius: Traditie en vernieuwing*, Antwerp, Lessius Hogeschool, 2005

Van Houdt, T., N. Golvers, and P. Soetaert, *Tussen woeker en weldadigheid: Leonardus Lessius over de Bergen van Barmhartigheid*, Leuven, Acco, 1992

Van Houdt, T. and F. Monsalve, "Usury and Interest," in H. Braun, E. De Bom, and P. Astorri (eds.), *A Companion to the Spanish Scholastics*, Leiden/Boston, Brill, 2022, pp. 475–497

Van Houtte A.J., "Les postes dans les Pays-Bas méridionaux sous la maîtrise des Tour et Taxis," in L. Janssens and M. Meurrens (eds.), *La poste des Tour et Taxis, 1489–1794*, Brussels, General State Archives, 1992

Van Sull, K., *Leonardus Lessius (1554–1623)*, Wetteren, 1923; French version: *Léonard Lessius, de la Compagnie de Jésus (1554–1623)*, Louvain/Paris/Brussels, 1930

Velardo T., "From the Primitive Mentality to the Civilization of Capitalism: Joseph Schumpeter, Reader of Lucien Lévy-Bruhl," *The European Journal of the History of Economic Thought*, published online 19 November 2024

Villey D., "Die Marktwirtschaft im katholischen Denken," *OrDO: Jahrbuch für die Ordnung von Wirtschaft und Gesellschaft*, 7 (1955), 23–69

Vismara P., *Oltre L'usura: La Chiesa moderna e il prestito a interesse*, Soveria Mannelli, Rubbettino, 2004

Waelkens L., *Amne adverso: Roman Legal Heritage in European Culture*, Leuven, Leuven University Press, 2015

Weber M., *The Protestant Ethic and the Spirit of Capitalism*, translated by Talcott Parsons, with a foreword by Richard H. Tawney, London/New York, Allen & Unwin/Scribner, 1930

Weber M., "Zur Psychophysik der industriellen Arbeit," in W. Schluchter and S. Frommer (eds.), *Schriften und Reden 1908–1912* (Max Weber Gesamtausgabe i/11), Tübingen, Mohr Siebeck, 1995

Weber M., *L'Éthique protestante et l'esprit du capitalisme*, translated and edited by Jean-Pierre Grossein, Paris, Gallimard, 2004

Wei I.P., *Intellectual Culture in Medieval Paris. Theologians and the University, c.1100–1330*, Cambridge, Cambridge University Press, 2012

Wijffels A.A., "Business Relations between Merchants in Sixteenth-Century Belgian Practise-Orientated Civil Law Literature," in Piergiovanni V. (ed.), *From Lex Mercatoria to Commercial Law*, Berlin, Duncker & Humblot, 2004, pp. 256–259

Wijffels A.A., "Argumentationsmuster in belgisch-niederländischen Konsiliensammlungen des 16. Jahrhunderts: Policy Considerations in der Ius commune-Tradition," in A. Cordes (ed.), *Juristische Argumentation—Argumente der Juristen* (Quellen und Forschungen zur höchsten Gerichtsbarkeit im alten Reich, 49), Köln-Weimar-Wien, Böhlau, 2006, pp. 55–73

Wijffels, A.A., "Policy considerations, en amont de l'argument conséquentialiste," conference held on 8 June 2017 at the Collège de France

Zwierlein, C., *The Political Thought of the French League and Rome (1585–1589): "De justa populi gallici ab Henrico tertio defectione" and "De justa Henrici tertii abdicatione" (Jean Boucher, 1589)*, Geneva, Droz, 2016

Index